FROM FARM TO FACTORY

The Development of Modern Society

Merrill Sociology Series

Under the editorship of
Richard L. Simpson
University of North Carolina, Chapel Hill
and
Paul E. Mott

FROM FARM TO FACTORY

The Development of Modern Society

Edited by

PAUL E. MOTT
HOWARD M. KAPLAN
GEORGE J. YELAGOTES
DONALD B. PITTENGER
MARC RIEDEL

Charles E. Merrill Publishing Company
A Bell & Howell Company
Columbus, Ohio

Published by
CHARLES E. MERRILL PUBLISHING CO.
A Bell & Howell Co.
Columbus Ohio 43216

ISBN: 0-675-09045-8

Library of Congress Catalog Card Number: 72-87429

1 2 3 4 5 6 7 8 / 77 76 75 74 73

Printed in the United States of America

THE EDITORS

Howard M. Kaplan is assistant professor of sociology and research associate in Institute for Social Research, Florida State University, Tallahassee, Florida.

George J. Yelagotes is assistant professor of sociology, Millersville State College, Millersville, Pennsylvania.

Donald R. Pittenger is associate demographer, Data and Systems Bureau, New York State Office of Planning Services, Albany, New York.

Marc Riedel is lecturer, School of Social Work, University of Pennsylvania, Philadelphia, Pennsylvania.

CONTENTS

PREFACE

Developing a series of readers for undergraduate sociology courses can be a very personal act. Every instructor has his own notions about what is valuable in his field and for his teaching. Some prefer the feisty stuff of so-called "pop" sociology; others want case examples of specific social problems. Classic-contemporary, functionalist-systemic, high brow-middle brow (no one will admit to less) are some of the more common forks in sociological highways.

The editors of these volumes are no exceptions. Generally dissatisfied with the readers that were available for introductory sociology, we tried to gather our own collection of articles for our introductory courses and make them available in the library. It was cumbersome and inconvenient. We sought an alternative approach, and the readers in this series are the result.

Reflected in them are our values of what is useful and important in undergraduate sociology, recognizing that these values are neither better nor worse than many others. Whenever possible we wanted to publish the whole article or the continuous book segment. The snippets of articles and patchwork abridgments of book excerpts found in many readers rob the student of a full understanding of how the author thought and worked. The figure of the idea presented is separated from its ground. Of course, we violated our intention sometimes when the article or the chapter was unusually long.

We feel that there are many old "standards" that still are key works in the field; still alive with their imaginative ideas. We included many of these. Our mix of old and new acknowledges that there is much useful sociology to be found in newspapers, magazines, and governmental reports. As the "popular" written media these sources may be viewed as barometers of contemporary concern. We borrowed liberally from them.

But we also confess to a bias concerning the importance of history to our field, embracing C. Wright Mills's charge to us to infuse our ideas and theories with the perspectives of history. We included a large dollop of historical materials in these readers. We hope that they demonstrate, however modestly, history's contribution to an understanding of the present. Finally, we aimed for the serious teacher and student, driving to the central ideas and concerns of the field.

In this, the second volume of the series, we offer a detailed look at the three major processes that have changed the nature of human relationships since ancient times: the development of cities, factories, and bureaucracies. The word "processes" is altogether inadequate to convey the pain, thought, and adjustment experienced by everyone who has been caught in these social forces. Take, for example, the process by which large, bureaucratic organizations developed and are developing. For over a hundred years people have been proclaiming the virtues of decentralization and the values of the humane community. Yet every reader of this book is affected by large organizations. Students try to cope with them while seeking to preserve their individuality in the midst of impersonal registration systems, large lecture courses and high-rise dormitories; the more introspective realize that most of their parents have been coping with bureaucracies throughout their adult lives. Efforts to make the bureaucracies respond are in many ways similar to an unfortunate family seeking aid from the county welfare office. The media, usually giant organizations, confront us at every turn with what we should want, enjoy, and believe. Preservation of self in the face of large organizations that seem impelled to prove the philosophy that the individual is one million divided by one million is _our_ trauma.

There have been others. The emergence of agriculture led to the demise of masculine hunting societies and ended an older ethos of nomadism and the freedom it implies. Trading spear for plow, and hunt for harvest, men's and women's adaptation to a settled agricultural life drastically changed their roles, their concepts of themselves, and their gods.

The emergence of the factory as the means to securing a living had similar effects. Having learned to love their land, to have their families near, and to exhort their god in the turning of the furrows, men and women had to leave their home to work for others in places that were palpably godless. The traumas of the present are not greater than these. Nor are they any less.

The stuff of social change is the upheavals that markedly alter the human situation. Each threatens the security of the individual and creates a crisis of values. Each leads to new levels of human organization, sophistication, and inevitably, new problems. We have tried to capture some of the hue and crash in this volume.

No preface is complete without an acknowledgment of intellectual and interpersonal debts. This is particularly true for the preface to introductory readers. Most obvious is our appreciation to the authors and publishers whose works appear here. Their permission to reprint the fruits of their scholarship gives substance to our otherwise abstract notions of what the field should offer to undergraduate sociology students. Less obvious, but no less important, is our continuing obligation to the students who have passed through our introductory sociology courses. Their demands for stimulating readings moved us to make this effort. Finally, we acknowledge the debt shared by all authors and editors fortunate enough to have concerned families, and thank them for their forbearance, assistance, and encouragement throughout this effort.

PEM
HMK
GJY
DBP
MR

PART I

Urbanization

THE WORLD IS URBANIZING FAR MORE
rapidly than it is increasing in total population. Between 1800
and 1850 the world's population increased 29 per cent, but
the proportion of people living in cities of 100,000 or more
increased 76 percent. In the next 50 years the figures were 37
and 222 percent respectively. During the first half of this
century the population increased 49 percent and the
proportion of people living in cities of 100,000 or more increased 254 percent. By 1960 one out of every five people
lived in localities of 100,000 or more people and almost one in
three lived in localities with 20,000 or more.

When sociologists use the term "urbanization" they have a
specific definition in mind: urbanization does not mean that
the number of people living in cities has increased, but rather,
that the proportion of the total population that is living in the
cities has increased. Urbanization is a world-wide
phenomenon; it is not found exclusively or primarily in
Europe and North America. In fact Asia has the highest
percentage of the total world population living in urban areas
of 100,000 or more people.

The urban trend is clearly visible in the United States. In 1840 this was a rural country with relatively primitive means of communication; over three-fourths of the population earned their living from agriculture. Since 1900 the American population has doubled, but at the same time the number of people living in metropolitan areas* has increased three and one-half times. Today two out of every three persons live in metropolitan areas. Most of this urban growth is occurring in the suburbs: between 1960 and 1968 the suburban population rose by 15 million people while the population of the central cities remained essentially unchanged. Today, over one-half of the population of the metropolitan areas lives in suburbs.

The first cities appeared almost 6000 years ago in Sumeria in what is now Iraq. By today's standards they were modest affairs, probably containing fewer than 25,000 residents. Still, many of the urban problems that concern us now were present in those precursors of metropolis. Air and water pollution were the rule and waste disposal was an unsolved problem. In other ways these ancient cities were radically different from their modern counterparts. Life was more ordered and constrained by an omnipresent value system. Gideon Sjoberg's article on the preindustrial city describes in detail the sources of that order. These constraints prevented ancient cities from exhibiting some of the worst excesses of their successors. For example, growth could be controlled by the simple expedient of not building a longer wall around the city. Urban planning and development were understood to be an obligatory function of the monarch rather than a job for largely ignored planning specialists.

Wade's study of the growth of five frontier towns illustrates again that many of the urban problems that concern us today were present even in relatively small communities more than 150 years ago. Pollution in many forms, slums, unplanned

---

*Metropolitan areas are dense urban conglomerates composed of a central city and the interdependent smaller cities and suburbs surrounding it.

growth, crime, racism seen particularly in the fear of blacks as perpetrators of criminal acts were already evident in these infant cities.

In other words urban blight is not a new problem; it is a very old one. What has happened is not merely that the swelling cities have compounded their problems and added a few new ones, but that more people now live in cities and thus more people are aware of the attendant problems. Urban problems existed in post-Revolutionary America, but since most Americans had little contact with the cities, they were not particularly concerned. Also, as cities have grown, the constraints of culture have fallen away giving rise to uncontrolled, unplanned growth. In the modern metropolis money can be spent for baseball stadia rather than for schools, for willy-nilly suburban development rather than for rehabilitation of the old city centers, and for highways rather than for mass transportation.

The record of urban growth in the 1960s is contained in Conrad Taeuber's article. The major themes are suburbanization and the first indications that immigration by blacks to the cities was declining. Since the majority of Americans now live in metropolitan suburbs, greater interest and concern for that style of life has developed. Stereotypes emerge from the popular literature picturing suburbia as a sterile, homogeneous subculture populated by bored, hard drinking, insular, wife-swapping middle-class Americans. If such stereotypes were true, then we would have a whole new set of serious social problems on our collective hands. In the selection by Gans, based on his experiences living in Levittown, the image of a homogeneous population is shattered at least for this particular suburb. Beneath a superficial homogeneity evoked by the similarities of houses, lawns, and styles of dress, Gans reveals a very diverse population. What then of other suburbs or of other parts of the stereotype? Just how different is suburban behavior from that in any other part of the metropolis?

Awareness of urban problems extends beyond the metropolitan areas. Smalltown, U.S.A. is mindful of these problems because the cities have penetrated these wayside places with television, newspapers, magazines, and books. Vidich and Bensman describe the variety of ways in which this penetration occurs in a small town they call "Springdale." Springdalers were aware of the intrusion of mass society, but the authors maintain that the intrusion was essential to the Springdale way of life.

Compare the situation of Springdale with that of Baghat, Turkey as it was coming into the orbit of Ankara, the capital city. The human dimensions of urbanization become apparent in Daniel Lerner's sensitive study of a community in transition from being a traditional, isolated, unchanging small town to being a part of the complex, cosmopolitan, fast moving world of a major metropolis.

We close this section with a look to the future with testimony before the U.S. Senate by the Greek urbanologist, Constantinos Doxiadis. Doxiadis reviews the problems of urbanism and proposes that the only way to solve them is to reestablish some of the controls that characterized ancient cities. Urban growth must be controlled by planning; further, it is inadequate to plan for only five or ten years ahead. Instead, if urban life in the future is to be humane, planning must begin now in order that developments in the city after the year 2000 may be controlled.

GIDEON SJOBERG

The
Preindustrial
City

In the past few decades social scientists have been conducting field studies in a number of relatively non-Westernized cities. Their recently acquired knowledge of North Africa and various parts of Asia, combined with what was already learned, clearly indicates that these cities are not like typical cities of the United States and other highly industrialized areas but are much more like those of medieval Europe. Such communities are termed herein "preindustrial," for they have arisen without stimulus from that form of production which we associate with the European industrial revolution.

Recently Foster, in a most informative article, took cognizance of the preindustrial city.[1] His primary emphasis was upon the peasantry (which he calls "folk"); but he recognized this to be part of a broader social structure which includes the preindustrial city. He noted certain similarities between the peasantry and the city's lower class. Likewise the present author sought to analyze the total society of which the peasantry and the preindustrial city are integral parts.[2] For want of a better term this was called "feudal." Like Redfield's folk (or "primitive") society, the feudal order is highly stable and sacred; in contrast, however, it has a complex social organization. It is characterized by highly developed state and educational and/or religious institutions and by a rigid class structure.

Thus far no one has analyzed the preindustrial city per se, especially as it differs from the industrial-urban community, although Weber, Tönnies, and a few others perceived differences between the two. Yet such a survey is needed for the understanding of urban development in so-called underdeveloped countries and, for that matter, in parts of Europe. Such is the goal of this paper. The typological analysis should also serve as a guide to future research.

Reprinted with the permission of the University of Chicago Press and the author from "The Preindustrial City," *American Journal of Sociology* 60 (March 1955): 438-45. Copyright © 1955 by the University of Chicago Press.

ECOLOGICAL ORGANIZATION

Preindustrial cities depend for their existence upon food and raw material obtained from without; for this reason they are marketing centers. And they serve as centers for handicraft manufacturing. In addition, they fulfill important political, religious, and educational functions. Some cities have become specialized; for example, Benares in India and Karbala in Iraq are best known as religious communities, and Peiping in China as a locus for political and educational activities.

The proportion of urbanites relative to the peasant population is small, in some societies about 10 percent, even though a few preindustrial cities have attained populations of 100,000 or more. Growth has been by slow accretion. These characteristics are due to the nonindustrial nature of the total social order. The amount of surplus food available to support an urban population has been limited by the unmechanized agriculture, transportation facilities utilizing primarily humans or animal power, and inefficient methods of food preservation and storage.

The internal arrangment of the preindustrial city, in the nature of the case, is closely related to the city's economic and social structure.[3] Most streets are mere passageways for people and for animals used in transport. Buildings are low and crowded together. The congested conditions, combined with limited scientific knowledge, have fostered serious sanitation problems.

More significant is the rigid social segregation which typically has led to the formation of "quarters" or "wards." In some cities (e.g., Fez, Morocco, and Aleppo, Syria) these were sealed off from each other by walls, whose gates were locked at night. The quarters reflect the sharp local social divisions. Thus ethnic groups live in special sections. And the occupational groupings, some being at the same time ethnic in character, typically reside apart from one another. Often a special street or sector of the city is occupied almost exclusively by members of a particular trade; cities in such divergent cultures as medieval Europe and modern Afghanistan contain streets with names like "street of the goldsmiths." Lower-class and especially "outcaste" groups live on the city's periphery, at a distance from the primary centers of activity. Social segregation, the limited transportation facilities, the modicum of residential mobility, and the cramped living quarters have encouraged the development of well-defined neighborhoods which are almost primary groups.

Despite rigid segregation the evidence suggests no real specialization of land use such as is functionally necessary in industrial-urban communities. In medieval Europe and in other areas city dwellings often serve as workshops, and religious structures are used as schools or marketing centers.[4]

Finally, the "business district" does not hold the position of dominance that it enjoys in the industrial-urban community. Thus, in the Middle East the principal mosque, or in medieval Europe the cathedral, is usually the focal point of community life. The center of Peiping is the Forbidden City.

ECONOMIC ORGANIZATION

The economy of the preindustrial city diverges sharply from that of the modern industrial center. The prime difference is the absence in the former of industrialism which may be defined as that system of production in which *inanimate* sources of power are used to multiply human effort. Preindustrial cities depend for the production of goods and services upon *animate* (human or animal) sources of energy—applied either directly or indirectly through such mechanical devices as hammers, pulleys, and wheels. The industrial-urban community, on the other hand, employs inanimate generators of power such as electricity and steam which greatly enhance the productive capacity of urbanites. This basically new form of energy production, one which requires for its development and survival a special kind of institutional complex, effects striking changes in the ecological, economic, and social organization of cities in which it has become dominant.

Other facets of the economy of the preindustrial city are associated with its particular system of production. There is little fragmentation or specialization of work. The handicraftsman participates in nearly every phase of the manufacture of an article, often carrying out the work in his own home or in a small shop near by and, within the limits of certain guild and community regulations, maintaining direct control over conditions of work and methods of production.

In industrial cities, on the other hand, the complex division of labor requires a specialized managerial group, often extra-community in character, whose primary function is to direct and control others. And for the supervision and co-ordination of the activities of workers, a "factory system" has been developed, something typically lacking in preindustrial cities. (Occasionally centralized production is found in preindustrial cities—e.g., where the state organized slaves for large-scale construction projects). Most commercial activities, also, are conducted in preindustrial cities by individuals without a highly formalized organization; for example, the craftsman has frequently been responsible for the marketing of his own products. With a few exceptions, the preindustrial community cannot support a large group of middlemen.

The various occupations are organized into what have been termed "guilds."[5] These strive to encompass all, except the elite, who are gainfully employed in some economic activity. Guilds have existed for merchants and handicraft workers (e.g., goldsmiths and weavers) as well as for servants, entertainers, and even beggars and thieves. Typically the guilds operate only within the local community, and there are no large-scale economic organizations such as those in industrial cities which link their members to their fellows in other communities.

Guild membership and apprenticeship are prerequisites to the practice of almost any occupation, a circumstance obviously leading to monopolization. To a degree these organizations regulate the work of their members and the price of their products and services. And the guilds recruit workers into specific occupations, typically selecting them according to such particularistic criteria as kinship rather than universalistic standards.

The guilds are integrated with still other elements of the city's social structure. They perform certain religious functions; for example, in medieval Europe, Chinese, and Middle Eastern cities each guild had its "patron saint" and held periodic festivals in his honor. And, by assisting members in time of trouble, the guilds serve as social security agencies.

The economic structure of the preindustrial city functions with little rationality, judged by industrial-urban standards. This is shown in the general nonstandardization of manufacturing methods as well as in the products and is even more evident in marketing. In preindustrial cities throughout the world a fixed price is rare; buyer and seller settle their bargain by haggling. (Of course, there are limits above which customers will not buy and below which merchants will not sell.) Often business is conducted in a leisurely manner, money not being the only desired end.

Furthermore, the sorting of goods according to size, weight, and quality is not common. Typical is the adulteration and spoilage of produce. And weights and measures are not standardized: variations exist not only between one city and the next but also within communities, for often different guilds employ their own system. Within a single city, there may be different kinds of currency, which, with the poorly developed accounting and credit systems, signalize a modicum of rationality in the whole of economic action in preindustrial cities.[6]

SOCIAL ORGANIZATION

The economic system of the preindustrial city, based as it has been upon animate sources of power, articulates with a characteristic class structure and family, religious, educational, and governmental systems.

Of the class structure, the most striking component is a literate elite controlling and depending for its existence upon the mass of the populace, even in the traditional cities of India with their caste system. The elite is composed of individuals holding positions in the governmental, religious, and/or educational institutions of the larger society, although at times groups such as large absentee landlords have belonged to it. At the opposite pole are the masses, comprising such groups as handicraft workers whose goods and services are produced primarily for the elite's benefit.[7] Between the elite and the lower class is a rather sharp schism, but in both groups there are gradations in rank. The members of the elite belong to the "correct" families and enjoy power, property, and certain highly valued personal attributes. Their position, moreover, is legitimized by sacred writings.

Social mobility in this city is minimal; the only threat to the elite comes from the outside—not from the city's lower classes. And a middle class—

so typical of industrial-urban communities, where it can be considered the "dominant" class—is not known in the preindustrial city. The system of production in the larger society provides goods, including food, and services in sufficient amounts to support only a small group of leisured individuals; under these conditions an urban middle class, a semileisured group, cannot arise. Nor are a middle class and extensive social mobility essential to the maintenance of the economic system.

Significant is the role of the marginal or "outcaste" groups (e.g., the Eta of Japan), which are not an integral part of the dominant social system. Typically they rank lower than the urban lower class, performing tasks considered especially degrading, such as burying the dead. Slaves, beggars, and the like are outcastes in most preindustrial cities. Even such groups as professional entertainers and itinerant merchants are often viewed as outcastes, for their rovings expose them to "foreign" ideas from which the dominant social group seek to isolate itself. Actually many outcaste groups, including some of those mentioned above, are ethnic groups, a fact which further intensifies their isolation. (A few, like the Jews in the predominantly Muslim cities of North Africa, have their own small literate religious elite which, however, enjoys no significant political power in the city as a whole.)

An assumption of many urban sociologists is that a small, unstable kinship group, notably the conjugal unit, is a necessary correlate of city life. But this premise does not hold for preindustrial cities.[8] At times sociologists and anthropologists, when generalizing about various traditional societies, have imputed to peasants typically urban kinship patterns. Actually, in these societies the ideal forms of kinship and family life are most closely approximated by members of the urban literate elite, who are best able to fulfil the exacting requirements of the sacred writings. Kinship and the ability to perpetuate one's lineage are accorded marked prestige in preindustrial cities. Children, especially sons, are highly valued, and polygamy or concubinage or adoption help to assure the attainment of large families. The pre-eminence of kinship is apparent even in those preindustrial cities where divorce is permitted. Thus, among the urban Muslims or urban Chinese divorce is not an index of disorganization; here, conjugal ties are loose and distinctly subordinate to the bonds of kinship, and each member of a dissolved conjugal unit typically is absorbed by his kin group. Marriage, a prerequisite to adult status in the preindustrial city, is entered upon at an early age and is arranged between families rather than romantically, by individuals.

The kinship and familial organization displays some rigid patterns of sex and age differentiation whose universality in preindustrial cities has generally been overlooked. A woman, especially of the upper class, ideally performs few significant functions outside the home. She is clearly subordinate to males, especially her father or husband. Recent evidence indicates that this is true even for such a city as Lhasa, Tibet, where women supposedly have had high status.[9] The isolation of women from public life has in some cases been extreme. In nineteenth-century Seoul, Korea, "respectable" women appeared on the streets only during certain hours of the night when men were supposed to stay at home.[10] Those women in preindustrial cities who evade some of the stricter requirements are members of certain marginal groups (e.g., entertainers) or of the lower class. The role of the urban lower-class woman typically resembles that of the peasant rather than the urban upper-class woman. Industrialization, by creating demands and opportunities for their employment outside the home, is causing significant changes in the status of women as well as in the whole of the kinship system in urban areas.

A formalized system of age grading is an effective mechanism of social control in preindustrial cities. Among siblings the eldest son is privileged. And children and youth are subordinate to parents and other adults. This, combined with early marriage, inhibits the development of a "youth culture." On the other hand, older persons hold considerable power and prestige, a fact contributing to the slow pace of change.

As noted above, kinship is functionally integrated with social class. It also reinforces and is reinforced by the economic organization: the occupations, through the guilds, select their members primarily on the basis of kinship, and much of the work is carried on in the home or immediate vicinity. Such conditions are not functional to the requirements of a highly industrialized society.

The kinship system in the preindustrial city also articulates with a special kind of religious system, whose formal organization reaches fullest development among members of the literate elite.[11] The city is the seat of the key religious functionaries whose actions set standards for the rest of society. The urban lower class, like the peasantry, does not possess the education or the means to maintain all the exacting norms prescribed by the sacred writings. Yet the religious system influences the city's entire social structure. (Typically, within the preindustrial city one religion is dominant; however, certain minority groups adhere to their own beliefs.) Unlike the situation in industrial cities, religious activity is not separate from the other social action but permeates family, economic, governmental, and other activities. Daily life is pervaded with religious significance. Especially important are periodic public festivals and ceremonies like Ramadan in Muslim cities. Even distinctly ethnic outcaste groups can through their own religious festivals maintain solidarity.

Magic, too, is interwoven with economic, familial, and other social activities. Divination is commonly employed for determining the "correct" action on critical occasions; for example, in traditional Japanese and Chinese cities, the selection of marriage partners. And nonscientific procedures are widely employed to treat illness among all elements of the population of the preindustrial city.

Formal education typically is restricted to the male elite, its purpose being to train individuals for positions in the governmental, educational, or religious hierarchies. The economy of preindustrial cities does not require mass literacy, nor, in fact, does the system of production provide the leisure so necessary for the acquisition of formal education. Considerable time is needed merely to learn the written language, which often is quite different from that spoken. The teacher occupies a position of honor, primarily because of the prestige of all learning and especially of knowledge of the sacred literature, and learning is traditional and characteristically based upon sacred writings.[12] Students are expected to memorize rather than evaluate and initiate, even in institutions of higher learning.

Since preindustrial cities have no agencies of mass communication, they are relatively isolated from one another. Moreover, the masses within a city are isolated from the elite. The former must rely upon verbal communication, which is formulated in special groups such as storytellers or their counterparts. Through verse and song these transmit upper-class tradition to nonliterate individuals.

The formal government of the preindustrial city is the province of the elite and is closely integrated with the educational and religious systems. It performs two principal functions: exacting tribute from the city's masses to support the activities of the elite and maintaining law and order through a "police force" (at times a branch of the army) and a court system. The police force exists primarily for the control of "outsiders," and the court supports custom and the rule of the sacred literature, a code of enacted legislation typically being absent.

In actual practice little reliance is placed upon formal machinery for regulating social life.[13] Much more significant are the informal controls exerted by the kinship, guild, and religious systems, and here, of course, personal standing is decisive. Status distinctions are visibly correlated, with personal attributes, chiefly speech, dress, and personal mannerisms which proclaim ethnic group, occupation, age, sex, and social class. In nineteenth-century Seoul, not only did the upper-class mode of dress differ considerably from that of the masses, but speech varied according to social class, the verb forms and pronouns depending upon whether the speaker ranked higher or lower or was the equal of the person being addressed.[14] Obviously, then, escape from one's role is difficult, even in the street crowds. The individual is ever conscious of his specific rights and duties. All these things conserve the social order in the preindustrial city despite his heterogeneity.

CONCLUSIONS

Throughout this paper there is the assumption that certain structural elements are universal for all urban centers. This study's hypothesis is that their form in the preindustrial city is fundamentally distinct from that in the industrial-urban community. A considerable body of data not only from medieval Europe, which is somewhat atypical,[15] but from a variety of cultures supports this point of view. Emphasis has been upon the static features of preindustrial city life. But even those preindustrial cities which have undergone considerable change approach the ideal type. For one thing, social change is of such a nature that it is not usually perceived by the general populace.

Most cities of the preindustrial type have been located in Europe or Asia. Even though Athens and Rome and the large commercial centers of Europe prior to the industrial revolution displayed certain unique features, they fit the preindustrial type quite well.[16] And many traditional Latin-American cities are quite like it, although deviations exist, for, excluding pre-Columbian cities, these were affected to some degree by the industrial revolution soon after their establishment.

It is postulated that industrialization is a key variable accounting for the distinctions between preindustrial and industrial cities. The type of social structure required to develop and maintain a form of production utilizing inanimate sources of power is quite unlike that in the preindustrial city.[17] At the very least, extensive industrialization requires a rational, centralized, extra-community economic organization in which recruitment is based more upon universalism than on particularism, a class system which stresses achievement rather than ascription, a small and flexible kinship system, a system of mass education which emphasizes universalistic rather than particularistic criteria, and mass communication. Modification in any one of these elements affects the others and induces changes in other systems such as those of religion and social control as well. Industrialization, moreover, not only requires a special kind of social structure within the urban community but provides the means necessary for its establishment.

Anthropologists and sociologists will in the future devote increased attention to the study of cities throughout the world. They must therefore recognize that the particular kind of social structure found in cities in the United States is not typical of all societies. Miner's recent study of Timbuctoo,[18] which contains much excellent data, points to the need for recognition of the preindustrial city. His emphasis upon the folk-urban continuum diverted him from an equally significant problem: How does Timbuctoo differ from modern industrial cities in its ecological, economic, and social structure? Society there seems even more sacred and organized than Miner admits.[19] For example, he used divorce as an index of disorganization, but in Muslim society divorce within certain rules is justified by the sacred literature. The studies of Hsu and Fried would have considerably more significance had the authors perceived the generality of their findings. And, once the general structure of the preindustrial city is understood, the specific cultural deviations become more meaningful.

Beals notes the importance of the city as a center of acculturation.[20] But an understanding of this process is impossible without some knowledge of the preindustrial city's social structure. Although industrialization is clearly advancing throughout most of the world, the social structure of preindustrial civilizations is conservative, often resisting the introduction of numerous industrial forms. Certainly many cities of Europe (e.g., in France or Spain) are not so fully industrialized as some presume; a number of preindustrial patterns remain. The persistence of preindustrial elements is also evident in cities of North Africa and many parts of Asia; for example, in India and Japan,[21] even though great social change is currently taking place. And the Latin-American city of Merida, which Redfield studied, had many preindustrial traits.[22] A conscious awareness of the ecological, economic, and social structure of the preindustrial city should do much to further the development of comparative urban community studies.

NOTES

1. George M. Foster, "What Is Folk Culture?" *American Anthropologist,* LV (1953), 159-73.

2. Gideon Sjoberg. "Folk and 'Feudal' Societies," *American Journal of Sociology,* LVIII (1952), 231-39.

3. Sociologists have devoted almost no attention to the ecology of preindustrial centers. However, works of other social scientists do provide some valuable preliminary data. See, e.g., Marcel Clerget, *Le Caire: Étude de géographie urbaine et d'histoire économique* (2 vols.: Cairo: E & R Schindler, 1934): Robert E. Dickinson. *The West European City* (London: Routledge & Kegan Paul, 1951); Robert Le Tourneau, *Fès: Avant le protectorat* (Casablanca: Société Marocaine de Librairie et d'Édition, 1949); Edward W. Lane, *Cairo Fifty Years Ago* (London: John Murray, 1896); J. Sauvaget, *Alep* (Paris: Librairie Orientaliste Paul Geuthner, 1941): J. Weulersse, "Antioche: Essai de géographie urbaine," *Bulletin d'études orientales,* IV (1934), 27-79; Jean Kennedy, *Here Is India* (New York: Charles Scribners Sons, 1945); and relevant articles in American geographical journals.

4. Dickinson, *op. cit.,* p. 27; O.H.K. Spate, *India and Pakistan* (London: Methuen & Co., 1954), p. 183.

5. For a discussion of guilds and other facets of the preindustrial city's economy see, e.g., J.S. Burgess, *The Guilds of Peking* (New York: Columbia University Press, 1928); Edward T. Williams, *China, Yesterday and Today* (5th ed.; New York: Thomas Y Crowell Co., 1932); T'ai-chu Liao, "The Apprentices in Chengtu during and after the War," *Yenching Journal of Social Studies,* IV (1948), 90-106; H.A.R. Gibb and Harold Bowen, *Islamic Society and the West* (London: Oxford University Press, 1950), Vol. I, Part I, chap. vi; Le Tourneau, *op. cit.;* Clerget, *op. cit.;* James W. Thompson and Edgar N. Johnson, *An Introduction to Medieval Europe* (New York: W.W. Norton Co., 1937), chap. xx; Sylvia L. Thrupp, "Medieval Gilds Reconsidered," *Journal of Economic History,* II (1942), 164-73.

6. For an extreme example of unstandardized currency cf. Robert Coltman, Jr., *The Chinese* (Philadelphia: F.A. Davis, 1891), p. 52. In some traditional societies (e.g., China) the state has sought to standardize economic action in the city by setting up standard systems of currency and/or weights and measures; these efforts, however, generally proved ineffective. Inconsistent policies in taxation, too, hinder the development of a "rational" economy.

7. The status of the true merchant in the preindustrial city, ideally, has been low; in medieval Europe and China many merchants were considered "outcastes." However, in some preindustrial cities a few wealthy merchants have acquired considerable power even though their role has not been highly valued. Even then most of their prestige has come through participation in religious, governmental, or educational activities, which have been highly valued (see, e.g., Ping-ti Ho, "The Sale Merchants of Yang-Chou: A Study of Commercial Capitalism in Eighteenth-Century China," *Harvard Journal of Asiatic Studies*, XVII [1954], 130-68).

8. For materials on the kinship system and age and sex differentiation see, e.g., Le Tourneau, *op. cit.*; Edward W. Lane, *The Manners and Customs of the Modern Egyptians* (3d ed.; New York: E.P. Dutton Co., 1923); C. Snouck Hurgronje, *Mekka in the Latter Part of the Nineteenth Century*, trans. J.H. Monahan (London: Luzac, 1931); Horace Miner, *The Primitive City of Bimbuctoo* (Princeton: Princeton University Press, 1953); Alice M. Bacon, *Japanese Girls and Women* (rev. ed.; Boston: Houghton Mifflin Co., 1902); J.S. Burgess, "Community Organization in China," *Far Eastern Survey*, XIV (1945), 371-73; Morton H. Fried, *Fabric of Chinese Society* (New York: Frederick A. Praeger, 1953); Francis L.K. Hsu, *Under the Ancestors' Shadow* (New York: Columbia University Press, 1948); Cornelius Osgood, *The Koreans and Their Culture* (New York: Ronald Press, 1951), chap. viii; Jukichi Inouye, *Home Life in Tokyo* (2d ed.; Tokyo: Tokyo Printing Co., 1911).

9. Tsung-Lien Shen and Shen-Chi Liu, *Tibet and the Tibetans* (Stanford: Stanford University Press, 1953), pp. 143-44.

10. Osgood, *op. cit.*, p. 146.

11. For information on various aspects of religious behavior see, e.g., Le Tourneau, *op. cit.*; Miner, *op cit.*, Lane, *Manners and Customs;* Hurgronje, *op. cit.*; André Chouraque, *Les Juifs d'Afrique du Nord* (Paris: Presses Universitaires de France, 1952); Justus Doolittle, *Social Life of the Chinese* (London: Sampson Low, 1868); John K. Shryock, *The Temples of Anking and Their Cults* (Paris: Privately printed, 1931); Derk Bodde (ed.), *Annual Customs and Festivals in Peking* (Peiping: Henri Vetch, 1936); Edwin Benson, *Life in a Medieval City* (New York: Macmillan Co., 1920); Hsu, *op. cit.*

12. Le Tourneau, *op. cit.*, Part VI; Lane, *Manners and Customs*, chap. ii; Charles Bell, *The People of Tibet* (Oxford: Clarendon Press, 1928), chap. xix; O. Olufsen, *The Emir of Bokkara and His Country* (London: William Heinemann, 1911), chap. ix; Doolittle, *op. cit.*

13. Carleton Coon, *Caravan: The Story of the Middle East* (New York: Henry Holt & Co., 1951), p. 259; George W. Gilmore, *Korea from Its Capital* (Philadelphia: Presbyterian Board of Publication, 1892), pp. 51-52.

14. Osgood, *op. cit.*, chap. viii; Gilmore, *op. cit.*, chap. iv.

15. Henri Pirenne, in *Medieval Cities* (Princeton: Princeton University Press, 1925), and others have noted that European cities grew up in opposition to and were separate from the greater society. But this thesis has been overstated for medieval Europe. Most preindustrial cities are integral parts of broader social structures.

16. Some of these cities made extensive use of water power, which possibly fostered deviations from the type.

17. For a discussion of the institutional prerequisites of industrialization see, e.g., Bert F. Hoselitz, "Social Structure and Economic Growth," *Economia internazionale*, VI (1953), 52-77, and Marion J. Levy, "Some Sources of the Vulnerability of the Structures of Relatively Non-industrialized Societies to Those of Highly Industrialized Societies," in Bert F. Hoselitz (ed.), *The Progress of Underdeveloped Areas* (Chicago: University of Chicago Press, 1952), pp. 114 ff.

18. *Op. cit.*

19. This point seems to have been perceived also by Asel T. Hansen in his review of Horace Miner's *The Primitive City of Timbuctoo, American Journal of Sociology*, LIX (1954), 501-2.

20. Ralph L. Beals, "Urbanism, Urbanization and Acculturation," *American Anthropologist*, LIII (1951), 1-10

21. See e.g., D.R. Gadgil, *Poona: A Socio-economic Survey,* (Poone: Gokhale Institute of Politics and Economics, 1952), Part II; N.V. Sovani, *Social Survey of Kolhapur City* (Poona: Gokhale Institute of Politics and Economics, 1951), Vol II; Noel P. Gist, "Caste Differentials in South India," *American Sociological Review,* XIX (1954), 126-37; John Campbell Pelzel, "Social Stratification in Japanese Urban Economic Life" (unpublished Ph.D. dissertation, Harvard University, Department of Social Relations, 1950).

22. Robert Redfield, *The Folk Culture of Yucatan* (Chicago: University of Chicago Press, 1941).

RICHARD C. WADE

The Growth of
Cities on
the American Frontier

The development of police and fire protection had long been a subject of official attention, and as the cities expanded both rapidly reached a critical phase. Like cleaning and paving programs, they caused a heavy drain on small budgets; hence many towns initially tried various expedients to avoid large expenditures. But the problems went beyond haphazard solutions. Increased population and wealth created greater inducements for criminals, while crowding and jerry-building enhanced fire risks. Though most towns had made important strides in securing life and property by 1815, all found the evils accumulated faster than the remedies.

All towns legislated very early to set up some police arrangement, but only those with large slave populations maintained men on the streets with any degree of regularity. In 1804 a wave of burglaries in Pittsburgh led to a temporary patrol, and a year later Cincinnati created a night watch in which all voters were forced to serve.[1] But both of these experiments lived only a short while, and protection and law enforcement reverted to county sheriffs and local constables. On the other hand, Lexington and Louisville organized systems supported largely or wholly by public funds. These were the most advanced in the West. Their purpose, however, was less the security of the inhabitants and their property than the control of slaves, and instructions to captains and men on the beat continually emphasized that function. Indeed, it was this fear of Negroes that provided Kentucky communities with the incentive, lacking north of the Ohio, to establish effective police.

As early as 1796 Lexington formed a modest watch, and four years later expanded it to cover nights and Sundays when citizens complained that "large assemblages of Negroes" had "become troublesome to the

Citizens." The trustees appointed two men to "parade at least three nights in the week from nine Oclock until six Oclock in the morning." A decade later an ordinance laid off the town into five districts, doubled the personnel and provided each policeman with a "Rattle." In 1813 two additional men joined the force, and the watch was put on a 24-hour basis. [2] Louisville's progress, while less impressive, followed a similar pattern, though a part of the support came from private subscription.

Other Western towns acted only sporadically, marshalling civic forces when crime rates rose, but generally leaving the problem to irregular constabularies. St. Louis institutionalized this partial system in an 1811 ordinance which declared that "whenever circumstances shall require," the chairman of the Board of Trustees or any two justices of the peace could call out a patrol in which all males over 18 had to serve. Though St. Louis's Negro population was small, the law gave the same instructions for the restraint of slaves as in Louisville and Lexington. Three years later Pittsburgh organized its first paid watch, raising nearly $3,000 on a special levy for its maintenance. [3] Yet, as late as 1815, Cincinnati, the fastest growing transmontane city, had no night patrol, and indeed was not to get one for over a decade.

Establishing a force was only the first step in assuring adequate protection and law enforcement. [4] Departments had to draw up their rules and procedures, contrive methods of operation, and build morale. This was not easy, since salaries were low, facilities poor, and evidently, temptations many, for often trustees had to shield the public from the police. Lexington authorities, for instance, received constant complaints about the "improprieties," "delinquency," and "sundry misdemeanors and neglect of duty" of their men. [5] Teen-agers and rowdies loved to "bait the watch," and even adults obstructed their work. In no town in 1815 were the police strong enough to quell riots or major disorders, or even to stop waves of vandalism.

Initially, municipalities used county jails, most of which contained only a few poorly kept and unhealthy cells where criminals and debtors, men, women, and children were indiscriminately mixed. Even "the calls of nature," charged the *Western Spy*, "are compelled to be answered...in the very apartment in which they are confined." [6] Discipline was impossible, and a Pittsburgh editor asserted that "instead of being places for correction and amendment, [they have] become scenes of debauchery, and means of corruption." Henry McMurtrie laconically described Louisville's jail as "a most miserable edifice, in a most filthy and ruinous condition, a first cousin to the black hole of Calcutta." [7] Their only redeeming feature lay in the fact that escape was possible, and every town had its spectacular breaks. Occasionally conditions became so bad that civic indignation demanded improvement, but in the fight that followed, advocates of economy prevented any real reform. Later, cities constructed their own prisons, which somewhat alleviated the crowding and promoted better sanitary facilities.

Police activity might have been greatly improved if street lighting in Western towns had been better. But until 1815 only Lexington provided its citizens with a public system. In 1812 the trustees authorized the erection of twenty lamps through the corporation, five of them along Main Street. Samuel Trotter traveled to Philadelphia at the treasury's expense "to examine the lamps in that City and have one made for this place." By the end of the year the Blue Grass metropolis became the first frontier city with night lighting. A year later municipal officials added to this service by offering free oil to those who put their own lamps on the street. [8]

In other communities taverns and homes provided the only illumination, but since lamp breaking was a popular outdoor sport of Western teen-agers, only a few householders risked it. McMurtrie observed that in Louisville "not a single lamp lends its cheering light to the nocturnal passenger, who frequently stands a good chance of breaking his neck." In Cincinnati, however, private lighting spread rapidly after 1810, developing so haphazardly that it created a fire risk, and the council moved in 1815 to establish some control. A fine of $50—one of the steepest penalties in local law—awaited any person erecting a lamp without official authorization. [9] But in general the new settlements lived in darkness after sundown, while criminals plied their trade under a black mantle which shielded them from both their victims and the police.

An ineffective police force not only left life and property insecure but weakened the defense of cities against fire. The evening watch was designed in part to be an alarm system, since the hazard greatly increased at nightfall when blazes could begin unnoticed and quickly get out of hand. Early urban history abounds with serious conflagrations. "We seldom pass a week," lamented an editor, "without reading some melancholy account of the disasters occasioned by the most destructive of all elements—fire." [10]

From the first days of settlement this danger haunted Western communities. Builders continued to use wood exclusively, though the number of brick and stone houses multiplied every year. As the towns grew, crowding increased, and it was difficult to confine the flames to a single shop or dwelling. Though it is impossible to estimate the total fire damage in these frontier communities, it must have been considerable, and was certainly greater than losses incurred in all other ways.

No city escaped its ravages. Small fires were so common that they received only passing notice in the newspapers, but each community had its spectacular blazes. In 1806 flames swept through Hart and Dodge's rope factory in Lexington, leaving an $8,000 establishment in ashes. Six years later a whole block in Pittsburgh was wiped out, with losses which would have been even greater if the evening had not been "remarkably calm." David Embree lost his brewery in Cincinnati in 1815, just a year after the court house burned down. Outbreaks became so frequent that many thought incendiaries were at work. The *Western Spy* charged in 1799 that "an association of wicked men" ignited four buildings a week, plundering homes while the citizens turned out for the emergency. More than a decade later when a "whole range of fine brick houses" on Pittsburgh's Wood Street caught fire, causing $35,000 loss, the authorities also suspected arson.[11]

Though large-scale destruction continued throughout this period, protection remained weak. A wave of excitement and agitation followed each big blaze, and constructive steps often resulted. But each new outbreak found the town somewhat unprepared. The engines worked badly or not at all, volunteers arrived too late, or bystanders preferred to watch the flames rather than fight them. Efforts to improve equipment and techniques could not be sustained after public interest lagged and money ran low. An old hand at fire reform finally became convinced that people enjoyed the spectacle and did not want improvement. Retreating into satire, he proposed two schemes to indulge their appetites. The first, called *"plan dilatory,"* required the government to burn all its apparatus so that no one need fear that the show might be stopped. His alternative, *"plan Immediate,"* stipulated that the city should buy twelve houses annually from a "conflagration fund," and light one every month as a kind of civic celebration.[12]

Though communities attacked the question along many fronts, the remedies never caught up with the problem. Municipal efforts were both public and private, involving the formation of largely self-governing companies using city funds and equipment and bolstered by ordinances designed to reduce risks. The charters of Louisville and Lexington forbade wooden chimneys within the corporation, and in the following years the trustees widened the prohibition to include shavings, more than twenty-eight pounds of gun powder, and frame and log houses that might be dangerous. In Pittsburgh, local authorities issued detailed regulations for stove pipes, the "Altitude of Chimneys," and bonfires.[13] Though some localities naturally emphasized their own peculiar dangers, by 1815 the codes of Western cities looked very much alike and contained similar restrictions.

Fires were considered a city emergency, and the whole community was expected to respond. Pittsburgh required all men living in the district to serve when called "unless a good and sufficient cause be offered." Failure to turn out led to a fine. A Lexington ordinance obligated those between sixteen and sixty to appear at every blaze and take orders from the Union Fire Company.[14] This system admirably suited the needs of small villages, but as settlements grew, it proved clumsy and outmoded, and the burden of firefighting fell more and more to volunteer companies. Though these associations had existed almost as long as the towns themselves, their activity did not take on great importance until the communities became too big to expect everyone to respond to an alarm. Then municipal authorities handed increased power to these quasi-official bodies. The relationship between the companies and the city was ambiguous. Local governments granted them charters and usually funds and equipment, but the organizations made their own rules and determined admission requirements. No question of jurisdiction or independence arose in this period because the same people who sat on official boards and councils were also prominent in the fire societies.

The public provided the volunteer organizations with equipment, either through subscriptions or from governmental funds. Communities further aided by providing hoses, hooks and ladders, and building stations to house the apparatus, and assuming the cost of repairs. Since engines were few and seldom really effective, great responsibility rested on the bucket brigades which brought water from wells or rivers to the fire by a human chain. Each city required householders and shopkeepers to have available at least two leather pails for immediate use, in addition to those furnished by local authorities. All these services constantly claimed about ten per cent of municipal budgets, and sometimes more when new equipment was purchased.[15]

Though some communities displayed more energy than others in tackling the fire problem, all lived under the fear that a windy night might reduce the town to ashes. The detailed accounts in the press of great conflagrations in other cities reflected the general anxiety of Western urbanites, while the rates of the Kentucky Mutual Assurance Fire Company, ranging from one to six per cent annually, testified to the local risks. By 1815 every municipality owned at least one engine, and Lexington and Pittsburgh had three. Legislation tended to outrun enforcement, and local inventories of equipment were never reassuring. In 1809 a Pittsburgh committee reported only 59 buckets in good repair in homes and shops, one engine "of which we can make no report," and some hooks and ladders "nearly compleated."[16] As residential building moved away from the river, hazards increased, and townspeople realized that future fire control would require a much greater supply of water.

Since all these cities except Lexington overlooked major rivers, the volume of water for town use was never a serious question. During the early days of settlement all buildings stood near the bank of a stream, and in case of fire plenty of water was available if it could be brought to the scene quickly enough. Later the population moved inland—which usually also meant upland—and new sources had to be found elsewhere, at least for emergency purposes. Public and private wells provided some, but this supply was uncertain, and soon discussion turned to the establishment of city-wide systems using steam power. As early as 1810 Calvin Adams petitioned the trustees of St. Louis for "exclusive privileges" for "bringing fresh water into the Town by Mean [*sic*] of Pipes." Though no community actually embarked on such an ambitious project, Pittsburgh and Lexington had similar suggestions under consideration before 1815.[17]

At the same time that adequate fire protection demanded more water, increasing populations required larger supplies for drinking. For this purpose Western townsfolk used springs, rivers or wells, depending on which was most accessible. Uninformed about germ theories, they chose by taste and appearance rather than purity. St. Louisans drank from the Mississippi, though they were careful to let the water stand in jars until the dirt settled. Henry McMurtrie thought the Ohio an "extremely pure" stream, but the people of Louisville preferred well water, which he claimed was "extremely bad, containing, besides a considerable quantity of lime, a large portion of decomposed vegetable matter."[18] Except for Lexington, which drew from the spring which had attracted the first settlers, the urban centers relied on both rivers and wells.

River water was free, but many wells were not. Some private owners, having incurred expenses in digging, sold water to users by the week or year, while vendors peddled it from door to door in carts. But generally, cities undertook to provide their citizens with water, and very early erected public wells. In 1802 Pittsburgh adopted an ordinance instructing the burgesses to build pumps "wherever they think most advisable," beginning with two on Market Street. It further provided for buying private wells "in useful and necessary parts of the Borough." As towns expanded, municipalities entered into this activity on a considerable scale, and in 1813 Cincinnati contracted to drill "possibly 30" in a single season.[19] Public control of the water supply, then, was firmly established in Western cities before 1815.

At the same time, local governments continually expanded their activity in protecting the health of their citizens. Epidemics, like fire, were among the hazards of urban living, and the image of Philadelphia's yellow-fever scourge in 1793 haunted Western townspeople. Fortunately, early charters granted municipal authorities broad powers to deal with problems of disease and sanitation. Nor was it long before conditions in the new settlements demanded their exercise. In 1802 a writer in the *Pittsburgh Gazette* charged that "the increase of diseases in this place, has of late been greater in proportion, than the increase of population," a fact he attributed to the "vitiated state of the air." "Narrow streets and alleys... filthy gutters, putrid vegetable and matter, the stench from the foul slaughter houses, the exhalations from ponds of stagnant water," all combined to threaten residents.[20]

No town was immune from these nuisances. Slaughtering inside the corporation limits led quickly to protests and municipal regulations.

Initially, local authorities established sanitary standards requiring butchers to keep their blocks and floors clean. But complaints continued, and soon most towns turned to licensing for control, restricting the number within the city, or at least within its center. Cincinnati's council went further, insisting that all meat be prepared at "a regular slaughter house" designated by the city.[21]

A more persistent and dangerous health hazard was stagnant water. All the river towns suffered from it, though only in Louisville and Cincinnati did it reach threatening proportions. In the former, larger ponds covered the outskirts of the city, while overflow from the river deposited a "creamy mantling surface" on the banks of the Ohio. In the summer these "depots of universal mischief" brought extraordinary sickness, giving Louisville the reputation of being the West's graveyard. The trustees constantly encouraged individuals to drain ponds on their property whenever possible, and in 1811 began a series of public projects to take water off Main and Jefferson Streets with brick sewers.[22] No other question bothered municipal officials quite so much, and Louisville records reveal constant concern with them. But the problem was too large for piecemeal solutions. It took an epidemic in 1817 to convince people that the situation had become intolerable.

Swamps and marshes imperiled Cincinnati in much the same way. The Ohio drowned the mouth of Mill Creek on the town's west end, and the low river bank along the city collected water which bred mosquitoes throughout the summer and accumulated filth the year round. In addition, the building industry complicated this drainage question by establishing brickyards, "every one of which," according to Daniel Drake, who counted nine in 1815, "is surrounded by several pools, which litterly consist of washings, of nearly the whole town." Rains cleaned the streets and alleys and then gravitated towards these pits, which became "hotbeds of corruption, the laboratories of poison, and the sinks of human life." In the even more grisly expression of "Sydeham" in *Liberty Hall,* they were a "rich solution of dead cats and pigs." In 1815 Cincinnati embarked on an extensive clean-up campaign—"the great purification," as Drake described it—but until that time progress had been "neither creditable to the energy of the corporation, honorable to the proprietors of those lots, nor beneficial to the public health."[23]

Sewage disposal also proved troublesome in the first years of urban living. Private vaults took care of family waste, while surface gutters carried away public and industrial garbage. Throughout this period towns contented themselves with the regulation of privies, requiring pits to be deep enough to prevent offensive odors, and outhouses to be cleaned regularly. Rapid building, however, led to carelessness in furnishing basic toilet facilities. The *Pittsburgh Gazette* charged in 1802 that "in all parts of the Borough there are tenements unprovided with Vaults—three or four families occupying buildings erected on a single lot of ground, are known to be without this necessary convenience...the dangerous consequences of which must be evident." In Lexington, the water table lay so close to the surface that cesspools threatened "to communicate with these wells...to jeopardise the health of our citizens," and soon the town limited their depth.[24] In no city did sewer improvement keep pace with increased population and building, and in each the situation by 1815 moved rapidly toward a crisis.

Inadequate sanitation generated a constant fear of disease, especially in summer months when the danger was greatest and when almost every death engendered anxiety. Though no town except Cincinnati tried to keep vital statistics, it is clear that smallpox, malaria, and influenza took many lives annually and occasionally reached epidemic proportions. Frequent newspaper accounts of sickness in the valley, though usually exaggerated, increased Western apprehensiveness, and the red flag of quarantine on housetops grimly reminded residents each year that the dreaded visitor was back in town. Against smallpox, the worst killer, local authorities encouraged vaccination, though initially there was some distrust. In 1804 a town meeting in Cincinnati forbade the new system, condemning any doctor using it as "an enemy to the health and prosperity of the town,"[25] but later the practice became an accepted medical weapon.

Quarantine laws, a much broader use of municipal power, enabled cities to remove the infected from the corporation, paying all expenses if necessary. Sometimes emergencies drove localities to more direct attacks on contagions. In 1809 the St. Louis council, hearing that a boat coming from Natchez carried a smallpox case and "being desirous to prevent the danger," authorized its chairman "to Call Out Such Members of Male Inhabitants...as he may deem necessary...to prevent the landing of said boat."[26] But not even task forces prevailed against influenza and malaria or the "fever and ague," which did their annual damage without fear of government intervention.

By 1815 Western towns had witnessed the appearance of all the urban problems which confronted Eastern cities, and already these questions exerted a growing pressure on local governments. In nearly every field of municipal authority—police, fire, streets, water, and health—conditions deteriorated so rapidly that a series of emergencies appeared, requiring decisive action. Any one of these was grave enough to tax the ingenuity of local authorities, yet the crises came on many fronts. Indeed, the multiplicity of issues was the real danger. Communities could handle some of the challenges, but not all. Yet their interrelatedness made success in any single one difficult.

This was an ironic situation, for in the first years of the nineteenth century the expansion of municipal power to cope with these problems constituted the central tendency of local government in the West. Having begun with extremely limited jurisdiction, towns managed to broaden their authority continually until it covered wide areas of town life. Some of this increased control was embodied in amendments to early charters, and the rest resulted from the cities' inching into the twilight zone which separated state and local power, pleading "necessity and immemorial usage as their authority."[27] By the end of the first generation of city life on the frontier, communities were largely self-governing, having appropriated either by grant or arrogation nearly all the necessary weapons to deal with problems arising from urban conditions.

One crucial weapon, however, was still lacking—the right to raise adequate revenues by taxation, which states continued to limit rigidly. The critical position of the cities demanded wide-scale improvements, all of which required funds greatly in excess of their annual income. In a desperate search for funds, municipalities resorted to borrowing, first modestly and later extravagantly. In addition some, like Pittsburgh and Cincinnati, sought to increase their corporate status from that of a borough or town to a city, hoping in this way to enhance their powers. By 1815 all these communities had become concerned about the problems mounting around them, and the minutes of local councils and boards breathed a new urgency that grew out of the impending crises. "It has become evident," the trustees of Lexington admitted, "that the present municipal regulations are insufficient in governing the place."[28] It was not that previous action had been fruitless, but rather that growth and expansion brought pain and sometimes peril. The burgeoning cities of the West had begun to feel both.

NOTES

1. *Pittsburgh Gazette,* November 25, 1803, August 31, 1804; *Liberty Hall* (Cincinnati), November 19, 1805.

2. Lexington, Trustees Book, July 7, 1800; September 25, 1801; January 4, 1812, February 13, 1812; June 17, 1813; January 20, 1814.

3. St. Louis, Ordinances, February 9, 1811; *Mercury* (Pittsburgh), March 28, 1815.

4. Poor enforcement was a familiar lament in every city. "We have had Hog Laws, Dog Laws, Theatre Laws, and Laws about Hay Scales...Kitchen Slops, Soap Suds, and Filth of every kind, and in no single instance have they been executed." *Kentucky Reporter,* August 26, 1809.

5. For these examples, see Lexington, Trustees Book, May 2, 1808, April 14, 1814, September 15, 1814. For charges against Pittsburgh's constable, see *Commonwealth* (Pittsburgh), September 24, 1813.

6. *Western Spy* (Cincinnati), March 31, 1817. A Pittsburgh grand jury in 1815 found the county jail "insecure" and objected to mingling debtors and criminals. *Pittsburgh Gazette,* December 2, 1815. A sheriff's investigation in St. Louis nine years earlier revealed similar conditions. Town of St. Louis, Court House Papers (MSS, Missouri Historical Society), VIII, 45.

7. *Pittsburgh Gazette,* June 8. 1793; McMurtrie, *Sketches of Louisville,* 122.

8. Lexington, Trustees Book, January 18. 1812; Lexington, Trustees Book, May 7, 1812; January 16, 1813.

9. McMurtrie, *Sketches of Louisville,* 143; Cincinnati, Ordinances, February 23, 1815.

10. *Liberty Hall* (Cincinnati), August 4, 1807.

11. *Kentucky Gazette,* June 24, 1806; *Pittsburgh Gazette,* July 31, 1812; *Liberty Hall* (Cincinnati), March 8. 1814, February 11, 1815; *Western Spy* (Cincinnati), December 17, 1799; *Pittsburgh Gazette,* October 23, 1815.

12. See "Admirer of a Fire," in *Pittsburgh Gazette,* January 18, 1809.

13. *Collection of the Acts of Virginia and Kentucky,* 3; Lexington, Trustees Book, November 22, 1796; February 17, 1808; April 8, 1815; Pittsburgh, Borough Papers, January 15, 1805; February 10, 1803. *Pittsburgh Gazette,* August 31, 1804.

14. Pittsburgh, Borough Papers, February 28, 1811; Lexington, Trustees Book, February 17, 1818.

15. See Lexington, Trustees Book, May 2, 1811, and *Liberty Hall* (Cincinnati), March 26, 1819.

16. *Kentucky Reporter,* April 9, 1814; Pittsburgh, Borough Papers, January 11, March 28, 1808.

17. St. Louis, Minutes, August 16, 1810; *Pittsburgh Gazette,* November 26, 1813, and Lexington, Trustees Book, November 4, 1813.

18. McMurtrie, *Sketches of Louisville,* 139.

19. *Western Spy* (Cincinnati), May 28, 1799, July 1, 1801; printed in *Pittsburgh Gazette,* August 9, 1802; *Western Spy* (Cincinnati), July 30, 1813.

20. *Pittsburgh Gazette,* July 23, 1802.

21. Louisville, Trustees Book, July 13, 1812; *Liberty Hall* (Cincinnati), March 16, 1803.

22. McMurtrie, *Sketches of Louisville,* 142; Louisville, Trustees Book, July 29, 1811, May 21, 1813, September 10, 1813.

23. Drake, *Statistical View,* 191; *Liberty Hall* (Cincinnati), January 31, 1810; July 28, 1812.

24. Pittsburgh, Borough Papers, September ?, 1803; Lexington, Trustees Book, May 5, 1814.

25. *Western Spy* (Cincinnati), December 13, 1804.

26. Lexington, Trustees Book, December 30, 1801; St. Louis, Minutes, December 16, 1809.

27. St. Louis, Minutes, May 3, 1824. See the speech by Mayor Carr Lane.

28. Lexington, Trustees Book, September 12, 1815.

CONRAD TAEUBER

The Growth of
American Cities:
1960-1969

In my testimony before this Committee on June 3, 1969, I pointed out some of the changes that have occurred in our population since 1960 with special reference to the changes in the numbers of Negroes and whites. Since that time, some additional observations on recent population changes have become available, providing new evidence on trends in the population of metropolitan areas. This new information indicates that in general the trends observed previously have continued. However, it also suggests some modifications of the conclusions based on the more limited data series which were used in the earlier testimony.

We have updated our information to 1969, and the overall picture of change since 1960 which I had given earlier remains much the same. Metropolitan areas have continued to grow more rapidly than the rest of the national population, and the increase has been primarily in the suburban areas. Between 1960 and 1969, central cities gained nearly three-quarters of a million people. This net change was the result of an increase of 2.6 million in the Negro population and a decline of 2.1 million in the white population. There was also some increase in the number of persons of other races. Nearly three-fourths of the total national growth in the Negro population since 1960 has occurred in the central cities of the metropolitan areas. As a result, 55 percent of the total Negro population now resides in central cities compared with 26 percent of the white population.

Most of the estimated 2.6 million increase in the Negro population in central cities is due to the natural increase of the population—that is, the excess of births over deaths. About one-third of the net gain—approximately 800,000 persons—is due to net in-migration. The decline in the white population of central cities, on the other hand, implies a substantial net out-migration of the white population during this period.

Reprinted and abridged with the permission of the author from an updated version of his Statement Before the House Committee on Banking and Currency, June 3, 1969.

In my earlier testimony, I had suggested that 1966 may have been a turning point, in that the net movement of the Negro population into cities was substantially slower after 1966 than in the earlier years and that the movement of the white population from central cities had been accelerated. As I pointed out then, it was difficult to know whether the figures represent anything more than a temporary aberration in long-term trends. New material now available clarifies the picture somewhat.

We have been able to extend the annual series back to 1964. The figures given in tables 1* and 2 are based on sample surveys and the year-to-year changes are subject to relatively large sampling errors. It is not possible with the data at hand to make certain that the figures for 1960-1964 are on an entirely comparable basis with those for later years. However, it is clear that from 1964 up to the present date there has been a steady, annual net population loss of whites in central cities. Since 1964 the overall loss of whites amounted to about 2.3 million. This figure implies that net out-migration of whites from the central cities has averaged about 800 to 900 thousand per year.

The year-to-year changes in the increase of the number of Negroes in central cities are subject to rather large sampling errors and one cannot be sure that the very low figure for the year 1966-67 provides an accurate reflection of what was happening. However, it is clear that since 1964 there has continued to be a large increase in the Negro population of the central cities and that any slowing down which may have occurred about 1966 has not continued to the more recent years. The increase of an average of about 300,000 per year has resulted from a net in-migration of about 100,000 per year and an annual excess of births over deaths of about 200,000 per year. The available evidence indicates some increase also in the number of Negroes in the suburban areas, but the numbers involved are still so small that it is difficult to establish the size of this increase.

More precise statements concerning the trends will have to await the results of the 1970 Census, which is to be taken beginning in April of next year. The sample data which are available at present do reflect trends generally, but they cannot adequately reflect small year-to-year changes and they do not provide any basis for statements about individual metropolitan areas.

Since my last appearance before this Committee, we have also secured data on changes that took place during the past year in family composition, education, income, and poverty. The results essentially bear out the conclusions reached from the data for other recent years.

FAMILY STRUCTURE IN CITIES AND SUBURBS

In comparing the types of families found in central cities and suburbs in 1968, it was observed that families with both a husband and wife present

---

* Editors' note: All of the tables from this statement have been deleted here.

were more typical of the suburban than the city family. About 8 out of every 10 families in major cities, and 9 out of every 10 families within the suburban rings, were headed by a man with his wife present. The proportion of families headed by women was twice as large in cities as in suburbs, and in both cities and suburbs they were more than twice as common among Negro than among white families. The most recent data indicate that no significant changes occurred between 1968 and 1969 in the family structure to be found in cities and suburbs among either whites or Negroes.

UNEMPLOYMENT IN METROPOLITAN AND NON-METROPOLITAN AREAS

Lower unemployment rates for men were found in metropolitan than in nonmetropolitan areas in 1969. Within metropolitan areas the unemployment rate for Negroes was about twice as high as that of whites in 1960, 1968, and 1969. Overall, the unemployment rate within metropolitan areas was less in March 1969 than in March 1968 for both whites and Negroes.

EDUCATION OF YOUNG ADULTS IN METROPOLITAN AND NONMETROPOLITAN AREAS

The educational achievement of young adults (25-29 years old in 1969) attests to the performance of our educational institutions for the generation recently exposed to the educational system. Metropolitan area residents had a higher level of educational attainment than residents of nonmetropolitan areas in 1969, 1968, and in 1960. About one-fifth of the whites 25 to 29 years of age living in metropolitan areas in 1969 had completed four years of college.

Negroes clearly lag behind whites in educational attainment in both metropolitan and nonmetropolitan areas. In metropolitan areas, as in nonmetropolitan areas, the educational attainment of young white adults in 1960 surpassed that of young Negro adults in 1969.

FAMILIES WITH HIGH INCOMES IN METROPOLITAN AND NONMETROPOLITAN AREAS

Some evidence of material progress is provided by observing how the proportion of families with incomes above $10,000 has grown since 1959. In 1968, 46 percent of the families residing in metropolitan areas had incomes providing the same purchasing power enjoyed by only 29 percent of all families residing in metropolitan areas in 1959. Between 1967 and 1968 there was continued growth in the proportion of families with high incomes. Among white families in the suburbs, about one-half had incomes above $10,000 and one-fifth had incomes above $15,000 in 1968. About one-fifth of Negro families in the central cities had incomes of $10,000 or over in 1968.

INCOME BY EDUCATIONAL ATTAINMENT OF MALES

The period between 1967 and 1968 was one of rapidly rising prices. Corresponding increases in income were not forthcoming at the same rate for all. During 1968, men between 25 and 54 years of age whose education ended with four years of high school or less, had incomes that advanced faster than the incomes of those who had attended college.

EARNINGS BY OCCUPATION IN METROPOLITAN AND NONMETROPOLITAN AREAS

In general, the earnings of year-round workers currently employed in nonagricultural occupation groups rose more rapidly between 1967 and 1968 than in previous years since 1959. The rate of increase in real earnings between 1967 and 1968 was double the average annual rate of change between 1959 and 1967 for male and female workers residing in metropolitan and in nonmetropolitan areas.

POVERTY

The increase in median income between 1967 and 1968 was associated with a decline of over 2 million persons having incomes below the poverty level. Although the poverty rate continued to be about twice as high among Negroes as among whites, the number of poor was reduced among both whites and Negroes in 1968. This reduction took place primarily in the central cities of large metropolitan areas and outside metropolitan areas. No significant reduction in the number of poor whites or Negroes were observed in central cities of smaller metropolitan areas or in the suburbs. There was a lower incidence of poverty in metropolitan areas (10 percent) than in nonmetropolitan areas (18 percent). Similar differences were observed in previous years.

POVERTY AREAS IN LARGE CITIES

Almost every major city has areas of concentrated poverty and physical deterioration. These "poverty areas" were defined in terms of selected socio-economic criteria in 1960 to provide a means of observing conditions in the poorest sections of metropolitan areas. Since 1960 the number of families residing in these areas has declined. In 1969 there were 30 percent fewer white families and 9 percent fewer Negro families in poverty areas than in 1960. Over half of all Negro families and 15 percent of all white families in the major cities lived in these areas in both 1968 and 1969. The racial composition within poverty areas reflects this uneven distribution of whites and Negroes. About one-half of all families in these poverty areas are Negro.

HERBERT GANS

Social Life
in
the Suburbs

The suburban critique is quite emphatic on the subject of demographic homogeneity. For one thing, homogeneity violates the American Dream of a "balanced" community where people of diverse age, class, race, and religion live together. Allegedly, it creates dullness through sameness. In addition, age homogeneity deprives children—and adults—of the wisdom of their elders, while class, racial, and religious homogeneity prevent children from learning how to live in our pluralistic society. Homogeneity is said to make people callous to the poor, intolerant of Negroes, and scornful of the aged. Finally, heterogeneity is said to allow upward mobility, encouraging working and lower class people to learn middle class ways from their more advanced neighbors. [1]

There is no question that Levittown is quite homogeneous in age and income as compared to established cities and small towns, but such comparisons are in many ways irrelevant. People do not live in the political units we call "cities" or "small towns"; often their social life takes place in areas even smaller than a census tract. Many such areas in the city are about as homogeneous in class as Levittown, and slum and high-income areas, whether urban or suburban, are even more so. Small towns are notoriously rigid in their separation of rich and poor, and only appear to be more heterogeneous because individual neighborhoods are so small. All these considerations effectively question the belief that before the advent of modern suburbs Americans of all classes lived together. Admittedly, statistics compiled for cities and suburbs as a whole show that residential segregation by class and by race are on the increase, but these trends also reflect the breakdown of rigid class and caste systems in which low-status people "knew their place," and which made residential segregation unnecessary.

Reprinted from *The Levittowners,* by Herbert J. Gans (New York: Random House, 1967), pp. 165-72. Copyright © 1967 by Herbert J. Gans. Reprinted by permission of Pantheon Books, a Division of Random House, Inc. and by Penquin Books, Ltd.

By ethnic and religious criteria, Levittown is much less homogeneous than these other areas because people move in as individuals rather than as groups, and the enclaves found in some recently built urban neighborhoods, where 40 to 60 percent of the population comes from one ethnic or religious group, are absent. Nor is Levittown atypically homogeneous in age; new communities and subdivisions always attract young people, but over time, their populations "age" until the distribution resembles that of established communities.[2]

Finally, even class homogeneity is not as great as community-wide statistics would indicate. Of three families earning $7000 a year, one might be a skilled worker at the peak of his earning power and dependent on union activity for further raises; another, a white collar worker with some hope for a higher income; and the third, a young executive or professional at the start of his career. Their occupational and educational differences express themselves in many variations in life style, and if they are neighbors, each is likely to look elsewhere for companionship. Perhaps the best way to demonstrate that Levittown's homogeneity is more statistical than real is to describe my own nearby neighbors. Two were Anglo-Saxon Protestant couples from small towns, the breadwinners employed as engineers; one an agnostic and a golf buff, the other a skeptical Methodist who wanted to be a teacher. Across the backyard lived a Baptist white collar worker from Philadelphia and his Polish-American wife, who had brought her foreign-born mother with her to Levittown; and an Italian-American tractor operator (whose ambition was to own a junkyard) and his upwardly mobile wife, who restricted their social life to a brother down the street and a host of relatives who came regularly every Sunday in a fleet of Cadillacs. One of my next-door neighbors was a religious fundamentalist couple from the Deep South whose life revolved around the church; another was an equally religious Catholic blue collar worker and his wife, he originally a Viennese Jew, she a rural Protestant, who were politically liberal and as skeptical about middle class ways as any intellectual. Across the street, there was another Polish-American couple, highly mobile and conflicted over their obligations to the extended family; another engineer; and a retired Army officer. No wonder Levittowners were puzzled when a nationally known housing expert addressed them on the "pervasive homogeneity of suburban life."

Most Levittowners were pleased with the diversity they found among their neighbors, primarily because regional, ethnic, and religious differences are today most innocuous and provide variety to spice the flow of conversation and the exchange of ideas. For example, my Southern neighbor discovered pizza at the home of the Italian-American neighbor and developed a passion for it, and I learned much about the personal rewards of Catholicism from my Catholic convert neighbors. At the same time, however, Levittowners wanted homogeneity of age and income—or rather, they wanted neighbors and friends with common interests and sufficient consensus of values to make for informal and uninhibited relations. Their reasons were motivated neither by antidemocratic feelings nor by an interest in conformity. Children need playmates of the same age, and because child-rearing problems vary with age, mothers like to be near women who have children of similar age. And because these problems also fluctuate with class, they want some similarity of that factor—not homogeneity of occupation and education so much as agreement on the ends and means of caring for child, husband, and home.

Income similarity is valued by the less affluent, not as an end in itself, but because people who must watch every penny cannot long be comfortable with more affluent neighbors, particularly when children come home demanding toys or clothes they have seen next door. Indeed, objective measures of class are not taken into account in people's associations at all, partly because they do not identify each other in these terms, but also because class differences are not the only criterion for association.[3] Sometimes neighbors of different backgrounds but with similar temperaments find themselves getting along nicely, especially if they learn to avoid activities and topics about which they disagree. For example, two women of diverse origins became good friends because they were both perfectionist housekeepers married to easy-going men, although they once quarreled bitterly over childrearing values.

But Levittowners also want some homogeneity for themselves. As I noted before, cosmopolitans are impatient with locals, and vice versa; women who want to talk about cultural and civic matters are bored by conversation about home and family—and, again, vice versa; working class women who are used to the informal flow of talk with relatives need to find substitutes among neighbors with similar experience. Likewise, young people have little in common with older ones, and unless they want surrogate parents, prefer to socialize with neighbors and friends of similar age. Some Levittowners sought ethnic and religious homogeneity as well. Aside from the Jews and some of the Greeks, Japanese, and the foreign-born women of other nations, observant Catholics and fundamentalist Protestants sought "their own," the former because they were not entirely at ease with non-Catholic neighbors, the latter because their time-consuming church activities and their ascetic life styles set them apart from most other Levittowners. They mixed with their neighbors, of course, but their couple visiting was limited principally to the like-minded. Because of the diversity of ethnic and religious backgrounds, the Philadelphia sample was asked whether there had been any change in the amount of visiting with people of similar "national descent or religious preference"; 30 percent reported a decrease, but 20 percent reported an increase.[4] Those doing less such visiting in Levittown also said they were lonelier than in Philadelphia.

Most people had no difficulty finding the homogeneity they wanted in Levittown. Affluent and well-educated people could move into organizations or look for friends all over Levittown, but older people and people of lower income or poorly educated women were less able to move around either physically or socially. Women from these groups often did not have a car or did not know how to drive; many were reluctant to use baby-sitters for their children, only partly for financial reasons. Heterogeneity then, may be a mixed blessing, particularly on the block, and something can be said for class and age homogeneity.

The alleged costs of homogeneity were also more unreal than the critics claim. It is probably true that Levittowners had less contact with old people than some urbanites (now rather rare) who still live in three-generation households. It is doubtful, however, that they had less contact with the older generation than urban and suburban residents of similar age and class, with the exception of the occupational Transients, who are far from home and may return only once a year. Whether or not this lack of contact with grandparents affects children negatively can only be discovered by systematic studies among them. My observations of children's relations with grandparents suggest that the older generation is strange to them and vice versa, less as a result of lack of contact than of the vastness of generational change.

This is also more or less true of adult relationships with the older generation. Social change in America has been so rapid that the ideas and experiences of the elderly are often anachronistic, especially for young mobile Levittowners whose parents are first or second generation Americans. Philadelphia women who lived with their parents before they moved to Levittown complained at length about the difficulties of raising children and running a household under those conditions, even though some missed their mothers sorely after moving to Levittown. A few found surrogate mothers among friends or neighbors, but chose women only slightly older then themselves and rarely consulted elderly neighbors. As for the husbands, they were, to a man, glad they had moved away from parents and in-laws.

That suburban homogeneity deprives children of contact with urban pluralism and "reality" is also dubious. Critics assume that urban children experience heterogeneity, but middle class parents—and working class ones, too—try hard to shield them from contact with conditions and people of lower status. Upper middle class children may be taken on tours of the city, but to museums and shopping districts rather than to slums. Indeed, slum children, who are freer of parental supervision, probably see more of urban diversity than anyone else, although they do not often get into middle class areas.

The homogeneity of Levittown is not so pervasive that children are shielded from such unpleasant realities as alcoholism, mental illness, family strife, sexual aberration, or juvenile delinquency which exist everywhere. The one element missing on most Levittown blocks—though, of course, in many city neighborhoods too—is the presence of Negro families. Although young Negro women came from nearby Burlington to work as maids, there were only two Negro families in the three neighborhoods built before Levittown's integration, and about fifty in the three built since then. Most Levittown children are unlikely to see any Negroes among them and will not have real contact with them until they enter junior high school. But it is not at all certain that mere visual exposure—to Negroes or anyone else—encourages learning of pluralism and tolerance. Children pick up many of their attitudes from parents and peers, and these are not necessarily pluralistic. If visual exposure had the positive effects attributed to it, city children, who see more Negroes than suburban children do, should exhibit greater racial tolerance. In reality they do not; indeed, the middle class child growing up in a white suburb may be more opposed to segregation than one raised in an integrated city. This is not a justification for segregation, but a suggestion that visual exposure is no sure means to integration.

A generation of social research has demonstrated that racial and other forms of integration occur when diverse people can interact frequently in equal and noncompetitive situations.[5] Here the suburbs are at an advantage when it comes to religious and ethnic integration, but at a disadvantage for racial and class integration, for aside from residential segregation, suburban high schools bring together students from a narrower variety of residential areas than do urban ones. Again, mere diversity does not assure the kind of interaction that encourages integration, and a school with great diversity but sharp internal segregation may not be as desirable as one with less diversity but without internal segregation. Judging by life on the block in Levittown, maximal diversity and extreme heterogeneity encourage more conflict than integration, and while conflict can be desirable and even didactic, this is only true if it can be resolved in some way. People so different from each other in age or class that they cannot agree on anything are unlikely to derive much enrichment from heterogeneity.

A corollary of the belief in diversity as a stimulant to enrichment holds that working class and lower class people will benefit—and be improved— by living among middle class neighbors. Even if one overlooks the patronizing class bias implicit in this view, it is not at all certain that residential propinquity will produce the intended cultural change. In Levittown, working class families living alongside middle class ones went their own way most of the time. For mobile ones, heterogeneity is obviously desirable, provided middle class people are willing to teach them, but nonmobile ones will react negatively to force feedings of middle class culture. Neighbors are expected to treat each other as equals, and working class residents have enough difficulty paying the higher cost of living among middle class people, without being viewed as culturally deprived. When working class organizations used middle class Levittowners for technical and administrative services, they rejected those who looked down on them and constantly tested the others to make sure they measured up to the norms of working class culture. For example, at a VFW softball game, two middle class members were razzed unmercifully for their lack of athletic skill. Children are not yet fully aware of class, so that they can be with (and learn from) peers of other classes, and there is some evidence that in schools with a majority of middle class children, working class children will adopt the formers' standards of school performance, and vice versa.[6]

By its very nature, demographic homogeneity is said to be incompatible with democracy, and advocates of diversity have emphasized that a democracy requires a heterogeneous community. However, as the description of Levittown's school and political conflict should indicate, bringing people with different interests together does not automatically result in the use of democratic procedures. Instead, it causes conflict, difficulties in decision-making, and attempts to sidestep democratic norms. If one group is threatened by another's demands, intolerance may even increase. Indeed, democratic procedure is often so fragile that it falls by the wayside under such stress, causing hysteria on the part of residents and the sort of panic on the part of the officials that I described. The fact is that the democratic process probably works more smoothly in a homogenous population. Absence of conflict is of course a spurious goal, particularly in a pluralistic society, and cannot be used as an argument for homogeneity. On the other hand, unless conflict becomes an end in itself, heterogeneity is not a viable argument for greater democracy,

Critics of the suburbs also inveigh against physical homogeneity and mass-produced housing. Like much of the rest of the critique, this charge is a thinly veiled attack on the culture of working and lower middle class people, implying that mass-produced housing leads to mass-produced lives. The critics seem to forget that the town houses of the upper class in the nineteenth century were also physically homogeneous; that everyone, poor and rich alike, drives mass-produced, homogeneous cars without damage to their personalities; and that today, only the rich can afford custom-built housing. I heard no objection among the Levittowners about the similarity of their homes, nor the popular jokes about being unable to locate one's own house.[7] Esthetic diversity is preferred, however, and people talked about moving to a custom-built house in the future when they could afford it. Meanwhile, they made internal and external alterations in their Levitt house to reduce sameness and to place a personal stamp on their property.[8]

NOTES

1. For an incisive critique of the balanced community ideal, see Harold Orlans, *Utopia Limited: The Story of the English Town of Stevenage* (New Haven: Yale University Press, 1953), pp. 88-94.

2. For a description of this trend in the first Levittown, see John T. Liell, "Social Relationships in a Changing Suburb: A Restudy of Levittown," paper presented at the 1963 meeting of The American Sociological Association. See also Peter Willmott, *The Evolution of a Community* (London: Routledge and Kegan Paul, 1963), p. 23.

3. For similar findings in Fairless Hills, Pennsylvania, see Ann Haeberle, *Friendship as an Aspect of Interpersonal Relations: A Study of Friendship among Women Residents of a Small Community,* unpublished Ph.D. dissertation, New York University, April 1956, p. 75.

4. Forty-four per cent said they had done "much" visiting with ethnic or religious peers in Philadelphia, and 52 per cent, "some." In Levittown, the percentages shifted slightly, to 37 and 66, respectively. Respondents were free to define what they considered "much" or "some." Jews and low-status people reported the most ethnic-religious visiting; Irish Catholics, the greatest increase after moving to Levittown.

5. See, e.g., Robin M. Williams, Jr., "Racial and Cultural Relations," in Joseph P. Cuttler, ed., *Review of Sociology: Analysis of a Decade* (New York: Wiley, 1957), pp. 437-447.

6. See, e.g., Alan B. Wilson, "Class Segregation and Aspirations of Youth," *American Sociological Review* 24 (December 1959): 836-845, but also the study by Sewell and Armer which questioned the impact of "neighborhood context" on educational aspirations. Of course, in school students are a captive audience, and school contacts among working and middle class students may evaporate after school hours.

7. A study of a Scottish new town reported that "only one-fifth of the tenants said they would prefer more variety and intermixture of house-types, while two-fifths regarded the row of identical buildings as a desirable feature," and that "a house which is one of many in a street can become personalized without much aid from the architect." See Vere Hole, "Social Effects of Planned Rehousing," *Town Planning Review* (London) 30 (July 1959): 161-173, esp. p. 169.

8. It is illuminating to compare the early popular writing about Levittown, New York, to more recent reports. Initially, the Long Island community was widely described (and decried) as a hideous example of mass-produced housing which would soon turn into a slum; twenty years later, journalists report the diversity produced by the alteration of houses, and the charm created by the maturing of trees and shrubbery—and, of course, the demand for the houses, which now sell for about twice their original price.

ARTHUR J. VIDICH
JOSEPH BENSMAN

Small Town
in
Mass Society

THE AMBIVALENT ATTITUDE
TO MASS SOCIETY

Springdalers have a decided respect for the great institutions that
characterize American society. The efficiency, organizational ability and
farflung activities of giant government and business enterprise inspire
them with awe. The military might of the nation and the productive
capacity of industry lend a Springdaler a sense of pride and security, and
the continuous development and successful application of science assure
him that he is a participant in the most forward-looking and progressive
country in the world. Anyone who would attack the great institutions of
America would have no audience in Springdale: "Everybody knows this
country wouldn't be what it is if it weren't for free enterprise and the
democratic form of government." When the Springdaler is on the
defensive he will tell the critic, "If you don't like it here you can go back to
where you came from."

The Springdaler also sees that the urban and metropolitan society is
technically and culturally superior to his own community. He sees this in
his everyday life when he confronts the fact that his community cannot
provide him with everything he needs: almost everyone goes to the city for
shopping or entertainment; large numbers of people are dependent on the
radio and television; and everyone realizes that rural life would be
drastically altered without cars and refrigerators. Springdalers clearly
realize how much of local life is based on the modern techniques,
equipment and products which originate in distant places.

The community is constantly dependent on cultural and material

Reprinted from Arthur J. Vidich and Joseph Bensman, *Small Town in Mass Society:
Class, Power and Religion in Rural Community* (Princeton, N.J.: Princeton University Press,
1958), pp. 79-86, 98-100. Copyright © 1958; rev. edition © 1968 by Princeton University
Press; Princeton Paperback, 1968. Reprinted by permission.

imports and welcomes these as a way of "keeping up with the times." However, they believe that the very technical and cultural factors that make for the superiority of the "outside" also account for the problems of living that cities exhibit. The "city masses," while they have easier access to progress, are also the ready-made victims of the negative aspects of progress. In contrast, rural life, because it is geographically distant, can enjoy progress and avoid the worst features of the industrial mass society; Springdalers can believe that they are in a position to choose and utilize only the best of two worlds, that the importations, if properly chosen, need not affect the inner life of the community.

Because it is possible to choose only the best, the Springdaler can believe, that in spite of some disadvantages, his is the better of two worlds. This belief in the autonomy or, at worst, the self-selective dependency of rural life makes it possible for the community member publicly to voice the following conceptions concerning the relationship between his town and mass society:

1. That the basic traditions of American society—"grass-roots democracy," free and open expression, individualism—are most firmly located in rural society. The American heritage is better preserved in the small town because it can resist bad city influences and thereby preserve the best of the past.
2. That the future hope of American society lies in rural life because it has resisted all "isms" and constitutes the only major bulwark against them.
3. That much of the progress of society is the result of rural talent which has migrated to the cities. In this way rural society has a positive influence on urban life; rural migrants account for the virtues of city life. "Everyone knows that most of the outstanding men in the country were raised in small towns" and Springdalers proudly point to several local names that have made good on the outside.
4. That "when you live in a small town you can take or leave the big cities—go there when you want to and always come back without having to live as they do." There is the belief that "if more people lived in small towns, you wouldn't have all those problems."

These summarize the types of beliefs that are frequently stated in public situations. The observer who is willing to go beyond the public statements discovers that Springdale has a great variety of direct and intimate connections with a wide range of institutions of the mass society. Moreover, these institutions affect many phases of the community, have consequences for its internal local functioning and in some ways control the direction of social change within it.

Springdale is connected with the mass society in a variety of different forms. The cumulative effect of these various connections makes possible the continuous transmission of outside policies, programs and trends into the community, even though the effects of the transmission and the transmitting agents themselves are not always seen. Outside influences can be transmitted directly by a socially visible agent such as the extension specialist who lives in the community for the purpose of acting upon it. Outside interests and influences can also be expressed indirectly through members of the community: policies and programs of relatively invisible outside interests are transmitted by *heads* of local branches of state and national organizations, by *heads* of local businesses dependent on outside resources and by *heads* of churches attached to larger organizations. In some instances the community is affected by the consequences of decisions made by business and government which are made with specific reference to the community, i.e., the decision to build a state road through the community or the decision to close down a factory. Plans and decisions that refer directly to the community are made from a distance by invisible agents and institutions. Perhaps most important are the mass decisions of business and government which are transmitted to the rural scene by the consequences of changes in prices, costs and communications. These affect the town even though they are not explicitly directed at it, and they comprise the invisible social chain reactions of decisions that are made in centers of power in government, business and industry. The invisible social chain reactions emanating from the outside no doubt alter the life of the community more seriously than the action of visible agents such as the extension specialist.

These types of transmission do not represent mutually exclusive channels, but rather exist in complex interrelationship with each other. They merely suggest the major ways in which the community is influenced by dynamics which occur in the institutions of mass society. How these combined dynamics in their various combinations affect the fabric of life in Springdale can be seen by examining the way in which cultural importations and economic and political connections shape the character of community life. In their net effect they influence the psychological dimension of the community.

CULTURAL IMPORTATIONS FROM MASS SOCIETY

The external agents of cultural diffusion range from specific observable individuals placed in the local community by outside institutions to the impact of mass media of communications and successive waves of migration. The consequence of these modes of diffusion lies in the effect which they have on local styles of living.

FORMAL IMPORTING ORGANIZATIONS
The adult extension program of the land grant college is mediated at the local level by the county agent and the home demonstration agent who

respectively are concerned with farming methods and production, and patterns of homemaking and family life. These agents carry out their program through the Farm and Home Bureau organizations. In Springdale township these agencies have a membership of 300-400 adults. The county agent is primarily concerned with introducing modern methods of farm production and operation and with fostering political consciousness among the farmers. As a type of executive secretary to the local Farm Bureau whose officers are local farmers, the agent acts as an advisor in planning the organization's program, which includes such items as production and marketing problems, parity price problems and taxation problems.

The organizational structure of the Home Bureau parallels the Farm Bureau. From skills and techniques and personnel available at the extension center, local programs consist, for example, of furniture refinishing or aluminum working as well as discussions on such topics as child-rearing, nutrition, penal institutions and interior design. The Home Bureau extension specialist trains a local woman in information and techniques which are reported back to the local club. This program, geared as it is to modern home-making, child-rearing and the feminine role, has the effect of introducing new styles and standards of taste and consumption for the membership.

Other institutional connectors similar to the above in organizational structure account for the introduction of still other social values and social definitions. The 4-H Club, the Future Farmers of America and the Boy and Girl Scouts, as well as the Masons, Odd Fellows, American Legion, Grange and other local branches of national organizations and their auxiliaries, relate the Springdaler to the larger society through the social meanings and styles of activity defined in the programs, procedures and rituals of the national headquarters. State and national conventions, but not office holding, of these as well as church organizations directly link individuals to the outside. In effect these arrangements regularize and institutionalize the communication and organizational nexus between the small town and the point of origin of new ideas and values.

New cultural standards are also imported by agents who are not permanent residents of the town or who have only a transient relationship with it. These include the teachers at the central school, many of whom view their jobs as a temporary interlude in a progression of experience which will lead to a position in a city system. The other agents of contact are a wide variety of salesmen and "experts" who have a regular or irregular contact with business, government and private organizations. From the surrounding urban centers and the regional sales offices of farm implement and automobile manufacturers and nationally branded products, modern methods of merchandizing and business practice are introduced. Experts in civil defense, evangelism, fire-fighting, gardening, charity drives, traffic control and youth recreation introduce new techniques and programs to the local community. This great variety and diversity of semi-permanent and changing contacts in their cumulative effect act as a perpetual blood transfusion to local society. The net effect that these agents have as transmitters of life styles depends in a measure on their position and prestige in the community. The differential effect of these cultural contacts is treated below.

THE UBIQUITY OF MASS MEDIA

Social diffusion through the symbols and pictorial images of the mass media of communications has permeated the community, reducing the local paper to reporting of social items and local news already known by everyone. Few individuals read only the local weekly paper; the majority subscribe to dailies published in surrounding cities and in the large metropolitan areas. This press, itself part of larger newspaper combines, presents an image of the passing scene in its news and nationally syndicated features to which the population of an entire region is exposed.

The mass culture and mass advertising of television and radio reach Springdale in all their variety. Television, particularly, is significant in its impact because for the first time the higher art forms such as ballet, opera and plays are visible to a broad rural audience. National events such as party conventions, inaugurations and investigative hearings are visible now to an audience which was previously far removed from the national centers of action and drama. Because of the relative geographic isolation of Springdale, television has made available entirely new areas of entertainment, information and education. It has created new leisure-time interests, has introduced new modes of leisure-time consumption and has led to the acceptance of standardized entertainment models. Wrestling, Arthur Godfrey and Howdy-Doody are common symbols of entertainment. Equally available and pervasive among the classes and individuals to whom they appeal are pocket books, comic books, and horror and sex stories. Micky Spillane, Willie Mays, Davy Crockett and other nationally prominent personages as well as nationally branded products are as well known and available to the small town as they are to the big city. The intrusion of the mass media is so overwhelming that little scope is left for the expression of local cultural and artistic forms.

However, the diffusion of the printed word is not limited to the mass media; it is present also in the realm of education, both religious and secular. The state department of education syllabus defines minimum standards and content for subject matter instruction. Courses of Sunday School instruction are available for all age levels, and each faith secures its material from its own national religious press. In each of these major institutional areas the standards and *content* of instruction are defined in sources available only in standardized form.

THE IMMIGRANT AS CULTURAL CARRIER

Specific individuals are carriers of cultural diffusion, and the volume and extent of migration in and out of the community suggests the degree and intimacy of its contact with the mass society. In a community which is regarded as stable and relatively unchanging by its own inhabitants, only 25 percent of its population was born locally. Another 25 percent has moved into the community since 1946 and 55 percent are new to the community since 1920. Moreover, of the 45 percent who have moved to the community since 1932, more than 30 percent have lived for a year or longer in cities with populations in excess of 25,000; 7 percent in cities with populations in excess of one-half million.

Each decade and each generation introduces a new layer of immigrants to the community. The agricultural and business prosperity of the 1940's and early 1950's has brought city dwellers to farms and to businesses on main street, and the housing shortage has led workers to reclaim long-abandoned farm dwellings. The 12 percent of new people who moved into Springdale in the Thirties came in response to the effects of the depression. From 1918 to 1928 the Poles moved onto farms abandoned by descendants of original settlers. Indeed, the ebb and flow of migration extends back to such eras of political and economic upheaval as the depression of the 1890's and the mass movement of people during the Indian Wars and the opening of the territory in the early 1800's. Each new wave of immigrants, bringing with it the fashions and thought styles of other places, influences the cultural development of the community.

The cumulative consequences of these channels of diffusion and the quantity and quality of the "material" diffused denies the existence of a culture indigenous to the small town. In almost all aspects of culture, even to speech forms, and including technology, literature, fashions, and fads, as well as patterns of consumption, to mention a few, the small town tends to reflect the contemporary mass society.

Basically, an historically indigenous local culture does not seem to exist. The cultural imports of each decade and generation and the successive waves of migration associated with each combine to produce a local culture consisting of layers or segments of the mass culture of successive historical eras. In the small town the remaining elements of the gay-ninety culture are juxtaposed against the modern central school. The newer cultural importations frequently come in conflict with the older importations of other eras. The conflict between "spurious" and "genuine" culture appears to be a conflict between two different ages of "spurious" culture.

THE POLITICAL SURRENDER TO MASS SOCIETY

Local political institutions consist of a village board, a town board and local committees of the Republican and Democratic parties. The jurisdiction of the village board includes powers of control and regulation over a variety of community facilities and services—street lighting, water supply, fire protection, village roads, street signs and parks. To carry out the functions empowered to it, it possesses the power of taxation. The town board is concerned chiefly with fire protection, the construction and maintenance of roads; through its participation on the county board of supervisors, it participates in programs connected with welfare, penal and other county services.

However, at almost every point in this seemingly broad base of political domain the village and town boards adjust their action to either the regulations and laws defined by state and federal agencies which claim parallel functions on a statewide or nationwide basis or to the fact that outside agencies have the power to withhold subsidies to local political institutions.

Local assessment scales and tax rates are oriented to state equalization formulas which partially provide the standardized basis on which subsidies are dispersed by the state. State highway construction and development programs largely present local political agencies with the alternative of either accepting or rejecting proposed road plans and programs formulated by the state highway department.

The village board, more than the town board, is dependent on its own taxable resources (taxes account for almost half its revenues) and best illustrates the major dimensions of local political action. The village board in Springdale accepts few of the powers given to it. Instead, it orients its action to the facilities and subsidies controlled and dispensed by other agencies and, by virtue of this, forfeits its own political power. Solutions to the problem of fire protection are found in agreements with regionally organized fire districts. In matters pertaining to road signs and street signs action typically takes the form of petitioning state agencies to fulfill desired goals "without cost to the taxpayer." On roads built and maintained by the state there is no recourse but to accept the state traffic bureau's standards of safety. A problem such as snow removal is solved by dealing directly with the foreman of the state highway maintenance crew through personal contacts: "If you treat him right, you can get him to come in and clear the village roads." In other areas of power where there are no parallel state agencies, such as for garbage collection or parks, the village board abdicates its responsibility.

As a consequence of this pattern of dependence, many important decisions are made for Springdale by outside agencies. Decisions which are made locally tend to consist of approving the requirements of administrative or state laws. In short the program and policies of local political bodies are determined largely by acceptance of grants-in-aid offered them—i.e., in order to get the subsidy specific types of decisions must be made—and by facilities and services made available to them by outside sources.

Psychologically this dependence leads to an habituation to outside control to the point where the town and village governments find it hard to act even where they have the power. Legal jurisdictions have been supplanted by psychological jurisdictions to such an extent that local political action is almost exclusively oriented to and predicated on seeking favors, subsidies and special treatment from outside agencies. The narrowing of legal jurisdictions by psychologically imposed limits leads to an inability to cope with local problems if outside resources are not available.

Power in local political affairs, then, tends to be based on accessibility to sources of decision in larger institutions. Frequently this accessibility consists merely of the knowledge of the source, or it may mean a personal contact, or an ability to correspond to get necessary information. Under these circumstances, power in the political arena is delegated to those with contacts in and knowledge of the outer world and to those who are experts in formal communication with impersonal bureaucratic offices. These are, on the individual level, the lawyer and, on an institutional level, the political party. The lawyer gains his paramountcy through technical knowledge and personalized non-party contacts up the political hierarchy with other lawyers. He is the mediator between the local party and the party hierarchy, and transforms his personalized contacts into political indispensability in the local community. His access to outside sources of power determines his power and predominance in the local community.

DANIEL LERNER

The Grocer and
The Chief:
A Parable

The Village of Balgat lies about eight kilometers out of Ankara, in the southerly direction. It does not show on the standard maps and it does not figure in the standard histories. I first heard of it in the autumn of 1950 and most Turks have not heard of it today. Yet the story of the Middle East today is encapsulated in the recent career of Balgat. Indeed the personal meaning of modernization in underdeveloped lands can be traced, in miniature, through the lives of two Balgati—The Grocer and The Chief....

BALGAT PERCEIVED: 1950

The interviewer who recorded Balgat on the verge—his name was Tosun B.—had detected no gleam of the future during his sojourn there. "The village is a barren one," he wrote. "The main color is gray, so is the dust on the divan on which I am writing now." Tosun was a serious young scholar from Ankara and he loved the poor in his own fashion. He had sought out Balgat to find the deadening past rather than the brave new world. He found it:

> I have seen quite a lot of villages in the barren mountainous East, but never such a colorless, shapless dump. This was the reason I chose the village. It could have been half an hour to Ankara by car if it had a road, yet it is about two hours to the capital by car without almost any road and is just forgotten, forsaken, right under our noses.

Tosun also sought and found persons to match the place. Of the five villagers he interviewed, his heart went straight out to the village shepherd. What Tosun was looking for in this interview is clear from his *obiter dicta:*

Abridged with permission of The Macmillan Company and the author from *The Passing of Traditional Society* by Daniel Lerner (New York: Free Press, 1958), pp. 19, 20-28, 33-38.© by the Free Press, a Corporation, 1958.

It was hard to explain to the village Chief that I wanted to interview the poorest soul in the village. He, after long discussions, consented me to interview the shepherd, but did not permit him to step into the guestroom. He said it would be an insult to me, so we did the interview in someone else's room, I did not quite understand whose. The Chief did not want to leave me along with the respondent, but I succeeded at the end. This opened the respondent's sealed mouth, for he probably felt that I, the superior even to his chief, rather be alone with him.

When the shepherd's sealed mouth had been opened little came out. But Tosun was deeply stirred:

The respondent was literally in rags and in this cold weather he had no shoe, but the mud and dirt on his feet were as thick as any boot. He was small, but looked rugged and sad, very sad. He was proud of being chosen by me and though limited tried his best to answer the questions. Was so bashful that his blush was often evident under the thick layer of dirt on his face. He at times threw loud screams of laughter when there was nothing to laugh about. These he expected to be accepted as answers, for when I said "Well?" he was shocked, as if he had already answered the question.

His frustration over the shepherd was not the only deprivation Tosun attributed to the Chief, who "imposed himself on me all the time I was in the village, even tried to dictate to me, which I refused in a polite way. I couldn't have followed his directions as I would have ended up only interviewing his family." Tosun did succeed in talking privately with two Balgat farmers, but throughout these interviews he was still haunted by the shepherd and bedeviled by the Chief. Not until he came to interview the village Grocer did Tosun find another Balgati who aroused in him a comparable antipathy. Tosun's equal hostility to these very different men made me curious. It was trying to explain this that got me obsessed, sleeping and waking over the next four years, with the notion that the parable of modern Turkey was the story of the Grocer and The Chief.

Aside from resenting the containment strategy which the Chief was operating against him, Tosun gave few details about the man. He reported only the impression that "the *Muhtar* is an unpleasant old man. Looks mean and clever. He is the absolute dictator of this little village." Nor did Tosun elaborate his disapproval of the *Muhtar's* opinions beyond the comment that "years have left him some sort of useless mystic wisdom." As a young man of empirical temper, Tosun might be expected to respond with some diffidence to the wisdom of the ancients. But the main source of Tosun's hostility, it appeared, was that the Chief made him nervous. His notes concluded: "He found what I do curious, even probably suspected it. I am sure he will report it to the first official who comes to the village."

Against the Grocer, however, Tosun reversed his neural field. He quickly perceived that he made the Grocer nervous; and for this Tosun disliked *him*. His notes read:

The respondent is comparatively the most city-like dressed man in the village. He even wore some sort of a necktie. He is the village's only grocer, but he is not really a grocer, but so he is called, originally the food-stuffs in his shop are much less than the things to be worn, like the cheapest of materials and shoes and slippers, etc. His greatest stock is drinks and cigarettes which he sells most. He is a very unimpressive type, although physically he covers quite a space. He gives the impression of a fat shadow. Although he is on the same level with the other villagers, when there are a few of the villagers around, he seems to want to distinguish himself by keeping quiet, and as soon as they depart he starts to talk too much. This happened when we were about to start the interview. He most evidently wished to feel that he is closer to me than he is to them and was curiously careful with his accent all during the interview. In spite of his unique position, for he is the only unfarming person and the only merchant in the village, he does not seem to possess an important part of the village community. In spite of all his efforts, he is considered by the villagers even less than the least farmer. Although he presented to take the interview naturally, he was nervous and also was proud to be interviewed although he tried to hide it.

All of this pushed up a weighty question: Why did the Chief make Tosun nervous and why did Tosun make the Grocer nervous? These three men representing such different throughtways and lifeways, were a test for each other. Looking for answers, I turned to the responses each had made to the 57 varieties of opinions called for by the standard questionnaire used in Tosun's interviews.

The Chief was a man of few words on many subjects. He dismissed most of the items on Tosun's schedule with a shrug or its audible equivalent. But he was also a man of many words on a few subjects—those having to do with the primary modes of human deportment. Only when the issues involved first principles of conduct did he consider the occasion appropriate for pronouncing judgment. Of the Chief it might be said, as Henry James said of George Eliot's salon style, *"Elle n'aborde que les grandes thèmes."*

The Chief has so little trouble with first principles because he desires to be, and usually is, a vibrant soundbox through which echo the traditional Turkish virtues. His themes are obedience, courage, loyalty—the classic values of the Ottoman Imperium reincarnate in the Atatürk Republic. For the daily round of village life these are adequate doctrine; and as the Chief has been outside of his village only to fight in two wars he has never found his austere code wanting. This congruence of biography with ideology explains the Chief's confidence in his own moral judgment and his short definition of a man. When asked what he wished for his two grown sons, for example, the Chief replied promptly: "I hope they will fight as bravely as we fought and know how to die as my generation did."

From this parochial fund of traditional virtues, the Chief drew equally his opinions of great men, nations, issues. The larger dramas of international *politique* he judged solely in terms of the courage and loyalty of the actors, invoking, to acknowledge their magnitude, the traditional rhetoric of aphorism. Generations of Anatolian *Muhtars* resonated as he pronounced his opinion of the British:

> I hear that they have turned friends with us. But always stick to the old wisdom: "A good enemy is better than a bad friend." You cannot *rely* on them. Who has heard of a son being friends with his father's murderers?

With his life in Balgat, as with the Orphic wisdom that supplies its rationale, the Chief is contented. At 63 his desires have been quieted and his ambitions achieved. To Tosun's question on contentment he replied with another question:

> What could be asked more? God has brought me to this mature age without much pain, has given me sons and daughters, has put me at the head of my village, and has given me strength of brain and body at this age. Thanks be to Him.

The Grocer is a very different style of man. Though born and bred in Balgat, he lives in a different world, an expansive world, populated more actively with imaginings and fantasies—hungering for whatever is different and unfamiliar. Where the Chief is contented, the Grocer is restless. To Tosun's probe, the Grocer replied staccato: "I have told you I want better things. I would have liked to have a bigger grocery shop in the city, have a nice house there, dress nice civilian clothes."

Where the Chief audits his life placidly, makes no comparisons, thanks God, the Grocer evaluates his history in a more complicated and other-involved fashion. He perceives his story as a drama of Self *versus* Village. He compares his virtue with others and finds them lacking: "I am not like the others here. They don't know any better. And when I tell them, they are angry and they say that I am ungrateful for what Allah has given me." The Grocer's struggle with Balgat was, in his script, no mere conflict of personalities. His was the lonely struggle of a single man to open the village mind. Clearly, from the readiness and consistency of his responses to most questions, he had brooded much over his role. He had a keen sense of the limits imposed by reality: "I am born a grocer and probably die that way. I have not the possibility in myself to get the things I want. They only bother me." But desire, once stirred, is not easily stilled.

Late in the interview, after each respondent had named the greatest problem facing the Turkish people, Tosun asked what he would do about his problem if he were the president of Turkey. Most responded by stolid silence—the traditional way of handling "projective questions" which require people to imagine themselves or things to be different from what they "really are." Some were shocked by the impropriety of the very question. "My God! How can you say such a thing?" gasped the shepherd. "How can I . . . I cannot . . . a poor villager . . . master of the whole world."[1]

The Chief, Balgat's virtuoso of the traditional style, made laconic reply to this question with another question: "I am hardly able to manage a village, how shall I manage Turkey?" When Tosun probed further ("What would you suggest for *your village* that you cannot handle yourself?"), the Chief said he would seek "help of money and seed for some of our farmers." When the Grocer's turn came, he did not wait for the question to be circumscribed in terms of local reference. As president of Turkey, he said: "I would make roads for the villagers to come to towns to see the world and would not let them stay in their holes all their life."

To get out of his hole the Grocer even declared himself ready—and in this he was quite alone in Balgat—to live outside of Turkey. This came out when Tosun asked another of his projective questions: "If you could not live in Turkey, where would you want to live?" The standard reply of the villagers was that they would not live, could not imagine living, anywhere else. The forced choice simply was ignored.

When Tosun persisted ("Suppose you *had* to leave Turkey?") he teased an extreme reaction out of some Balgati. The shepherd, like several other wholly routinized personalities, finally replied that he would rather kill himself. The constricted peasant can more easily imagine destroying the self than relocating it in an unknown, i.e. frightful, setting.

The Chief again responded with the clear and confident voice of traditional man. "Nowhere," he said. "I was born here, grew old here, and hope God will permit me to die here." To Tosun's probe, the Chief replied firmly: "I wouldn't move a foot from here." Only the Grocer found no trouble in imagining himself outside of Turkey, living in a strange land. Indeed he seemed fully prepared, as a man does when he has already posed a question to himself many times. "America," said the Grocer, and, without waiting for Tosun to ask him why, stated his reason: "because I have heard that it is a nice country, and with possibilities to be rich even for the simplest persons."

Such opinions clearly marked off the Grocer, in the eyes of the villagers around him, as heterodox and probably infidel. The vivid sense of cash displayed by the Grocer was a grievous offense against Balgat ideas of tabu talk. In the code regulating the flow of symbols among Anatolian villagers, blood and sex are permissible objects of passion but money is not. To talk much of money is an impropriety. To reveal excessive *desire* for money is—Allah defend us!—an impiety.[2]

Balgati might forgive the Grocer his propensity to seek the strange rather than reverse the familiar, even his readiness to forsake Turkey for unknown places, had he decently clothed these impious desires in pious terms. But to abandon Balgat for the world's fleshpots, to forsake the ways of God to seek the ways of cash, this was insanity. The demented person who spoke thus was surely accursed and unclean.

The Grocer with his "city-dressed" ways, his "eye at the higher places" and his visits to Ankara, provoked the Balgati to wrathful and indignant restatements of the old code. But occasional, and apparently trivial, items in the survey suggested that some Balgati were talking loud about the Grocer to keep their own inner voices from being overheard by the Chief—or even by themselves.

As we were interested in knowing who says what to whom in such a village as Balgat, Tosun had been instructed to ask each person whether others ever came to him for advice, and if so what they wanted advice about. Naturally, the Balgati whose advice was most sought was the Chief, who reported: "Yes, that is my main duty, to give advice. (Tosun: *What about?*) About all that I or you could imagine, even about their wives and how to handle them, and how to cure their sick cow." This conjunction of wives and cows, to illustrate all the Chief could imagine, runs the gamut only from A to B. These are the species that the villager has most to do with in his daily round of life, the recurrent source of his pains and pleasures and puzzlements. The oral literature abounds in examples of *Muhtar* (or his theological counterpart, the *Hoca*) as wise man dispensing judgment equally about women and cows.

Rather more surprising was Tosun's discovery that some Balgati went for advice also to the disreputable Grocer. What did they ask *his* advice about? "What to do when they go to Ankara, where to go and what to buy, how much to sell their things." The cash nexus, this suggested, was somehow coming to Balgat and with it, possibly, a new role for the Grocer as cosmopolitan specialist in how to avoid wooden nickels in the big city. Also, how to spend the real nickels one got. For the Grocer was a man of clear convictions on which coffee-houses played the best radio programs and which were the best movies to see in Ankara. While his opinions on these matters were heterodox as compared say, to the Chief's, they had an open field to work in. Most Balgati had never heard a radio or seen a movie and were not aware of what constituted orthodoxy with respect to them. Extremists had nonetheless decided that these things, being new, were obviously evil. Some of them considered the radio to be "the voice of the Devil coming from his deep hiding-place" and said they would smash any such "Devil's-box" on sight.

At the time of Tosun's visit, there was only one radio in Balgat, owned by no less a personage than the Chief. In the absence of any explicit orthodox prohibition on radio, the Chief, former soldier and great admirer of Atatürk, had followed his lead. Prosperous by village standards, being the large landowner of Balgat, he had bought a radio to please and instruct his sons. He had also devised an appropriate ceremonial for its use. Each evening a select group of Balgati foregathered in the Chief's guest room as he turned on the newscast from Ankara. They heard the newscast through in silence and, at its conclusion, the Chief turned the radio off and made his commentary. "We all listen very carefully," he told Tosun, "and I talk about it afterwards." Tosun, suspecting in this procedure a variant of the Chief's containment tactics, wanted to know whether there was any disagreement over his explanations. "No, no arguments," replied the Chief, "as I tell you I only talk and our opinions are the same more or less." Here was a new twist in the ancient role of knowledge as power. Sensing the potential challenge from radio, the Chief restricted the dangers of innovation by partial incorporation, thus retaining and strengthening his role as Balgat's official opinion leader.

Tosun inquired of the Grocer, an occasional attendant at the Chief's salon, how he liked this style of radio session. The grocer, a heretic perhaps but not a foolhardy one, made on this point the shortest statement in his entire interview: "The Chief is clever and he explains the news." Only obliquely, by asking what the Grocer liked best about radio, did Tosun get an answer that had the true resonance. Without challenging the Chief's preference for news of "wars and the danger of wars"—in fact an exclusive interest in the Korean War, to which a Turkish brigade had just been committed—the Grocer indicated that after all *he* had opportunities to listen in the coffee-houses of Ankara, where the audiences exhibited a more cosmopolitan range of interests. "It is nice to know what is happening in the other capitals of the world," said the Grocer. "We are stuck in this hole, we have to know what is going on outside our village."

The Grocer had his own aesthetic of the movies as well. Whereas the Chief had been to the movies several times, he viewed them mainly as a moral prophylactic: "There are fights, shooting. The people are brave. My sons are always impressed. Each time they see such a film they wish more and more their time for military service would come so that they would become soldiers too." For the Grocer, the movies were more than a homily on familiar themes. They were his avenue to the wider world of his dreams. It was in a movie that he had first glimpsed what a *real* grocery store could be like—"with walls made of iron sheets, top to floor and side to side, and on them standing myriads of round boxes, clean and all the same dressed, like soldiers in a great parade." This fleeting glimpse of what sounds like the Campbell Soup section of an A & P supermarket had provided the Grocer with an abiding image of how his fantasy world might look. It was here, quite likely, that he had shaped the ambition earlier confided to Tosun, "to have a bigger grocery shop in the city." No pedantries intervened in the Grocer's full sensory relationship to the movies. No eye had he, like the Chief, for their value as filial moral rearmament and call to duty. The Grocer's judgments were formed in unabashedly hedonist categories. "The Turkish ones," he said, "are gloomy, ordinary. I can guess at the start of the film how it will end. . . . The American ones are exciting. You know it makes people ask what will happen next?"

Here, precisely, arose the local variant of a classic question. In Balgat, the Chief carried the sword, but did the Grocer steer the pen? When Balgati sought his advice on how to get around Ankara, would they then go to movies that taught virtue or those that taught excitement? True, few villagers had ever been to Ankara. But things were changing in Turkey and many more Balgati were sure to have a turn or two around the big city before they died. What would happen next in Balgat if more people discovered the tingle of wondering what will happen next? Would things continue along the way of the Chief or would they take the way of the Grocer?

(Editors' note: In 1954 Lerner visited Balgat to see what changes, if any, had occurred in the community since the first set of interviews. He took with him one of the original interviewers (Tahir S.) and a new interviewer (Zilla K.). The effects of urbanization were apparent immediately on his arrival in the village: there was regular bus service to the capitol, telegraph lines ran above many of the streets, and there were now 500 houses where there had been 50. Lerner went immediately to call on the old chief to win his permission to interview the villagers. The necessary permission was given. We rejoin the author's narrative as he reviews his notes from his conversation with the chief.)

As I review my notes on that tour of monologue-with-choral-murmurs, he appears to have certified the general impression that many changes had occurred in Balgat. His inventory included, at unwholesome length, all the by-now familiar items: road, bus, electricity, water. In his recital these great events did not acquire a negative charge, but they lost some of their luster. The tough old farmer did not look shining at new styles of architecture, nor did he look scowling, but simply looked. Under his gaze the new roofs in Balgat were simply new roofs. The wonder that these new roofs were *in Balgat* shone in other eyes and cadenced other voices.

These other voices were finally raised. Either the orator had exhausted the prerogative of his position (he had certainly exhausted Tahir S., whose eyes were glazed and vacant) or the issue was grave enough to sanction discourtesy toward a village elder. The outburst came when the quondam farmer undertook to explain why he was no longer a farmer. He had retired, over a year ago, because there was none left in Balgat to do an honest day's work for an honest day's lira. Or rather two lira (about 36 cents)—the absurd rate, he said, to which the daily wage of farm laborers had been driven by the competition of the voracious Ankara labor market. Now, all the so-called able-bodied men of Balgat had forsaken the natural work praised by Allah and swarmed off to the Ankara factories where, for eight hours of so-called work, they could get five lira a day. As for himself, he would have none of this. Rather than pay men over two lira a day to do the work of men, he had rented out his land to others and retired. He was rich, his family would eat, and others might do as they wished.

The protests that rose did not aim to deny these facts, but simply to justify them. Surprised, we asked whether it was indeed true that there were no farm laborers left in Balgat any more. "How many of you," we quickly rephrased the question, "work on farms now?" Four hands were raised among the 29 present, and all of these turned out to be small holders working their own land. (These four were sitting together and, it later turned out, were the only four members of the *Halk* Party among the group, the rest being vigorous *Demokrat* men.)

Galvanized by the intelligence now suddenly put before us (even Tahir S. had reawakened promptly upon discovering that there were hardly any farmers left in Balgat), we started to fire a battery of questions on our own. As this created a din of responding voices, Tahir S.—once again the American-trained interviewer—restored order by asking each man around the circle to tell us, in turn, what he was now working at and how long he had been at it. This impromptu occupational census, begun on a leisurely Sunday, was never quite completed. As it became clear that most of the male population of Balgat was now in fact working in the factories and construction gangs of Ankara—*for cash*—our own impatience to move on to our next questions got the better of us.

How did they spend the cash they earned? Well, there were now over 100 radio receivers in Balgat as compared to the lone receiver Tosun had found four years earlier. There were also seven refrigerators, four tractors, three trucks, and one Dodge sedan. Most houses now had electric lights and that had to be paid for. Also, since there was so little farming in Balgat now, much of the food came from the outside (even milk!) and had to be bought in the grocery stores, of which there were now seven in Balgat. Why milk? Well, most of the animals had been sold off during the last few years. What about the shepherd? Well, he had moved to a village in the east a year or so ago, as there were no longer any flocks for him to tend. How was the Grocer doing? *"Which one?"* The original one, the great fat one that was here four years ago? "O, that one, he's dead!"

THE PASSING OF BALGAT

While dressing slowly, the next morning, I planned my strategy for lunch with the Chief. Had he learned anything from the Grocer? Clearly his larger clues to the shape of the future had come from Atatürk, whose use of strong measures for humane new goals had impressed him deeply as a young man. But surely he had also responded to the constant stimuli supplied by the Grocer, whose psychic antennae were endlessly *seeking* the new future here and now. The Chief, rather consciously reshaping his ways in the Atatürk image, had to be reckoned a major figure in the Anatolian transformation. But the restless sensibility of the Grocer also had its large, inadequately defined, place. Whereas the masterful Chief had been able to incorporate change mainly by rearranging the environment, the nervous Grocer had been obliged to operate through the more painful process of rearranging himself. Most villagers were closer to his situation than to the

Chief's. The Grocer then was my problem and, as symbol of the characterological shift, my man. It was he who dramatized most poignantly the personal meaning of the big change now under way throughout the Middle East.

I recalled Tosun's unflattering sketch of him as an anxiety-ridden pusher, an "unfarming person" who "even wore some sort of necktie." What had located these details, what had made the Grocer a man I recognized, was Tosun's acid remark: "He most evidently wished to feel that he is closer to me than he is to [other villagers] and was curiously careful with his accent all during the interview." Tosun had seen this as vulgar social climbing, but there was something in this sentence that sounded to me like History. Maybe it was the 18th century field-hand of England who had left the manor to find a better life in London or Manchester. Maybe it was the 19th century French farm lad, wearied by his father's burdens of *taille* and *tithe*, who had gone off to San Francisco to hunt gold and, finding none, had then tried his hand as mason, mechanic, printer's devil; though none of these brought him fortune, he wrote home cheerfully (in a letter noted by the perspicacious Karl Marx) about this exciting new city where the chance to try his hand at anything made him feel "less of a mollusk and more of a man." Maybe it was the 20th century Polish peasant crossing continent and ocean to Detroit, looking for a "better 'ole" in the new land.

The Grocer of Balgat stood for some part of all these figures as he nervously edged his psyche toward Tosun, the young man from the big city. I'm like you, the Grocer might have been feeling, or I'd like to be like you and wish I could get the chance. It was harsh of Tosun, or perhaps only the anti-bourgeois impatience of an austere young scholar looking for the suffering poor in a dreary village, to cold-shoulder this fat and middle-aged man yearning to be comfortably rich in an interesting city. But the Grocer had his own sort of toughness. He had, after all, stood up to the other villagers and had insisted, even when they labeled him infidel, that they ought to get out of their holes. Though dead, he had won an important victory. For the others, despite their outraged virtues, *had* started to come around, once they began to get the feel of Ankara cash, for advice on *how* to get out of their holes. Had they also acquired along with their new sense of cash, some feel for the style of life that Grocer had desired? That was what I wanted to find out in Balgat today....

In Balgat I reported directly to the Chief. He appeared, after a few minutes, steaming and mopping his large forehead. He had been pruning some trees and, in this warm weather, such work brought the sweat to his brow. This was about the only work he did any more, he explained, as he had sold or rented most of his land in the last few years, keeping for himself only the ground in which he had planted a small grove of trees that would be his memorial on earth. Islamic peoples regard a growing and "eternal" thing of nature, preferably a tree, as a fitting monument, and a comfortable Muslim of even diffident piety will usually be scrupulous in observing this tradition—a sensible one for a religion of the desert, where vegetation is rare and any that casts a shade is especially prized. The Chief agreed to show me his trees and as we strolled away from the house he resumed his discourse of yesterday.

Things had changed, he repeated, and a sign of the gravity of these changes was that he—of a lineage that had always been *Muhtars* and landowners—was no longer a farmer. Nor was he long to be *Muhtar*. After the coming election, next month, the incorporation of Balgat into Greater Ankara was to be completed and thereafter it would be administered under the general municipal system. "I am the last *Muhtar* of Balgat, and I am happy that I have seen Balgat end its history in this way that we are going." The new ways, then, were not bringing evil with them?

> No, people will have to get used to different ways and then some of the excesses, particularly among the young, will disappear. The young people are in some ways a serious disappointment; they think more of clothes and good times than they do of duty and family and country. But it is to be hoped that as the *Demokrat* men complete the work they have begun, the good Turkish ways will again come forward to steady the people. Meanwhile, it is well that people can have to eat and to buy shoes they always needed but could not have.

And as his two sons were no longer to be farmers, what of them? The Chief's voice did not change, nor did his eyes cloud over, as he replied:

> They are as the others. They think first to serve themselves and not the nation. They had no wish to go to battle in Korea, where Turkey fights before the eyes of all the world. They are my sons and I speak no ill of them, but I say only that they are as all the others.

I felt at this moment a warmth toward the Chief which I had not supposed he would permit himself to evoke. His sons had not, after all, learned to fight bravely and die properly. His aspiration—which had led him, four years earlier, to buy a radio so his sons would hear the Korean war news and to see movies that would make them "wish more and more their time for military service would come"—had not been fulfilled. Yet the old Chief bore stoically what must have been a crushing disappointment. These two sons through whom he had hoped to relive his own bright dreams of glory had instead become *shopkeepers*. The elder son owned a grocery store and the younger one owned Balgat's first clothing store. . . .

NOTES

1. Under the Ottoman Empire, a traditional Turkish phrase for referring to the glory of the Sultan was "master of the whole world." The shepherd, like his elders, apparently falls back on the old imagery in a moment of crisis.

2. Silence does not obviate desire. In Turkish villages it is customary for the head of household to bury his hoard of metal coins in a secret garden spot; when he dies there is a frenzied treasure hunt for the cache. Tabu on talk, as Freud suggested, is a way of inhibiting the passage from desires to deeds. Traditional men, like the wise monkeys, find it safer to see no evil, speak no evil, hear no evil. This particular custom has the practical merit of restricting plans for a treasure hunt while papa is still alive.

CONSTANTINOS A. DOXIADIS

The Urban Condition: Present and Future

1. THE HUMAN SETTLEMENTS ARE VERY COMPLEX ORGANISMS

Mankind began the effort of solving the recent problems of cities by considering the problems of buildings only, then it moved to transportation and especially highways; today it is considering people and social problems. In every such attempt at placing emphasis on one element of the human settlement, mankind went astray, since all human settlements consist of five interconnected elements which cannot be separated. These are: Nature, in which we live, Man, Society, which Man forms, Shells (buildings, etc.) and Networks which he constructs. They are all indispensable.

Our concern is Man alone; but in order to serve himself, he has built his own cosmos which consists of five elements whose separation would mean the destruction of his whole system of life. We must deal with the system of the world of Man, and develop it for his benefit. In order to deal with it, we must study the 26 combinations of its five elements.

It is wrong, however, to assume that we have only 26 combinations to study, since our elements can be studied in five radically different ways— as economic, or social, or political, technological or cultural phenomena. It would certainly be wrong to assume that to look at the five elements in five different ways leads to 25 combinations. Their actual number is 33,554,431.

Even this number, however, is very small when compared to that of the actual *personal* points of view, since each person will judge his city in terms of his home, neighborhood, community, metropolis, or even the megalopolis, and the region or the nation to which it belongs. This idea

Reprinted with the permission of the author from his Statement Before the Subcommittee on Executive Reorganization, Committee on Government Operations, United States Senate, December 5, 1966, in Part 8 of the Hearings on the *Federal Role in Urban Affairs* (Washington, D.C.: U.S. Government Printing Office, 1967), pp. 1720-27, 1735-63.

forces us to understand a scale of units to which we all belong, ranging from our personal space, through units such as room, and house, to the whole earth. We can judge our position in terms of a total of 15 units and therefore the previous 33 million ways of looking at our cities reach mythical numbers of billions and trillions.

It is clear that our settlements and the ways of looking at them are very complex. When we now take into consideration the very great changes that have occurred in all elements (since Nature, Man, Society, Shells and Networks all change continuously) and the increasing numbers and sizes of all cities, we realize that not only are our settlements complex, but they are becoming more so with every day that passes.

In spite of their complexity, mankind, after dealing with them for thousands of years, had learned by trial and error to handle them successfully. Today, because of the explosive changes which have taken place, this is no longer true. The situation of all elements of settlements is becoming progressively worse.

2. CONDITIONS OF LIFE IN HUMAN SETTLEMENTS ARE GETTING WORSE

In order to understand the truth of this statement we must examine all five elements of the settlements.

Nature, the basic element of the world of Man is being spoilt, natural resources of vital importance for Man, plants and animals, soil and ores, are decreasing, water is being polluted, air is being contaminated—when we purify it inside buildings we empty it into the streets to be inhaled when we go out for some fresh air; we are doing what they did in the Middle Ages with sewage. Natural beauty is spoilt, the surface of the earth is gradually being covered by all sorts of man-made works (Networks of all kinds, Shells, etc.) many of which do not contribute to its meaningful development.

Man is losing his importance. In his conflict with the machine his position quite often recedes. He loses his place in the city, becomes nervous, develops phobias and becomes a displaced person. In large urban areas he encloses himself in insulated buildings—he turns into a troglodyte, or he flees the city and turns into a nomad. In doing so, he may gradually turn into a centaur, half man and half car.

In the process he loses contact with nature, he loses age-old values like contact with art, he spends many hours commuting. The maning of so many additional hours for leisure changes if we think of: how Man spends them and where he spends them.

Society in several respects is disintegrating. Social contacts are being reduced, because of the lower densities in which we live. It is wrong to assume that we are living in high densities. Of course it is true that more people are living in urban areas; but within these areas the density is now about one third of what it was 40 years ago. It is a fact that there are areas of higher densities; nevertheless, for the average urban dweller densities have dropped, while distances dividing people have increased enormously.

Of course we now have cars, but the underprivileged do not, while children, the aged, and the infirm cannot drive even though they may be the ones who need the contacts more.

Of course we now have telecommunication media, but they cannot replace the contacts between members of the two sexes, or the relationship between parents and children. Neither do they allow for the necessary dialogue upon which progress and democracy are based. We can send messages to distant places but we lose in personal communications.

We are building multi-story residences and although we achieve higher densities we are increasing the distances between people in what really counts, in time. People cannot come into contact easily when we pile them one on top of another; they prefer the head-to-head, feet-to-feet communication to the head-to-feet superimposition.

The structure of our cities is such that social and racial segregation are accentuated if not directly caused; but these are only facets of the overall problem, and they cannot be dealt with separately.

Man, in order to facilitate his life within his world, has created social units which provide the opportunity for closer ties which make him an integral part of the whole. Such units are the family, the neighborhood, and the small city. By our action, we have now destroyed the small city, and we are in the process of destroying the neighborhood and threatening even the family. Needless to say we have no proof that what we are doing is good for Man—on the contrary we could easily prove the opposite.

The school of thought which insists that the community of locality is not necessary has no proofs to offer.

Transportation systems within the city are not better for Man today; he crosses a metropolitan area at an average speed of 9 miles/hour, and that was the speed of horse-drawn carts at the beginning of our century. As a result, Man who is living at much greater distances than before, is forced to spend much more time commuting. In this respect, Man has moved backwards: the higher the speed of his machines the longer it takes him to reach the center of his towns.

The transportation systems which we have today do not correspond to modern technology, and do not serve Man as they could. Many other networks of facilities, such as water and sewerage, are not properly interconnected to form a national whole, or are not sufficient, since the cost of building them for people living in low densities is very high.

Houses and buildings though very elaborate in their technology and appliances, are inadequate when it comes to serving Man's need for isolation as well as that for contact with other men.

As an example of the first case I mention the post-war elimination of the compound wall, and the emergence of the picture window, both of which forced people towards exhibitionism or deprived them of the use of open space. The overall result was a loss of privacy.

As an example of the second case I mention the elimination of the small road and small square where children could play and people could congregate.

What we have achieved is a confusion of private and public space; we have opened the private space to the public, while we have made the public space unattractive.

I think that we can say with certainty that contemporary Man has failed completely in forming a proper settlement for a normal satisfactory life. Because of great new forces, people are tending to come close together in major settlements; but in doing so they have not managed to create a better way of life, and they are doing themselves more harm than ever before.

In order to enjoy the benefits of many facilities they are depriving themselves of many values.

The social problems have been aggravated, new major economic problems have arisen (the city has not enough revenue and the central city has no way of financing its central role), business is declining in many downtown areas, major administrative and political problems are arising.

Our cities are weaker than in the past. They are gradually becoming irrational. Is it not characteristic that the highest traffic is found in the more congested, more densely-built parts with the narrowest streets? They are shapeless, and ugly; the parking lot has come to replace public gardens and squares.

In the meantime, we are destroying the values which existed in old cities, and in a very few years it will be too late! The balance is upset: Society as a whole loses (less service at higher cost); Man as an individual loses (less facilities at higher cost); local government in most instances loses (greater responsibility at highest cost); state and federal government in most instances loses (much greater responsibility at much higher cost); many private owners lose (decay and depression in their areas). *Versus:* Very few people who profit (where settlements expand at no cost to them).

3. THE PRIMARY CAUSE OF OUR PROBLEMS IS THE DYNAMIC CHANGE OF SETTLEMENTS

If we now try to understand why the situation and the problems have been aggravated, we will find that the primary cause is the dynamic change of settlements. The explosion of population, and the economic and technological forces of which we speak, has caused problems not so much because of its size, but because it is continuous, and it causes a constant change in the whole structure of settlements and in the relationship between their elements and parts.

If we look at the whole national scene we will recognize that movements of people and distribution of projects take place in a relatively reasonable way. Under the pressure of needs, people and activities are being continuously redistributed, and there are no major hindrances.

If we look at the very small scale of architectural projects we find many that make sense, increasingly so with every day that passes.

If however, we look at the scale of cities and metropolitan areas we will see that the forces are in great conflict and are causing numerous problems. The reason is, that the forces which are being continuously and dynamically added, come up against the existing structure; the result is great conflict. As a consequence many parts and elements suffer enormously.

The settlements with all the forces they contain grow, the central areas are choked to death, and the people escape to outlying areas without having any proper conception of what it is they are doing. As a result we have two types of areas which are suffering—the central ones from great pressures, and the peripheral ones from low densities.

Life in major settlements means more services for Man(1) at lower cost in relation to same services provided in the countryside (and of course this is why people move to urban areas), but(2) at higher costs in relation to previous conditions without such services.

Since, however, people tend to live at lower densities, they increase the cost much more than is necessary, and make the burden unbearable; this increases the confusion and dissatisfaction.

Whereas problems are being continuously aggravated, we are trying to deal with them by way of insufficient means and static programs and plans. By the time these are implemented—if they are—the situation will have been aggravated even further. Obviously we are moving in a vicious circle. Only as a small example I would like to remind you of something that was mentioned by the Mayor of New York: that in spite of the implementation of housing programs the number of unsound housing units increased in New York from 420,000 in 1960 to 520,000 in 1965, that is by 25 percent in 5 years.

We have lately become convinced, in Detroit, that by the time the present urban renewal programs will have been implemented, much greater areas will be in need of urban renewal.

Within these unreasonably growing organisms, Nature, Man, Society, Shells, and Networks are suffering enormously. We are creating areas of stresses and pressures which are holes and pits in the urban tissue; those in need, those who are the weakest, fall into these pits and once inside are unable to get out. We looked at their color, their race, or their religion, and we connect the problems with these causes, when the real cause is the fact that we have allowed our cities to develop such pits in the first place.

4. CONFUSED BY THE GREAT PROBLEMS,
WE ARE NOT ACTING WISELY

The Chairman of this committee has stated that "we are apt to see the answer before we really understand the problem." I would like to confirm this on the basis of my experience. In most of the cases I am familiar with, we have acted unwisely in terms of the overall problem of our settlements. I have not yet seen any city in the world where the responsible officials can claim that the situation tomorrow will be better than it is today.

The Chairman has asked "why, when massive resources of our government have been poured into the cities***do we have an urban crisis?" On this I must point out that perhaps the cause lies in this very fact, that we *are pouring* resources *into* the cities. The solution may lie exactly in the opposite direction, that of using resources *outside* the cities. When we have an organism which is suffering from great pressures should we be allowed to add resources and pressures to it? Is a surgeon allowed to operate on a heart without first recommending a loss of weight, and generally a lessening of the pressures being exercised on it?

I think that we must understand that the solution may lie in creating new settlements to relieve those suffering from pressures, in which case we can hope to remodel the initial ones in a reasonable way.

We have failed to do this, and as a result of aggravation of the situation, we either tend to become adjusted to the existing city and gradually lose the courage to protest—we may even become adapted to it—or we try to escape.

As an example of the first case I will mention the scholars who are fighting any attempt at changing the structure of the present metropolis, as if this were the correct one.

As an example of the second case I will mention the escape into suburbs and new towns conceived not as part of a whole settlement but as isolated units for a certain economic, social or racial group.

The situation is so bad that even in the studies we make in trying to face it, we make three grave mistakes:

1. We overlook the real physical dimensions of phenomenon and the problem and always select smaller areas for our studies.

2. We overlook the real time dimensions of our subject and the physiological rhythm of its development and try to handle it with annual budgets or 5-year plans.

3. We lay great emphasis on the extrapolation of present trends as if these were correct and their continuation beneficial.

Looking now at the efforts of the past and present generations I think that we can accuse ourselves of lack of understanding, lack of goals and lack of courage.

The lack of understanding is so intense that only today are responsible leaders beginning to dedicate their time to the overall problem and speak of a *crisis*. This was a most repulsive idea in the fifties, and even in 1963 when we were preparing the Declaration of Delos to mobilize public opinion, it caused great opposition.

The lack of understanding is so intense that we have neither proper programs nor goals to be attained, nor the courage to define any. As far as I know only the city of Dallas, Texas has opened any discussion of goals and issued its first report.

We do not have any overall long-term views and policies. We are overworking several possibilities, such as investments in the existing older structures of the cities, which we are tending to destroy before they are amortized. We are not incorporating those programs we do implement into an overall policy.

Consequently, we are spending considerable amounts which, however, do not yield enough, since there is no proper research, experimentation, follow through, conclusion, feed-back of information.

Our attitude is really narrow-minded and because of this we do not preserve values (which is a well-intentioned conservatism). Instead we destroy values (in nature, buildings, cities and culture).

We are finally beginning to be conscious of our failure, and prefer to place the blame on politicians, business and financial leaders, planners and architects, builders, speculators—depending on who is speaking—not recognizing that the failure is one of our whole society—a failure to realize what is happening and to act accordingly.

In fact, it is time for us to understand that we do not act in order to face the crisis, we simply react on a small scale, in a negative way, and thus we fail.

5. WE ARE IN A CRISIS AND WE ARE HEADING TOWARDS DISASTER

We are in the middle of a crisis. We are entitled to speak about a crisis because the present dynamic situation does not show any tendency of amelioration. Almost every measurable aspect of our life in the city proves that the situation is getting worse.

The programs that we implement are insufficient to face our problems. Public housing first, which is being implemented for 33 years and, after that, urban renewal for 17 years, have not saved the situation. In spite such attempts it is getting worse. The newest program of all, the Demonstration Cities Program, is only a small beginning in the direction of coordinated action, small in size and small as compared to the areas it must cover.

If this is the situation today, it is going to be much worse in the next 5, 10, even 15 and 20 years for many cities and definitely for many aspects of our problems. Even if the best legislation is passed this year by Congress, it will be several decades before it can have direct impact on a great scale.

Action taken today means results in 10, 15 years, and major changes by the end of our century.

We must be prepared for an aggravation of the crisis since the real forces that shape the dynamically changing settlements are deployed years before they become physically apparent. We have been able to demonstrate this, by the changing patterns of non-farming land in the Urban Detroit Area, in the project which was conceived by Walker Cisler and sponsored by the Detroit Edison Company and Wayne State University.

Study of the changing patterns has demonstrated that many urban decisions have been taken by private people, industry, and authorities, many years before actual construction started. They anticipated growth and they bought land where they thought they would need it. They invested in land, thinking, planning and designing. To ascribe these early decisions to land speculation would be naive oversimplification. When municipal authorities came with their planning they met the resistance of those who preceded them.

It is a fact that today, because of the lack of proper policies, we are wasting land which is an irreplacable commodity and then take planning action after the facts occur.

The situation is going to become even worse in the future since there is no visible indication of a change for the better.

By the year 2000 urban population will be at least doubled and urban land will be many times more extensive. The number of machines in our cities will increase immensely. All this means that the greatest pressures will be on our cities, pressures which they cannot stand. A century from now the situation will be disastrous.

By the end of the century the structure of our society will be different. 91% of the population will be urban, and this percentage will continue to rise. The remaining 9% will have many characteristics of an urban population. This entitles us to say that by the end of the century 95% of the population will belong to an urban society, and this percentage will continue to increase. We are heading toward a completely urban society, and we overlook this fact.

Pressures on natural resources are going to increase enormously. Human settlements in the U.S.A. cover, and will cover, the following percentages of the total inhabitable area: 1% today, 4% or more in 2000 A.D.; 10% or more in 2066 A.D. Water and air pollution will prevail in much larger areas, agricultural land will be critically reduced, natural beauty will be destroyed in many parts of the territory.

Man is going to turn into a misguided, displaced person, hiding in the depths of buildings, fleeing the most developed parts, spending perhaps all his spare time commuting to work and traveling to and from points of interest, trying to communicate with others. He is going to have more characteristics of a nomad and troglodyte than of a citizen.

Society will be confused, the multiplication of contacts between persons and groups may well lead to confusion in communication. Today we may know little, and tomorrow even less, in terms of the total knowledge of man, compared to what we knew a generation ago. The conflict between a changing Society and a more stable Shell is going to result in a weaker overall relationship.

Expanding networks are going to lead us towards a chaotic synthesis of which Man will be a very small and unimportant component.

The cities will become worse. We will be spending more, in urban renewal for example, and achieving less, and people will flee these areas more than they are doing at present since pressures on the existing centers will increase continuously.

These trends will lead towards a new system of interconnected settlements forming a new universal city as we can see by studying the trends of the Eastern Megalopolis which is already taking shape, those of the Great Lakes Megalopolis which is beginning to take shape, the trends within the U.S.A. or in the world.

The difference between this universal city (to be completed in the 21st century), and the city of the past will be greater than that between the village and the city of today. In the history of man we will recognize the great phases of: nomadic life—temporary settlement, rural society—villages, rural and urban society—villages and cities, scientific society—the universal city or Ecumenopolis.

The dimensions of the city are completely inhuman, and, if present trends continue, life in this city will be completely unbearable.

Many people, threatened by this world city, try to avoid it through several means of escape. But the bare facts show that the coming of the universal city is inevitable; our real challenge, if we are to create a better way of living, is not to avoid the universal city, but to make life in it human.

If we do not achieve this in time, then the present crisis will lead to disaster for Man, to an inhuman, undemocratic Society.

6. WE MUST CHANGE PRESENT TRENDS BY DEFINING OUR HUMAN GOALS

This is our only way of reacting to present trends which inevitably lead to disaster: change them so that we strive towards human goals, leading to a better quality life.

It is time we defined what we want to achieve, what our goals are: we must set up these goals before we proceed to planning. One of our unreasonable actions today is that while we are preparing plans, programs and budgets, they do not indicate what their realization will mean for each one of us. If we go to a businessman with such a proposal he will throw it away, because what he wants to know is the direct results of the implementation of any proposal. Where cities are concerned we do not define these results. We propose, for example, transportation systems representing revolutionary changes, but we do not indicate what their impact on our way of living will be.

It is time we asked ourselves what we mean by a better quality of life, what is the "best" that we expect the City of Man to offer him. I am glad that your committee decided to question "all past assumptions and concepts previously taken for granted," "what are the basic facts of urban life" and what the "actual needs."

I will try to answer such difficult questions by presenting a few thoughts which may be of interest to those who are trying to clarify basic facts and actual needs.

If we start from the basic facts we have to realize that instead of being guided by the production of income we should be more interested in the way of living which is the only justification even for the production of income. We then have to ask ourselves what kind of life do we need, what is the goal of the city?

I cannot give any better answer than the age-old definition of Aristotle's, that the goal of the city is to make Man happy and safe. We used to smile at the mention of happiness and we thought that safety would be studied only in a case of war. Now we are beginning to understand that an internal balance of all the elements is of primary importance for the quality of our life.

This alone can be our goal but we have to find ways of measuring this happiness and safety. We must learn how to do this. As a first step I propose that we measure happiness by the satisfaction we experience at each moment of our life. Our most important commodity is our life-time, measured in units of time.

Today we are beginning to develop systems for the best circulation of cars, for the best use of such commodities as minerals or water and for measuring our benefits from them; but we do not do this for our most important commodity—that of time.

Now, if we attempt to formulate time budgets, our thought will proceed as follows: Man, in this case the average American citizen, spends 76% of his life-time at home, (males 69% and females 83%), and 24% away from it. He spends 36% sleeping, 20% working, and 10% eating, dressing and bathing. He is left 34% or 1/3 of his life, for leisure, pleasure, thought, etc. It is this 1/3 which constitutes the basic difference between man and animal. But males between 20 and 59, have only 20% of free time, of which one third is spent in commuting. This means 90 minutes; but for some people it means 3 hours or two thirds of their free time. On the basis of such calculations we can develop a time budget, which is more important than any other budget for Man, and estimate how much time each Man can afford to spend on each of his activities.

If man spends 76% of his time in his home, how much should we spend for it and for its surrounding? If he wastes 12% of his total time commuting and if this represents two-thirds of his free time, how much are we prepared to spend for its reduction?

In order to answer these questions we must define the satisfaction that Man derives from each type of action. Does he prefer to walk for 10 minutes or to drive for 30 minutes in a small car or 60 minutes in a luxurious one? In this way we have the total value of his time expressed in minutes multiplied by satisfaction.

Satisfaction should be measured for all aspects of Man—for his body, his senses, his mind and his soul; and this can be gradually achieved. Such satisfaction at every moment of his life, multiplied by the time during which this satisfaction is felt will give the total satisfaction possible, which we can compare with economic feasibility and reach the conclusions about what is preferable at what cost, about how much time for what satisfaction, at what expenditure.

We can also attempt to measure safety in terms of accomplishment. Is it worth increasing the operating speed on highways if this means a decrease of safety? Should we be satisfied with the present threat of our life from the exhaust of cars and the cancer of the lungs caused by industrial smog? Should we or should we not attempt to change this situation, and at what cost?

If we now begin to judge the existing situation in such terms, we will begin to understand how we must deal with several of our problems.

7. WE HAVE THE OBLIGATION TO GUIDE THE FORMATION OF BETTER SETTLEMENTS

Some people are completely opposed to prescriptive and normative action in the field of human settlements and support the approach of non-interference with the action of each community for its settlements.

This attitude is completely wrong. The question is not whether people will be free to ultimately decide about their actions; this is a basic right in a democracy and nobody should deprive them of it. The question is whether Society and Government and Science have the obligation to warn the citizens about the dangers involved in letting their settlements follow the wrong course. I think that this obligation is just as valid as that of a doctor, surgeon, or psychiatrist to recommend very positively the necessary action.

I think that we are making a grave mistake in avoiding to acquaint people with the problems created by their ways of living. It is up to them to decide whether they will follow our lead, but it is the great responsibility of experts and Government to tell the truth about problems and solutions.

It is time for contemporary Man to decide whether his settlements will take shape at random or whether he is going to guide their formation. If he believes in letting them take shape anyhow, he should do the same for highways, otherwise he would be inconsistent, foreseeing for the arteries and not for their nodal points where the settlements are, foreseeing for the bones and not for the flesh.

An example of the necessity for action is given by the selection of proper densities for every type of settlement. In the past, by trial and error the built-up part of settlements reached a density of between 40 and 100 inhabitants per acre. Today the densities are much lower to the detriment of the economic base, the social operation of the community and the aesthetic value of the settlements. It is time we clarified our attitude on this and other points.

Man must act in order to create his settlements and not let them take shape at random. He must act in a normative and prescriptive way.

Society must protect Man from his own mistakes. Why do we protect our people from unfit food and drugs and not from the unfit social structures being imposed on them by unfit human settlements?

It is time we acted for Man's protection from an unfit settlement. All my considerations are based on this idea.

8. WE HAVE TO CONCEIVE THE TOTAL FRAME OF OUR SETTLEMENTS

The fact that we see the coming of the universal settlement obligates us to conceive it properly and take action for its rational implementation.

When a settlement is very small, one dwelling for example, there is no reason for Society to interfere with its formation. When it consists of a few houses the local community can take care of it. The larger it is however the more it demands action at a higher level.

It is the Government of the United States which has to conceive the total frame of all its settlements and create their basic features. It has to create the basic networks *before* private individuals take the initiative, because otherwise planning becomes negative in many respects.

In the same way in which the Government took over the initiative of creating a pattern for the distribution of rural land and another for the first American cities, the Government now has the obligation to create the pattern of the developing urban areas in as big a scale as possible and as early as possible.

Creation of the proper frame means a conception of (1) a whole system of Networks from transportation to telecommunications and a definition of the rights-of-way for the generations to come, by planning for certain speeds and anticipating even higher ones; (2) the whole system of basic functions within the areas created by major arteries.

Creation of the proper frame is necessary so that the inhuman city can operate in as reasonable way as possible making the maximum use of present day technology. The fact that Congress has authorized research in high speed connections between Boston and Washington is characteristic of the present trends; such action can lead to success if no decision is taken without proper study of its consequences for the whole settlement of which it is a part.

Within the great frame, local authorities and private initiative can and must play their role in the creation of as diverse communities as possible expressing in their own way the desires of their inhabitants for their way of life.

No government is rich or strong or wise enough to act for all its citizens in building the human settlements, but no government can avoid the responsibility of creating the frame for the total settlements, which is something the citizens cannot undertake.

In this way the creation of the settlements will be divided between government, which will set the frame, and local authorities, cities and citizens who will construct the total. The real question is not whether government or private citizens should act for the settlements, but where and to what extent each does it.

9. WE MUST BUILD HUMAN COMMUNITIES WITHIN AN INHUMAN FRAME

A conception of the total frame of our settlements requires its organization by proper units; the larger it is the more the levels of its organization by spatial units.

It is imperative for us to understand the necessity of a system of responsibilities, and decisions by level of communities, if the organization of our life is to succeed.

It is fashionable nowadays to speak of the shrinking earth and to imply that we all belong to one very small universal community; the truth is that we belong to such a community *as well*. There is however no reason at all why we should allow the creation of new scales in the space which is of interest to us, to eliminate the scales of lower order to which we belong anyhow. The fact that flying brings us closer to Europe, does not eliminate the need to walk to the corner store, or look at the gardens of our neighborhood, in the same way in which it does not eliminate the need to kiss our wives and children goodbye.

Our new task is not to live in a shrunken world, but to live in many scales simultaneously.

The fact that we must create the frame of an inhuman universal city does not eliminate the need for human values in a human scale. We have to create around us communities in a human scale, of the type taught to us in the great laboratory in which Man is both the research director and the guinea pig for thousands of years.

The human city does not shrink, it is always there, in human scale and it will be there for as long as Man retains his natural characteristics; it is as real a need as that for his clothing and his home.

We must acquire once again the courage to create the cells of our social life which are as indispensable as our homes for the family life. Many of them together will then form the major inhuman urban areas.

The basic part, and the cell of our cities is the community of locality, and its basic dimensions are those corresponding to Man. It is mainly a residential community but it can also be commercial, educational, etc. It should be such that Man can walk in it easily, can be served easily, can develop connections due to locality.

All these lead to a community (not crossed by a car but served by it) with a length of no more than one mile, within which Man can move without meeting cars, where human scale can be reestablished at its best.

10. WE NEED PREVENTIVE, POSITIVE AND CREATIVE DEVELOPMENT POLICIES

Policies must define dynamic action and be dynamic in content which means leading towards development. We should therefore speak of development and have: development policies, development programs, development plans.

They must all be dynamic in process, which means we must cover as much time in the future as possible. In the light of this, to plan for the year 2000 is too short a period for our preparation. We must think and project for longer periods, even when we express ourselves with plans for the year 2000.

The realization of the meaning of dynamic policies leads to the conclusion that we must foresee and guide evolution. A single example of how this should operate is the following: we always speak of de-centralization, but it no longer leads anywhere as the new parts still exercise pressures on the suffering center, and it is only a matter of time when they will be overtaken.

What we need instead of de-centralization is new-centralization, or the creation of new centers of a higher order, which alone can save existing cities, guarantee growth for every part. Only then can action in existing centers have any meaning.

The method by which we develop our policies must be scientific. We must find the truth and we must tell the truth. Our present action resembles medieval attitudes in medicine (not to dissect the human body nor touch it). Now we are even worse, for we do not touch the city, the administration, the boundaries, the architecture and plans.

Our policies should not be limited to surgery, as in urban renewal, nor to curative measures. They should be preventive ones; only in cases where prevention was not started on time, should they be curative and only in exceptional cases should they allow for surgical operations.

Our policies should not be negative (how to change parts of the city) but definitely positive ones—how to create new parts in new areas and by doing so create solutions for problems that appear unsolvable in certain locations with too great an investment in interests and values of all sorts.

Humanity has always reached the heights of civilization by creating the new, not by remodeling the old. Today, because of the very great investment which has taken place in our settlements we have to remodel them as well, but this action will not succeed unless we create new areas to relieve the existing ones, and save them from death.

What we need is preventive policies, and curative and surgical operations only where they are imperative, and positive creative policies, to save the cities which exist and are now in great danger.

PART II

Industrialization

UNLIKE URBANIZATION, INDUSTRIALIZATION
is a fairly recent development; it began to affect seriously the
traditional way of life less than 150 years ago. That way of life
had been primarily agricultural with a modest amount of
craft production and commerce. It was a way of life that faded
only very slowly and grudgingly in the face of mass production
technologies.

Industrialization has occurred by two somewhat different
methods. In western Europe and the United States it evolved
naturally with a minimum of centralized planning. In its early
stages it blended very closely into the agrarian way of life:
merchants sold raw materials to farmers who with their
families converted them into finished products (woolens or
cotton products primarily). But as rudimentary but larger
machines were developed to produce the goods more rapidly,
production moved out of the cottage and into a barn or
warehouse. Continued improvements in technology eventually
led to the modern factory organization. More recently, mass
production industries manned by human beings are yielding
to automated enterprises with decidedly different requirements for human skills.

The gradual, evolutionary industrialization occurs today in underdeveloped countries, but it is more often guided by centralized state planning for economic growth. Because they exist in a world where the highly industrialized societies use very sophisticated and complex technologies, these countries encounter some problems that western Europe and the United States did not. To compete successfully in world markets the developing countries must adopt the same highly efficient technologies, but those technologies require a host of smaller supporting independent enterprises to supply tools, parts, and power. These smaller, but vital factories are referred to as the infrastructure of the industry. The developing nations cannot simply install an oil refinery or an automotive assembly plant and expect to produce the desired product: they must also develop the necessary infrastructures and this is very difficult to do because the skills and resources often do not exist in sufficient quantity. In western Europe no such problem arose because the technology developed slowly and was never much ahead of the competencies of the people. Another important difference is that industrialization in developing nations can occur readily only in the large cities while in western Europe it happened in numberless small towns. The Europeans did not need very much power or water to operate their simple machines, so industry could develop almost anywhere. But in developing nations the larger towns are the only places where sufficient power and transportation are available to meet the needs of the large, complicated technologies being adopted. Also, many of these countries are urbanizing very rapidly and industrializing the cities can provide the migrants with employment.

But by whatever means it has developed, industrialization has been a painful process for many of the human beings involved. In this section we will look at the process of industrialization, some of its effects, and the directions in which it may develop in the future.

It all began in England, and the selection from Mabel

Buer's book describes the processes involved. Her chapter conveys two important propositions from social change theories. First, that events of the enormity of industrialization occur when a number of ultimately interrelated but immediately independent activities occur in appropriate sequence. Second, that since the parts of society are interrelated to some extent, changes in one part will cause changes in other, related parts.

The next four articles are about the impact of industrialization on the traditional culture in which it occurs and on the worker and his family. Warner and Low record the loss of a sense of craftsmanship and creativity among shoemakers as they moved from their small shops where they made shoes from scratch to the factory where they and their machines performed only one step. The authors trace the development of a shoemakers' union from the insecurity induced by their new situation.

Blumer argues for a more balanced view of the impact of industrialism. Certainly it can have destructive effects, but it can also have supportive consequences. Against this plea for balanced interpretation, we offer Polanyi's famous discussion of some of the economic consequences of *capitalist* forms of industrialization. In such economies land, labor, goods, and money are organized into markets where the only operative rules are those of supply and demand. The mutual responsibilities of manor lord and his peasant are torn away and replaced by a new rule that says the owner owes only the market price of the work of his laborers and nothing more. Here and elsewhere in his book *The Great Transformation* Polanyi traces some of the consequences of the culture of classic capitalism.

In a short selection from his book William Goode makes the important point that while it is customary to discuss the effects of industrialization on the family and the worker, any adequate theory of social change must look at the reverse of this relationship. The type and structure of the family, the

existence of rules like primogeniture, or customs that con-
strain young people to leave home and make a life of their
own rather than stay on the family farm can facilitate or
discourage efforts to industrialize.

The final two articles are about a future that has begun.
William Letwin makes the ironic point that industrial
societies need not be wealthier or blessed with better living
standards than agricultural societies. The point is ironic
because so many underdeveloped societies assume that they
must industrialize if they are to enjoy a high standard of
living.

Robert Theobald discusses the consequences of the
cybernetic revolution. He believes that we are moving into a
technological era in which self-correcting machines will do
more and more of the work now done by human beings. Large
sections of the population will be unemployable. Theobald
proposes that a sufficient share of the national wealth be
given to these people to insure them an economically
satisfying life.

MABEL C. BUER

Industrialization
in
England

Up to the middle of the 16th century England was a poor and backward country, her finance and foreign commerce in the hands of foreigners, her natural resources largely undeveloped. The discovery of the New World and of the ocean routes to the East inevitably shifted the world's economic centre of gravity; the prosperity of the Mediterranean countries tended to decline and that of the Atlantic countries to rise. England shook off the foreign yoke and began to attempt long distance foreign trade and to be less dependent upon foreign finance. Slow, but perceptible, progress was made under the Tudors and Early Stuarts but then came civil disorder, disastrous foreign wars, plague and fire. All this held back economic development, though some progress was made in spite of adverse circumstances, but it was not until 1688 that continuous advance was possible. The 18th century may be said in many respects to have begun in 1688; 18th century writers date everything from "The Revolution." In that year the constitutional question was settled in a manner favourable to the only class that counted politically and internal peace was only slightly interrupted after this date. The national finances were placed upon a secure basis; the device of a perpetual national debt, the interest upon which was a first charge upon national revenue, not only added elasticity to the State finances but educated its citizens in investment. The foundation of the Bank of England (1694) and its successful management, gave additional stability to both public and private finance. There can be no doubt that the Dutch connection was extremely advantageous to England at this juncture. Holland was at that time the leading commercial and financial nation of Europe and was viewed by Englishmen with jealous admiration and dislike. Nevertheless they learnt much from Holland in agriculture and in gardening, in commerce and shipping, but more

Reprinted with the permission of the publisher from *Health, Wealth, and Population in the Early Days of the Industrial Revolution* (London: George Routledge and Sons, Ltd., 1926) and (New York: Howard Fertig, Inc., 1968), pp. 47-62.

especially in finance. Moreover, Dutch investments contributed substantially to the successful launching of the Bank of England and
otherwise supported English government borrowings.

Two important financial devices were developed in England in the first
part of the 17th century and substantially improved after 1688, namely
banking and joint stock trading. Both these devices were dangerous in
ignorant and inexperienced hands, and numerous banking runs and crises
on the one hand, and commercial crashes, from the famous Bubble on-
wards, on the other, proved this to the full during the next two hundred
years. Yet without these devices it is difficult to conceive of modern
commerce and industry. They are an essential part of the world as we
know it. The first successful application of the Joint Stock principle was to
distant and foreign trade, of which the East India Company was the most
famous example. Such an enterprise would have been impossible for the
individual merchant. The possibility of distant trade was also dependent
upon the development of sea transport. By 1760 land transport had improved little but sea transport had already made considerable advance.
The mariner no longer, as in ancient and medieval times, had to hug the
coast nor seek a port at night nor lay up his ship in winter. Sea transport
continued day and night, summer and winter. Great improvements in ship
building and the art of sailing enabled the sailor to contend against
tempestuous seas and contrary winds. The adoption of the compass and
the invention of the quadrant,[1] the log line, and, at last, the
chronometer[2] enabled him safely to leave the sight of land and to find a
path across vast oceans. The development of foreign trade directly
stimulated many branches of industry while the profits from it were largely
invested in land and so indirectly stimulated the improvements in
agriculture.

Joint Stock enterprise was centred in London and trading by joint stock
and regulated companies tended to the concentration of commerce in that
city.[3] London was never so predominant as during the 17th and the first
half of the 18th centuries. Greater London contained one-tenth of the total
population of the country and probably over half of the urban
population.[4] The major proportion of the foreign trade passed through
London; Bristol and Norwich were stationary and Liverpool had hardly
begun to be, at a time when the capital was developing rapidly. London
was the great collecting and distributing centre for the foreign trade of the
country and in the 18th century she further developed a great entrepôt
trade for the Continent. As a result of these activities London possessed a
great shipping and ship building industry. The East Indiamen, the largest
merchant ships afloat, were built on the Thames. In connection with the
flourishing commerce, banking and finance developed. Until the second
half of the 18th century nearly all the banking of the country was concentrated in London. Burke stated that in 1750 there were not twelve

banks outside London but by 1793 there were over 400 country banks. In the 18th century London began to rival Amsterdam as the financial centre of Europe. A specialized class of stock jobbers arose and insurance for sea, fire and other risks was also developed. London was also the administrative center of the country and, though the Civil servants at that date were an extremely small body, yet Parliament and its numerous hangers on and the administrative branches of the Army and Navy formed a not inconsiderable body. As the seat of government London was necessarily, in the absence of police, a large garrison town. Lastly, it was the centre of the world of fashion and of the intellectual and artistic activities which were dependent upon the patronage of that world. A large part of the great population of London consisted of persons employed in subordinate capacities in these various activities. There must have been a very large army of porters, warehousemen, lightermen, and clerks attached to shipping and commerce and numerous clerks and messengers in finance. Shipbuilding gave employment to various subsidiary industries such as rope making, barrel making and so on. Shipping provided for all those who live, honestly or dishonestly, by the sailor, from the marine storekeeper to the crimp. As to the world of fashion, moralists were never tired of inveighing against the armies of idle footmen it supported and, in addition, there were more active domestics and hosts of chairmen, link boys and hangers on.

London was also a great industrial city. Besides shipbuilding and its numerous subsidiary industries, it was a great centre of luxury trade which had naturally developed near its market. Apart from the important silk industry it was famous for watches, leather goods, jewellery, furniture, plate, coach building and so on, not to mention such obvious things as the various branches of the clothing industry. Concentration of population is cumulative; all this mass of persons needed an army of traders to serve them, from the high class shop-keeper to the petty huckster, from the wealthy wholesale merchant to the pedestrian market woman, there were also the carters, horse tenders, road menders and scavengers who directly or indirectly assisted in transport. There were besides the various branches of the building trade which provided it with shelter. Lastly, London like other great cities, supported a large number of parasites; prostitutes, beggars, thieves and rogues of every description.

This great city, containing one-tenth of the population of the country and a considerably greater proportion of the wealth, had to be fed and provided with the fuel and raw materials necessary for its industry. The repercussion of the necessary organization upon the economic life of the country as a whole was far reaching. The economic life of the country immediately surrounding London was subordinate to it. In the immediate vicinity prosperous villages depended upon market gardening, which by the middle of the 18th century had reached a very high standard; while in

Middlesex many farmers devoted themselves to producing hay upon an intensive system for the numerous London horses.[5] The farmers of Kent especially those near the river, raised fruit for the London market. All these persons had to buy corn, meat and other necessaries, London had made specialization in agriculture lucrative. Less beautiful than the market gardens were the numerous brick fields to be found in many directions, on the outskirts of the town. Timber mainly came by sea from Scotland or the Baltic, coal by sea from Newcastle, this latter being a highly organized and lucrative trade. Corn was brought in by river or sea; poultry was brought by cart from as far as Norfolk, geese are even said to have been driven in flocks from that county. Milk, notoriously adulterated, was supplied by dairy farmers, whose herds grazed in Hyde Park and other open spaces, but less perishable dairy produce came from a distance. The meat trade needed an elaborate organization. Cattle walked from all parts of the country, even from the Highlands of Scotland, to be slaughtered in London. On the cattle routes many farmers made a lucrative living by letting temporary grazing for the travelling droves, while fattening them after their long trek was another paying branch of the trade. Adam Smith mentioned the importance of the London meat market in improving Scottish agriculture, and the part which it played in Highland farm economy has been well brought out in a recent study.[6] By relieving the extreme poverty of the Highlands it was, perhaps, a factor in their final pacification. At any rate it gave the Highlands, what they had not possessed before, an economic interest in the English connection. The repercussion of the London market on English agriculture is dealt with more fully in the next chapter.

As London grew in wealth and population, so her needs led to greater calls over wider areas upon the agriculture and industry of the rest of the country. As the rest of the country grew in wealth, it made greater demands upon the luxury products of London and upon the foreign products for which London was the distributing centre. In the second half of the 18th century, when the new industries of the North and the Midlands were developing, the London market was of great importance. It was that market which stimulated the early cotton industry[7] and gave an outlet for the products of Birmingham, Sheffield and of the Potteries. London merchants, instead of expecting credit from the manufacturers, appear to have given it and, in some cases, the London banks also gave credit to provincial enterprise. The country banks, which developed after 1750 and which did much to finance improvements in agriculture and industry were themselves very dependent upon their London agents and upon the Bank of England. Thus the foreign trade of London caused the growth of that city in wealth and population and that growth in its turn stimulated improvement in the rest of the country.

There was, however, another stimulating influence which acted upon certain industries, especially in the second half of the 18th century, and that was war. The war demand had an important reaction upon agriculture,[8] and also upon that typical war industry—iron making. Iron making in the 18th century was even more dependent upon the demand for armaments than it is to-day. The multifarious modern uses for the metal had not arisen and, apart from armaments, the sole demand was for a few tools and domestic utensils most of which required little material. Domestic utensils were generally of wood, pewter, bronze or copper, though iron pots were used to a limited extent. Ships were built of wood, bridges of stone, water pipes were of wood, such simple machinery as existed was made of wood and most tools were of the same material. Timber was thus one of the most important raw materials, but in this country the supply of it was becoming very limited. This shortage had been an important factor in the widespread substitution of brick as a building material while coal had replaced wood as fuel in all places to which it was possible to transport it. Coal was also being used in many industrial processes such as brick making, pottery making, brewing and the work of the forge. It was natural that many attempts, though unsuccessful, had been made to overcome technical difficulties and to use coal instead of charcoal in the processes of iron making. These processes were very greedy of fuel and the iron industry was considered a dangerous rival of ship-building; so much so that it was restricted within a certain distance of the coast. The iron industry, in fact, was threatened with extinction and the country was faced with dependence upon foreign supplies for an important munition of war. Between 1730 and 1784, however, a series of inventions were made which not only rendered possible the use of coal for all the processes of iron making but enormously cheapened and simplified those processes. A necessary concomitant of the development of the iron making was the improvement of the steam engine, which made the necessary blast possible for the furnaces and rendered the industry independent of water power. The primary impetus for the improvement of the steam engine was the relative exhaustion of the Cornish tin mines, the continued working of which was only rendered possible by more powerful pumps. Pumping was also becoming necessary in many of the coal fields, and indeed without the steam engine the supply of coal for the new industries would have been lacking; though it might be added that the demand would also, to a great extent, have been lacking too. The earliest use of the steam engine was for blast furnaces and for mining, and the adaption of it as the motive power for machinery came later.[9] The cheapening of iron and the possibility of its production upon a large scale, led to its utilization for many new purposes; bridges, water pipes, machinery and so on, and thus ushered in a true iron age.

The growth of internal trade, with the consequent movement of both goods and persons, brought into prominence the vital problem of transport. In the early part of the 18th century regular facilities by coach and wagon began to be organized between London and important provincial centres. The services, however, were slow and uncertain owing to the appalling condition of the roads. The problem of the roads was partly technical and partly administrative. A new technique of road planning and road making had to be evolved to meet the enormous increase of wheeled traffic. Gradients which had been easily surmounted by horsemen and pack horses were a great strain for wheeled traffic, and grassy ways which had met the needs of a few pedestrians and horsemen became impossible quagmires when used by vehicles. The administrative unit was the parish and small rural areas were naturally unwilling to incur expense for the benefit of through traffic. The administrative problem was partly solved by the development of the turnpike system, and the science of road planning and road making was gradually improved to meet the new needs.

Road transport, however, was unsuitable for the long distance transport of heavy goods. For this sea transport was used to a great extent and the advantage which this country enjoyed, at this stage of economic development, from its long and indented coast line, can hardly be overestimated. Sea transport, however, was subject to considerable delays from adverse weather and was, of course, not available between some important sources of raw material. The growing need for coal both for domestic and industrial uses made particularly urgent some new method of transport, and the first canal in this country (Manchester to Worsley 1760) was constructed for the transport of coal. The success of this undertaking led its promoter to plan the Manchester and Liverpool Canal. This project was carried through in the face of enormous difficulties, but its outstanding success led to the rapid encouragement of canal making by the manufacturing class and nothing less than a canal mania followed. Many of the projects were foolish and uneconomic but others led to a great volume of traffic and during its short reign the canal had a revolutionary effect upon the economic development of the country. It made possible the large scale movement of heavy and bulky goods such as coal and iron and led to the utilization over wide areas of coal for fuel and of iron for various purposes. It rendered possible a greater localization of industry and wider markets, with a consequent larger scale of production. It made possible the development of many new industrial centres which, though well situated in regard to coal and raw materials, had inadequate river transport. By canal such towns were provided with necessary food and building materials on the one hand and could dispose of their products on the other. The canal stimulated agriculture by providing the farmer with a wider market for many of his products and by enabling him to obtain manure and coal. The development of road and canal transport was undoubtedly due to the pressing needs of industry and commerce. But when that development had taken place, it equally undoubtedly reacted upon industry and commerce and caused a stupendous increase in production and exchange of all kinds. It is unnecessary to enlarge upon this fact, it is a matter of common knowledge and agreement.

The controversial question is the effect of this increased production upon the mass of the population. It has frequently been held that the effect was harmful, that the increased output made the rich richer and the poor poorer. The popular picture of the Industrial Revolution may perhaps be not unjustly summarized as follows:

Before 1760 the major portion of the people of this country were independent small farmers, who probably also engaged in some industrial occupation, such as woollen weaving. They were independent and enjoyed considerable prosperity and security owing to their double occupation. A picture is suggested, if not actually described, of well built, rose covered cottages, of well tilled fields and cheerful, unhurried industry; the people strong and healthy and living to a good old age. Not very much is said about the towns. They are assumed to be small, sanitary and peopled by well-to-do shop keepers and independent craftsmen. London is totally ignored though, as a matter of fact, it contained one-tenth of the population and its social condition is well known to readers of 18th century fiction, if not to those of economic history. Then, continues this unconvincing history, about 1760 Watt unhappily invented the steam engine and numerous other persons invented various mechanical devices, especially in connection with the cotton industry. These inventions, it is admitted, enormously increased production but they also entailed the control of industry by capitalists who, it is alleged, alone benefited by the changes. The mass of the people not only lost their former independence and their chance of rising in the world, but were subjected to low wages, unemployment and general exploitation. They were herded into insanitary factories and unhealthy towns. The condition of the towns led to constant epidemics of typhus and cholera, which evils were viewed with supreme indifference by the governing classes. It was a little surprising that population increased rapidly under these conditions whereas under the old idyllic ones it had increased very slowly. But this phenomenon is glibly explained by an increased birth rate, the increase being due to misery and the unhealthy herding into factories. All these changes are supposed to have been effective between 1760 and 1815-25.

Recent research has modified almost to the point of destroying this picture. In the first place it has shown that the essential change in economic life in the period 1760-1815 was not the introduction of steam motive power or machinery. These inventions were not really effective until after 1815.[10] The essential changes before that date were the improvements in, and the changed organization of, agriculture, the chief industry of the country, and the improved transport facilities (roads and canals) which were also prime factors in the agricultural changes. The increased use of coal as a fuel, again due to transport changes, was also important. The changes in the iron industry were mainly important in cheapening an essential war material. The many new uses for iron were developed after 1815, as a remedy for the peace depression in the industry. Up to 1800 the steam engine was almost entirely a servant of the iron and mining industries.[11]

The establishment of factory industry was a very much slower process than used to be supposed. The tendency of many historians to ante-date the general adoption of machinery is due to ascribing too much importance to the actual date of an invention. Early machinery was clumsy, costly[12] and greedy of fuel. Constant breakdowns caused endless trouble and it was difficult to find skilled workers for repairs. Many employers were men of small means and most of them were conservative minded. The scales were heavily weighted against machinery and it is not surprising to find that in most industries its adoption was relatively slow. Even in cotton spinning, the earliest machine industry, machinery did not finally displace hand work in fine muslins until the decade 1850-60. There was no power loom weaving for wool (as opposed to worsted) until 1839 and wool weaving was not a predominantly machine industry until the '60s. The new methods were difficult to adopt and changes in other industries were equally gradual. The change from home to factory industry was by no means catastrophic.[13] In regard to the alleged effect of the factory upon the growth of population, a rapid increase in the population occurred long before factory industry and machinery had affected any but a very small part of the workers.

Secondly, capitalism was not the result of machinery, it was rather, perhaps, one of its causes. The life of Europe was not revolutionized because a genius watched a kettle boiling over, but because a social organization had been evolved which encouraged invention instead of punishing it as treachery or witchcraft. That organization, which can be briefly described as capitalistic, had its beginnings in Italy in the 13th century and in England at least as early as the 15th century and possibly earlier. Broadly speaking it may be defined as the system under which the handicraftsman does not own the raw material or the finished article, nor does he decide the quantity or quality of goods to be made. These decisions are made by the owner of the goods, known to economists as the capitalist or entrepreneur. The early capitalist was usually a trader and capitalistic organization tended to arise in industries which became dependent on distant trade, either for their raw material or for markets for their finished products. The small handicraftsman, working either independently or as a member of a Guild, was incapable of calculating the chances of distant and uncertain trade and sank naturally into the position of an employee of the trader. Some luxury employments (for instance those of gold and silversmiths and tailors) early became capitalistic because, from their nature, they were combined with money lending. Though foreign trade in 1760 was small compared with that of the present day, yet a large and wealthy merchant class with capital to venture existed and our most important industries were dependent to a considerable extent upon distant markets. As a natural consequence the organization of these industries had become capitalistic. The greater part of the woollen industry was capitalistic in its organization, while the cotton industry had been so from its origin. In the hosiery industry of the eastern counties the employers even owned the tools and simple machines. Mining enterprise usually originated as capitalistic enterprise on the part of the landowner, the organisation of the Cornish Stannaries and the Forest of Dean was exceptional. Iron making[14] in all its branches was early organized on a capitalistic basis, so was shipbuilding. Turning to the luxury industries of London, these were nearly all carried on under the capitalistic out-work system.

Capitalistic enterprise was, therefore, not invented about 1760, while factory organization did not become the predominant form of organization until 80 or 90 years after that date. The change from home to factory was slow. Though like all changes in organization, it brought hardship to individuals, that hardship was mitigated by the slowness of the change. The amount of unemployment caused by machinery seems to have been grossly exaggerated; much of the misery due to the aftermath of war being incorrectly ascribed to the new methods. The economic history of the period was first written in a time of profound peace, when the extent of the reaction after a long and exhausting war was little understood. That mistake is less likely to be made now. It can even be argued that the new methods of production were an important element in the ultimate recovery from the after effects of war. A better knowledge of the period anterior to 1760 is teaching us that unemployment, low wages and child labour were no new phenomena at that date. All these evils were likely to be worse with an out-work system than with a factory system. The factory, indeed, in the long run probably tended to mitigate these evils rather than to increase them.

The growth of towns showed itself before the advent of the factory or machinery. The changes in transport led to a rapid increase of trade and facilitated localization of industry. The towns as distributing centres, therefore, increased in importance. There also seems to have been some concentration of hand workers in the towns. In the old days the workers necessarily lived near the sources of food and fuel and the more portable manufactures were transported. Increased transport facilities made it more economic to employ the worker near the market for raw material and finished goods, since it was possible to bring food and fuel in large quantities to the towns. Though the use of water power was a factor tending to the decentralization of industry, the centralizing forces were sufficiently strong to lead to a rapid urban growth in the second half of the 18th century. But though the towns were growing their condition was not, as is often supposed, deteriorating. Insanitary towns are not an invention of modern times. On the contrary, the towns of the Middle Ages were disease ridden and insanitary to a degree that is indescribable. Those of the 17th century were little better. Far from the middle of the 18th century marking the beginning of an era of town degradation, it marks the beginning of an era of town improvement. Incredible as the statement may appear to many persons, the towns, particularly London, were becoming more healthy in the second half of the 18th century. Streets were being widened and paved, drains covered in, water supply improved, houses rebuilt, with an astonishing effect upon the death rate.

Growing commerce led to the demand for wider and better paved streets; it also provided the money for these improvements. Growing commerce had led to improved transport. Improved transport led to cheaper paving stones and building materials. The substitution of brick for timber was a factor favourable to health, tending to a more hygienic architecture and giving less harbourage to vermin. Bricks were sometimes transported by canal, but as a rule, brick works were established in close vicinity to the district which they served, coal however had to be carried to them. Improved transport led to cheap and plentiful fuel which, besides cheapening many industrial processes, made possible better warmed houses, better cooked food and greater cleanliness. Cleanliness was also aided by iron pipes and steam pumps which made possible a plentiful, if often impure, water supply. The development of the cotton industry also tended in the same direction. At first this industry was a luxury one, catering only for the well-to-do, but the rapid cheapening of its product by the application of machinery soon led to production for the masses. Cotton cloth was a cheap material suitable for women's dresses and for body and household linen; it wore less well than stout woollen material but that was advantageous from the health point of view since it could be cheaply renewed. Cotton washed easily and therefore its use much encouraged cleanliness. The cheapening of iron led to cheaper household utensils, while the substitution of the iron bedstead for the old vermin-ridden wooden one was important from the hygienic point of view, though, at first this change was mainly confined to institutions. The substitution of china crockery for the old wooden, earthenware or pewter utensils was generally held to have led to greater cleanliness. Even the cheap china ornament may have had its uses in fostering house pride among the very poor.

The growth of foreign trade had directly added two very important items to the national food supply, namely sugar and tea. The native country of the sugar cane is unknown but it was cultivated in Asia from great antiquity. It was introduced by the Arabs from Persia into Egypt, Sicily and South Spain. As early as 1319 a Venetian merchant shipped

100,000 lbs of sugar to London, but it remained a costly luxury and an article of medicine in this country until the 18th century. The Spanish and Portuguese colonists had introduced the plant to the West Indies and to the American continent and it was from the West Indies that 18th century England drew her supplies. The growth of the trade can be gauged from the fact that in 1700 the import into Great Britain was only 10,000 tons but that in 1800 it was 150,000 tons.[15] Pringle[16] believed that the increased use of sugar had been a factor very favourable to public health and apart from anything else its increased use must have encouraged the consumption of fruit, much of which never becomes pleasantly sweet in this northern climate. It also made possible the preservation of fruit for winter use in the form of jams and conserves.

Tea was brought by the East India Company from China. In the middle of the 17th century it was still an expensive luxury and by the end of that century the annual import was only about 20,000 lbs; but by the end of the 18th century the rate of consumption exceeded two lbs. per person per annum. The importance of tea lay in the fact that it was a substitute for alcohol and it must have been an important factor in the increased sobriety, which all authorities are agreed took place at the end of the 18th century and the beginning of the 19th century. Though both these commodities were dear according to modern notions, yet early 19th century writers always considered both tea and sugar to be necessaries of life for the working classes. They were, apparently, consumed by all classes, though doubtless in small quantities by the least well off.[17]

The most important effect of the growth of commerce was, however, upon the home food supply. A new demand for agricultural products was created which stimulated agricultural improvements and the improvements in transport helped both to create and to satisfy this demand. The agriculture of the country passed rapidly from being largely communal and for subsistence to being almost entirely capitalistic and for a market. Whatever may be thought of the social consequences of these changes the effect upon agricultural output was entirely favourable. The high death rate of the Middle Ages was very largely due to the frequent recurrence of famines and food scarcities: deaths from actual starvation being added to by those from disease due to the consumption of unsuitable food; while the general malnutrition increased the numbers of victims of epidemic disease, so prevalent from other causes. A subsistence system of agriculture is not only necessarily unprogressive but also necessarily insecure. This insecurity is the more serious in so far that a community that is normally self sufficing will have great difficulty in obtaining supplies from the outside. Trade and transport will be unorganized and moreover the community will have nothing to offer in exchange for food. A community which normally imports its food supply can turn with comparative ease to other sources should the normal source fail. The wider the area from which its supplies are normally drawn, the less the inconvenience which will be felt from the failure of one source. On the other hand, a community which normally exports food can cease to do so, temporarily, in case of harvest failure and, should the failure be severe, the normal lines of trade and transport for export can be utilized for import and the future crop can be mortgaged in payment. It is commonly represented that international interdependence in regard to food supply represents insecurity. This is only true from a military point of view and even in this respect there is perhaps a tendency to over-stress it. Apart from war, international trade in food has enormously increased the security of mankind. Few countries are large enough to give security from famine by home trade, since weather conditions tend to be similar over wide areas. If this is the case with modern countries it was still more so with the smaller national units of the Middle Ages, and much more so of the economic units, which were often only tiny villages with their surrounding fields. The natural hindrances to territorial exchange were added to by the foolish policy of local exclusiveness which often prevented the transport of food between neighbouring areas. So that in addition to the great and widespread scarcities and famines which were frequent in the Middle Ages, local famines and acute scarcities often occurred. The growth of commerce thus directly added to the security of the national food supply but it also led to a revolution in agricultural organization and production.

NOTES

1. The sextant was not invented until 1761.

2. In 1735.

3. Cunningham. *Industry and Commerce.* 4th ed., 1905.

4. In 1811 London still contained about 2/5 of the urban population and the northern towns had grown rapidly in the second half of the 18th century.

5. Kalm. *Visit to England.* 1748. Reprinted 1892. Also others.

6. Grant. *Highland Farm.* 1924.

7. Unwin, *op. cit.*

8. See note to Chapter VI of *Health, Wealth, and Population.*

9. Ashton. *Iron and Steel in the Industrial Revolution.* 1924.

10. Apart from coarse cotton spinning.

11. Ashton, *op. cit.*

12. Machinery only became relatively cheap with the development of the machine tool industry in the '20's.

13. Knowles. *Industrial and Commercial Revolutions.* 1st ed., 1921.

14. Ashton, *op. cit.*

15. Enc. Brit. "Sugar."

16. Pringle. *Diseases of the Army.* Appendix. 1752.

17. At any rate in London and the South.

W. LLOYD WARNER
J.O. LOW

The Shoe Industry in Yankee City

During the first years of the settlement of Yankee City and New England and in the earliest phase of shoemaking, families made their own shoes. The second phase of the first stage was characterized by the itinerant shoemaker who, owning his own tools, made shoes in the kitchen of his customer, using materials supplied by the customer. In this process, the shoemaker was assisted by his customer's family and received his compensation largely in the form of board and lodging. Many families in Yankee City and in the outlying communities, particularly those dwelling on the north bank of the river, became proficient in the art of shoemaking at this stage. They made their own shoes during the winter months, passing down the art in the home from generation to generation. This section of New England has, therefore, a strong tradition of shoemaking.

The next stage began (*circa* 1760) when the shoemaker set up a small shop and made shoes to order for his local customers. These shops were known as "the ten-foot shops," and the customer's order was known as "bespoke." During the first part of this period, the shoemaker still made the complete shoe, but his relation with the market became indirect. The entrepreneur appeared. He was a capitalist shoemaker, hiring workers in their homes to make boots and shoes for him to sell at retail or wholesale. In the second phase of the period the central shop developed where materials were sorted. The parts were cut in the shop, distributed and served in the homes, then collected and the soles joined to the uppers in the shop. Machines were used scarcely at all. The processes of shoemaking were divided, and workmen specialized in one or more operations. Jobs were thus defined within the industry; for the most part, the worker no longer faced his customers.

During this period the market remained local, and the interests of the merchant-master and the journeyman were the same. When improved land and water transportation brought about an expansion of the market, the merchant became an increasingly dominant figure. The bargain became one of price as well as quality, and the interest of the merchant to produce cheaply in order to undersell competitors began to conflict with the maker's desire to earn as much as he could from his labor.

Professor John R. Commons, in an article entitled "American Shoemakers 1648-1895," traced the evolution of the industry in this country from court records of cases involving conflicting interests both within and without the industry. He reports that the first guild of shoemakers, known as the "Shoomakers of Boston," was granted a charter of incorporation in October 1648. Since the days of the "Shoomakers of Boston" other formal organizations have come into existence and left concrete evidence of the various conflicts of interests within the industry.

Before 1852, the menaces to the industry and to the groups within it resulted mainly from the expansion of markets. Until this time all shoes were made by hand, and each craftsman owned his own set of tools. But to meet the increasingly exacting demands of an expanding market, as to both price and quality, it was inevitable that the growing technological knowledge would be utilized to mechanize some phases of shoe manufacture. In 1852 a sewing machine for stitching uppers was invented, and the following decade saw the mechanization of many other processes. This development intensified the split in interests between the owner-control group and the operatives; it also established the subordinate position of the latter which they have occupied ever since. Accelerated mechanization of the industry in the decades after the Civil War occasioned changes in the social structure of the shoe factory.

One of the most important results of the introduction of machinery into shoemaking was the enormous decrease in labor costs. The cost per one hundred pairs was reduced by the machine to well under one-tenth of the costs of 1850, and the average labor cost in 1932, we were told, had dropped to forty cents per pair. Another result was the great potential increase in production. For example, an expert hand laster produced fifty pairs a day; a lasting machine, from three hundred to seven hundred per day. A welt machine is fifty-four times as fast as welt sewing by awl and needle. The introduction of machines into shoemaking converted it from a strictly hand trade to one of the most specialized of machine industries. The position of labor was greatly modified by the technical revolution. The production has changed only in detail, but the process of manufacture has changed from a single skilled trade, carried on by a craftsman from start to finish, to one of two to three thousand operations in greater part done by machine.

The security of the workers as craftsmen was threatened by the new developments. The shoe workers did not make the machines they were suddenly forced to operate, and they had no way of predicting what jobs would next be mechanized. The owning group had in the machines an effective weapon to lessen the value of the worker's craftsmanship.

Out of this situation arose the Knights of St. Crispin, active from 1868-1872, the most powerful labor organization known up to that time and probably the most important one previous to the modern labor unions. The Knights were organized to protest against the substitution of many "green hands" for the old-time craftsmen, which was made possible by the new use of machines. It was a violent protest, but its life was short.

Since the collapse of the Knights of St. Crispin there have been few effective labor organizations among New England shoe operatives and none in Yankee City until the strike of 1933. Mechanization, however, did not cease, and with it went the subjugation of the workers. Several complete processes of shoemaking were standardized in the course of time. One of them was the "turn" process, particularly adapted to the manufacture of high-quality women's shoes. This process, one of the oldest of modern shoe-building techniques, was standard in Yankee City at the time this study was made in 1931-35.

The turn process has given way, in Yankee City as elsewhere, before the inroads of price competition. Cheaper shoes for women are replacing those made by more complicated and costly processes such as the welt. McKay, and turn methods. Cement and lockstitch processes were evolved to produce shoes that could be sold at a lower retail price. These changes also permit great factory flexibility in adjusting to style variations, an important consideration to the modern manufacture of women's shoes. The rapidity with which styles change has created rush work demands, necessitating speed in manufacturing processes and a quick and ready adaptability to change. When an order is received, the factory must push production so that the order may be completed before the style changes. With the changing styles, there is a decreasing demand for standardized types of shoes. The result is alternation between rush work and lay-offs. This trend in the manufacture of women's shoes induces a greater than average fluctuation in employment. These factors have contributed to the instability of employment in Yankee City shoe factories.

Another factor in the instability of the shoe factories is the practice of leasing machines. The leasing system was first introduced by Gordon McKay in 1861 and was continued by the larger shoe-machinery companies. The machine manufacturers adopted a royalty system in which the rates per unit of output were the same to both large and small manufacturers. This worked to the disadvantage of the former, who preferred a sliding scale. The small entrepreneur who had been attracted by this feature of shoe manufacture seldom had sufficient capital investment to insure success. The relatively small initial cost of establishing shoe factories resulted in a high mortality among these enterprises.

With the development of a large market in the West and South, the shoe industry has moved many of its production units away from the New England states and closer to the markets. One entire NRA hearing in January 1935 was devoted to a study of the migration of the boot and shoe industry from Massachusetts, and showed that state's share in the national production of shoes to have declined from 47.13 per cent in 1899 to 20.05 per cent in 1934, while its volume of production had diminished— in spite of the increase in national production—from 103 million pairs in 1899 to 71 million in 1934. Some of the important factors contributing to the migration of the shoe industry were the following:

(1) labor disturbances;

(2) the necessity to reduce manufacturing expenses and obtain lower labor cost, in order to meet severe price competition;

(3) the location of manufacturing plants in or near the principal markets;

(4) inducements offered to Massachusetts manufacturers by cities and towns located in other states to move to their localities. Such inducements take the form of freedom from taxes, free rent, donations of factory sites and/or property, and, frequently, cash subsidies.

The conditions which we have described (national, state, and local) have placed the Yankee City shoe worker in a precarious position. Changing methods of production and the vicissitudes of the trade itself have led to instability among shoe-manufacturing enterprises. Yankee City is in no position to absorb the output of its factories, and the latter have become more and more dependent on the large chain stores for retail distribution. The number of shoe companies operating in Yankee City and the number of employees have varied from year to year. In 1929, sixteen shoe factories were operating in Yankee City—the largest number operating at one time. The peak in actual employment was reached in 1926 when 2,060 individuals were employed in the shoe factories in the city.

The shoe industry, not only in Yankee City, but throughout the country, was one of the first to suffer before the general depression of 1929, showing a decline from a 1923 peak in value of product. During the period of high production, the shoe workers were in a position to dictate their own wages, but during the period of decreasing employment the manufacturers held the dominant position in the internal factory organization and gradually forced down the price of labor.

This pressure, deriving ultimately from retail-price competition, stimulated a concentrated effort on the part of the workers to organize in order that they might resist the manufacturers' desire to reduce costs by reducing wages.

THE STRIKE AND THE EVOLVING SOCIAL
AND ECONOMIC SYSTEMS

Before we ask ourselves what this economic history has told us about the causes of the strike, let us re-assess our findings. We have spoken of an economic history. However, we do not have one history but several—at least six histories can be traced. We can conveniently divide the technological history of Yankee City's shoe industry into five phases (see Chart I). At least two important stories are to be found here; the tools change from a few basic ones entirely hand-used to machines in an assembly line, and the product from a single pair of shoes to tens of thousands in mass production.

The changes in the form of division of labor (see Chart I) are another story of the utmost importance. In the beginning, the family made its own shoes, or a high-skilled artisan, the cobbler, made shoes for the family. In time, several families divided the high-skilled jobs among themselves, and later one man assigned the skilled jobs to a few men and their families. Ultimately, a central factory developed and the jobs were divided into a large number of systematized low-skilled jobs. The history of ownership and control is correlated with the changes in the division of labor. In early days, tools, skills, and materials were possessed by the family; eventually, the materials were supplied by the owner-manager, and soon he also owned the tools and machines. The sequence of development of producer-consumer relations tells a similar story. The family produced and consumed its shoes all within the circle of its simple unit. Then, the local community was the consumer-producer unit, and ultimately the market became national and even world-wide. Worker relations (see Chart I) changed from those of kinship and family ties to those of occupation where apprenticeship and craftsmanship relations were superseded and the individual unit became dominant in organizing the affairs of the workers. The structure of economic relations changed from the immediate family into a local hierarchy and the locally owned factory into a vast, complex system, owned, managed, and dominated by New York City.

With these several histories in mind (and with the help of Chart I) let us ask ourselves what would have happened if the strike had taken place in each of the several periods. In period one, with a family-producing and consuming economy, it is obvious that such a conflict would have been impossible. The social system had not evolved to sufficient complexity; forces had not been born which were to oppose each other in civil strife. In the second phase, several families in a neighborhood might have quarreled, but it is only in one's imagination that one could conceive of civil strife among the shoemakers.

In the third phase, however, there appears a new social personality, and an older one begins to take on a new form and assume a new place in the

CHART I   *The History of the Differentiation of the Yankee City Shoe Industry.*

	Technology	Form of Division of Labor	Form of Ownership and Control	Producer-Consumer Relations	Worker Relations	Structure of Economic Relations
IV The Present (1920-1945)	Machine Tools mass production, assembly line methods	Nearly all jobs low skilled; a very large number of routinized jobs	Outside ownership and control of the factory (tools leased)	Very few retail outlets; factory merely one source of supply for chain stores	Rise of industrial unions, state supervised...	Center of dominance New York. Very complex financial producer and retail structure. Local factory not important in it
III Late Intermediate Period (approximately to World War I)	Machine Tools machines predominate; beginning of mass production through use of the machine (McKay)	A central factory still high degree of skill in many jobs	First small, and later large local men of wealth own or lease the tools and machines	National market and local capitalist; many outlets	Craft and apprenticeship (St. Crispin's Union)	Center of dominance local factory; complex hierarchy in local factory system
II Early Intermediate Period (approximately to the Civil War)	Machine Tools few machines first application (Elias Howe, etc.)	One man assigns highly skilled jobs to few men; highly skilled craftsmen ("letting out" system)	Small, locally controlled manufacturers; tools still owned by workers, materials by capitalist, market controlled by "owner"	Owner and salesmen to the consumer regional market	Informal apprenticeship and craft relations	Simple economic no longer kinship; workman subordinate to manager.
I The Beginning (early 1600's)	Hand Tools increasing specialization and accumulation of hand tools	Specialization among several families; a few highly skilled jobs	Local Control: not all shoemakers need own tools; beginning of specialization	Local buyer from several producer families sells products (no central factory)	Kinship and neighbors among workers	Semi-economic but also kinship and neighborliness
	Hand Tools few, basic and simple	All productive skills in family, including making of shoes; a few cobblers for the local market	Local Control: skills, tools, and materials owned and controlled by each family; or by the local cobbler	The family produces and consumes shoes and most other products	Largely kinship and family relations among workers	Very simple non-economic; the immediate family

94

community. The capitalist is born and during the several periods which follow he develops into full maturity. Meanwhile the worker loses control and management of his time and skills and becomes a subordinate in a hierarchy. There are, thus, distinct and opposing forces set up in the shoemaking system. What is good for one is not necessarily good for the other, but the interdependence of the two opposing groups is still very intimate, powerful, and highly necessary. The tools, the skills, and the places of manufacture belong to the worker; but the materials, the place of assembly, and the market are now possessed by the manager. Striking is possible but extremely difficult and unlikely.

In the fourth period, full capitalism has been achieved; the manufacturer is now the owner of the tools, the machines, and the industrial plant; he controls the market. The workers have become sufficiently self-conscious and antagonistic to machines to organize into craft unions. Industrial warfare still might prove difficult to start, although it did occur, because in a small city where most people know each other the owner or manager more often than not knows "his help" and they know him. The close relation between the two often implies greater compatibility and understanding, which cut down the likelihood of conflict. But when strikes do occur the resulting civil strife is likely to be bitter because it is in the confines of the community.

In the last period, the capitalist has become the supercapitalist; the workers have forgotten their pride in their separate jobs, dismissed the small differences among themselves, and united in one industrial union with tens and hundreds of thousands of workers throughout the country combining their strength to assert their interests against management. In such a social setting strikes are inevitable.

HERBERT BLUMER

Industrialization and the Traditional Order

What does the introduction of industrialization do to the traditional order of preindustrial societies? The conventional answer of sociologists is that industrialization undermines the traditional order. Industrialization is regarded as displacing existing occupations, shifting production from the home and the village, producing migration and urbanization, fostering social mobility, introducing monetary and contractual relations, arousing new wishes and expectations, and promoting secular and rational perspectives. The impact of such changes is alleged to break down the existing family system, disrupt the prevailing class structure, disintegrate status and role arrangements, undermine paternalistic relations, weaken the established system of authority, transform traditional tastes, and erode established values. My studies convince me that this widely held view is markedly inaccurate. I wish to sketch its major deficiencies and suggest a more balanced conception.

One outstanding deficiency arises from the common tendency to ascribe to industrialization social changes that are due to other factors. Some of these nonindustrial factors antedate early industrialization. Every society into which modern industrialization enters has a preceding history of exposure to Western culture. The play of such varied influences as missionary activity, foreign trade, colonial domination, plantation systems, military aggression and control, alien governmental administration, programs of foreign education, and the introduction of diverse technological products induce appreciable disintegration of indigenous cultures. Such influences set into play many forms of continuing social change and produce many lines of strain and conflict. All too frequently students of early industrialization overlook or underestimate the significance of these previously implanted influences toward change. Students should be careful not to attribute to early industrialization a

Reprinted with the permission of the publisher and the author from "Industrialization and the Traditional Order," *Sociology and Social Research* 48, No. 2 (January 1964): 129-38.

body of social disintegration which has arisen from prior nonindustrial sources.

In a similar manner, it is necessary to perceive clearly the sizable number of factors of social change which may accompany early industrialization. It is a gross mistake to think that the industrializing process enters preindustrial societies by itself. Early industrialization is always a period of incorporation into a wider outside world. The doors are opened to a host of influences such as new political systems, new political doctrines, ideas of nationalism, new laws, new financial arrangements, new transport systems, new schemes of medicine and sanitation, new forms of schooling, new conceptions of rights and privileges, and new wishes and aspirations. Such nonindustrial influences may lead to profound changes in the prevailing order in life. That such influences are not an intrinsic part of industrialization is clearly revealed by their separate operation today in many "underdeveloped" regions which are undergoing great change but little or no industrialization. The fact that weighty nonindustrial influences usually accompany industrialization is no excuse for confusing them with industrialization. Indeed, the conscientious scholar interested in studying the effects of early industrialization has precisely the task of disjoining industrialization from nonindustrial influences. Current scholarly thought is seriously perverted by the failure to do so.

Having noted the widespread yet needless confusion of industrialization with large numbers of other agencies of social change, I wish now to consider a number of important features of both industrialization and the traditional order of life. This consideration will reveal other deficiencies in current thought on early industrialization.

The chief observation to be made in the case of industrialization is that it is a very heterogeneous process. To be true, one can specify in abstract form certain typical elements of industrialization—the use of power driven machines, factories in which to house them, workers with requisite skills to operate them, management to direct operations, power facilities for the machines, a system of procurement of the materials entering into the manufactured products, a system for the distribution of products to the market, and a set of supplementary facilities such as transport, communication, banking and credit, purchasing and selling. However, this abstract sketch of the skeletal features of industrialization gives no idea of the immense range of difference in the concrete forms which it may take. The industrializing process may vary greatly in such significant matters as size and type of industrial establishment, form of ownership, policies of management, system of factory operation, composition of the labor force, manner of recruiting and allocating workers, levels of industrial skills, levels of wage payments, availability of markets, and the character of the supplementary facilities mentioned above. It is a mistake to assume that the industrializing process enters preindustrial societies with a uniform makeup, impinging on them at the same points, imposing the same demands and introducing the same kind of situations.

In considering the nature of traditional societies we need to note similarly a picture of diversity. There is an obvious diversity in the cultural makeup of such societies, as for example between a primitive tribe and a feudal agricultural society. But this kind of difference is not of special importance to our present discussion. Our concern, instead, is with the character of their traditional orientation, since it is an attachment to the past which leads us to classify these societies as being traditional. We find great differences in the nature of their traditional orientations. Some of the traditional societies may be deeply entrenched in attachment to the social order which has come to them from the past, whereas other societies may be much more receptive to innovation and change. This observation leads us to what is of primary interest, namely, that within each traditional society there is likely to be appreciable difference from point to point in commitment to the traditional order. No traditional society presents itself as a solid and uniform block in attachment to traditional forms. Attachment may be great in some parts, moderate in others, and negligible in still other parts. Further, the parts differ in the ways in which they buttress one another or impose strain on one another. A traditional society, consequently, should be viewed in terms of the pattern of traditional attachment—its spread, its intensity, its interbuttressing, its anchor points, its areas of toughness, its areas of weakness, and its lines of strain. Admittedly, so-called traditional societies are seldom depicted in this way and then only in a fragmentary manner. Yet, it is precisely this kind of depiction that is required in order to deal sensibly with a question of how such societies will respond to an outside influence, such as the industrializing process. Viewed in this way, there is great difference between preindustrial societies in terms of their respective structures of traditionalism. The pattern of fixed or instable parts, strong or weak areas, and resistant and receptive points varies significantly from one society to another. Any treatment of traditional societies should respect this important fact.

These few remarks suggest the need of recognizing that both the industrializing process and the traditional order are heterogeneous. As we inspect instances of their contact we find that they meet each other at differing points, and they bring to these points of contact differing social forms with different degrees of strength and vigor. Given this variable character of their confrontation, it is a grievous mistake to presume uniform happenings when industrialization enters a traditional society.

A further deficiency in current views lies in the failure to see that the traditional order is active and selective *vis-a-vis* the industrializing process. People in the traditional society meet the situations introduced by industrialization in terms of the advantages and disadvantages which the situations offer. Their responses are selective. They may defer to the demands of the industrial situations or force modification on them. They may seize and exploit the opportunities which the situations offer for the pursuit of their own interests. Thus, they weave divergent patterns of activity around the industrializing process and bring it inside of the context of their collective life. It is false to view industrialization and the traditional order as naturally standing and moving in opposition to each other. It is more realistic to see their points of contact as occasions for diversified accommodations or diversified modifications of both of them. Such a view should supplant the largely mythical notion that industrialization intrudes as a unitary structured force which pushes aside and displaces the traditional order.

My studies compel me to recognize at least five significantly different ways in which a preindustrial society may respond to the industrializing process. I label these five responses as "rejective," "disjunctive," "assimilative," "supportive," and "disruptive."

REJECTIVE RESPONSE

A traditional society may reject incoming industrialization or parts of it. Such rejection may occur at many different points and in many different ways. Powerful groups, such as a landed aristocracy, a commercial class, or a governmental oligarchy may discourage and curb industrialism in the interest of protecting vested advantages. Social prejudices, special interests, and firm attachments to given forms of traditional life may lead certain sets of people to reject key features of the industrializing pattern. Industrial owners may be shunned, industrial managers refused acceptance, industrial employment may be avoided or never embraced as a career, people may refuse to enter into the residential mobility which industrial employment requires, they may reject free contractual relations in favor of paternalistic fealty, factory regimens may be consistently resisted or sabotaged, rigid obstacles may be placed before the free operation of a training or promotion system, manufactured products may be heavily taxed and their marketing may be restricted. These are a few of the ways in which the industrializing process may be repelled.

Such forms of rejection are much more common than is realized by even the more knowledgeable scholars. Some attention has been given to this rejective response in treating what is frequently referred to as "resistance" to industrialization; but this treatment is usually focused on the problem of how to overcome resistance. I wish instead to call attention to the fact that the rejective response represents one important way by which a traditional society may meet and deal with incoming industrialization. Various groups in the traditional society may be completely out of sympathy with those portions of the industrializing process with which they are confronted and may, indeed, succeed in blocking their entrance and operation. At such points the traditional order is effectively protected and maintained instead of crumbling or giving way.

DISJUNCTIVE RESPONSE

A disjunctive response occurs when the industrializing process, or parts of it, even though in no sense rejected by the society, operate as a detached development without incorporation in traditional life. For example, an oil refinery in a preindustrial society may remain apart, its ownership may be absentee, its managerial and technical personnel may form an insulated community, the native working force may be small, the manufactured products may not enter into the domestic market, and industrial income may not flow into the local area. In such a disjunctive relation, the industrializing operation may have essentially no connection with the established order, may impose no strain on it, and constitute no threat to it. Admittedly, total disjunction in the sense of covering the full industrial operation is rare, and the few instances of its happening have been short lived. But partial disjunction occurs repeatedly at different points of the industrial apparatus and may persist in many instances as a set of regularized arrangements. The disjunctive response has scarcely been noticed by scholars, much less studied by them. Yet to one who is sensitized to perceive it, it becomes evident that its occurrence is frequent— sufficiently frequent that it must be recognized not as an oddity but as an important way in which a traditional order may meet, with toleration and sympathy, various parts or features of the industrializing process without being affected by them or affecting them. The features do not enter into traditional life but merely exist alongside of it in a disparate fashion.

ASSIMILATIVE RESPONSE

This is a very common and a very important manner by which a traditional order may respond to an inthrust of industrialization. It consists of an absorption of the industrializing process or of its parts by the traditional order without disruption of its own organization and patterns of life. Let me recite a variety of illustrative instances. Industrial owners may accept the ideology and modes of life of the established elite groups; managerial personnel may be given niches inside of the existing status structure; industrial workers even though having new occupations and incomes may cling to their traditional forms of life; their new residential settlements may perpetuate the essential forms of traditional village organization; employer-employee relations may follow traditional status patterns; industrial income may be expended in traditional manner; and industrial interests may be incorporated inside of the prevailing pattern of traditional interests.

The descriptive accounts in the literature present innumerable instances of such types of assimilation by established traditional societies. In some cases, the absorption may be confined to but a few scattered parts of what is introduced by industrialization. In other cases, the whole system of industrial organization may be made to fit and operate inside of the traditional framework; we see this vividly when industrialization is introduced into a firmly established racial order. It should be evident to the perceptive student that the assimilative response is by and large very common in early industrialization. Nor should its occurrence be viewed as strange or unexpected. To the contrary, it is usual for people with firmly established social arrangements, buttressed by sentiments and a body of secure beliefs, to so mould what they adopt that it fits inside of their normal and natural order of life. The people of a traditional order are not passive and helpless before the entrance of early industrialization; they meet it with their own interests and bents. At countless points of contact they shape it to be congenial to their customary arrangements. In this way the industrializing process, or many of its parts, may come to be woven into the traditional order without endangering or affecting the basic character of that order.

SUPPORTIVE RESPONSE

We are forced to recognize another and quite different way in which a traditional order may respond to early industrialization. This response takes the form of a strengthening or reinforcement of the traditional order or of significant parts of it. This may seem odd in the light of the conventional notion of disintegration which has become so deeply entrenched in sociological thought; but its occurrence is again frequent, even though sadly overlooked by scholars. The strengthening of the traditional order to which I refer does not come from some kind of intensified resistance to industrialization. Instead, it takes the form of different traditional groups and institutions using the opportunities presented by industrialization to pursue more effectively traditional interests and to maintain traditional positions more firmly. Let me mention several typical kinds of instances to give an idea of this type of response. Industrialization may lead to a strengthening of the position of a ruling class, increase the power of the military establishment, fortify the central government, reinforce traditional ownership and authority, strengthen families by supplying steady income, reinforce local schools and other institutions, and reinvigorate hopes and plans for traditional careers. To see more clearly how industrialization may conduce to such strengthening effects on different parts of a traditional society, one should bear in mind that in traditional orders various groups and institutions are frequently limited in realizing traditional goals because of a scarcity of resources and facilities. Industrialization may provide a greater measure of such resources and facilities than are available under traditional arrangements. Here and there a group or an institution finds a situation of advantage or acquires fuller means for furthering traditional interests. Such buttressing and reinvigoration of different parts of the traditional order is one of the most interesting yet least studied happenings under industrialization.

DISRUPTIVE RESPONSE

Since the disintegrative influence of industrialization on traditional orders has been dealt with so extensively in the literature there is no need to describe and illustrate this type of response, as has been done in the case of the other four. The conventional thoughts with regard to it are stated in the opening paragraph of the present essay. Suffice it to say that the traditional order or parts of it may be undermined at many points by the adjustments which are made to the situations introduced by industrialization. Since the central aim of the present essay is not to deny the occurrence of the disruptive response but to put the response in proper perspective, no identifying treatment of it is required.

In the foregoing discussion I have sought to designate five important ways in which traditional orders respond to early industrialization. It is very rare, indeed, that a traditional order will respond in only one of the five ways; where such a single type of response seems to occur it is short lived. In the typical case, several and usually all five of the responses take place, side by side, in different parts of the traditional order and in different combinations. Thus, early industrialization may undermine the traditional order in some areas, strengthen it in other areas, be rejected at certain points, be absorbed at other points, and in other parts exist in a disparate fashion without affecting the traditional order.

Several matters need to be observed in the play of the five types of response over the expanses of the traditional order. First, it would be a mistake to assume that the picture of differential responses is to be found only at some initial stage of early industrialization, only to pass over subsequently into a single current of descriptive response. To the contrary, each one of the five responses may be a continuing affair, maintaining itself during decades of contact with the industrializing process. Second, it should not be thought that the rejective, disjunctive, assimilative, and supportive responses take place only in scattered and insignificant parts of the traditional order. They may cover broad and important areas of the social order. They operate in all of the major areas on which sociologists are prone to fasten their concern—such areas as the class structure, the authority system, the organization and life of families, the structure of social roles and status systems, the institutional organization, the system of values, and the array of tastes and aspirations. Traditional arrangements in such areas do not merely disintegrate or fade away before the imputed onslaught of the industrializing process; they may meet industrialization in any or all of the other four ways, with great frequency and with great vigor. Third, we have no evidence to support a claim that the disruptive response—or for that matter any of the other four—is in some ultimate sense the most important or the most dominant of the five responses. The idea, in itself, of trying to rank them in an order of comparative importance is probably meaningless because of the great variety of the situations in which they occur. But even if we entertain the idea we must note that we have no comparative studies of the five responses. Indeed, scholars are so ill cognizant of the rejective, disjunctive, assimilative, and supportive responses that they have not even singled them out for individual study.

Enough has been said, I trust, to belie the conventional idea of industrialization which is so deeply embedded in both scholarly and lay thought. The idea that industrialization is a massive force which proceeds relentlessly to undercut the pillars of the traditional order into which it is introduced is false. The blithe way in which the idea has been taken for granted by scholars and the tenacity with which they cling to it tell a great deal about peculiarities of scholarly thought but nothing reliable about the empirical world onto which the idea is projected. The idea, it may be mentioned in passing, seems to have originated in the colorful and largely inaccurate depictions of the Industrial Revolution in England; and to have subsequently taken root largely because of involvement in the political and social agitation of the 19th century. Whatever may have been its history, the idea has become fixed in sociological lore. Yet, despite its axiom-like status the idea turns out to be untrue when matched against empirical reality.

The proper perspective, in my judgment, is to see traditional orders as being essentially active and selective with regard to the industrializing process and to what it introduces. In using this metaphor I refer to the fact that the differentiated groups of people who belong to the traditional order *act toward* the multiplicity of situations which industrialization introduces and seek to fashion lines of activity in response to the invitations, opportunities, threats, perils, compulsions or detached character which these situations seem to offer. The postures which are taken and the lines of activity which are developed toward the situations are governed in very large measure by traditional preferences, interests, and values. That there should be the variety of responses which we have sketched is easily understandable. The defining process which takes place may lead people in some situations to cling resolutely to established practices, in others to adopt new ways but bring them smoothly inside of the framework of traditional life, in others to seize on opportunities to fortify their traditional interests and objectives, and in still others to branch out in new and unconventional ways. There should be nothing strange in this picture of divergent responses.

This view of what happens in general when industrialization enters a traditional order should have a wholesome corrective influence on current scholarly thought on this topic. It should lead scholars to modify drastically the long-standing belief that industrialization acts solely or predominantly to undermine the traditional orders of preindustrial societies. It should lead theorists to be more careful in formulating their schemes concerning the influence of early industrialization on such matters as class structure, family organization, race relations, systems of authority and power, role relationships, and value systems. It should lead research workers to ferret out what actually happens in this area of contact of industrialization with traditional societies in place of organizing their approaches on the basis of a pre-established answer. And it should lead teachers to refrain from perpetuating in their instruction the long-standing fictitious image that the impact of industrialization on traditional societies is naturally one of extensive disintegration.

I wish to close with a brief comment on a point made early in this paper, namely, that the industrializing process is typically accompanied by many other agents of social change. Scholars seem prone to overlook these other agents and, consequently, to attribute to industrialization the changes induced by such other agents. This proneness is evident in the treatment of disintegration of traditional orders in periods of early industrialization. Appreciable disintegration is indeed likely to occur in such periods in response to the play of a complex of influences, of which the industrializing process is only one. Since the disintegration occurs *in a period* of industrialization it is easy to ascribe it to industrialization even though much of it arises from other influences. I suspect that the disposition to do this explains in major measure why industrialization is seen almost exclusively as an undermining agent and why little note is taken of the other ways in which the traditional order may respond to its play.

KARL POLANYI

The
Great
Transformation

This cursory outline of the economic system and markets, taken separately, shows that never before our own time were markets more than accessories of economic life. As a rule, the economic system was absorbed in the social system, and whatever principle of behavior predominated in the economy, the presence of the market pattern was found to be compatible with it. The principle of barter or exchange, which underlies this pattern, revealed no tendency to expand at the expense of the rest. Where markets were most highly developed, as under the mercantile system, they throve under the control of a centralized administration which fostered autarchy both in the households of the peasantry and in respect to national life. Regulation and markets, in effect, grew up together. The self-regulating market was unknown; indeed the emergence of the idea of self-regulation was a complete reversal of the trend of development. It is in the light of these facts that the extraordinary assumptions underlying a market economy can alone be fully comprehended.

A market economy is an economic system controlled, regulated, and directed by markets alone; order in the production and distribution of goods is entrusted to this self-regulating mechanism. An economy of this kind derives from the expectation that human beings behave in such a way as to achieve maximum money gains. It assumes markets in which the supply of goods (including services) available at a definite price will equal the demand at that price. It assumes the presence of money, which functions as purchasing power in the hands of its owners. Production will then be controlled by prices, for the profits of those who direct production will depend upon them; the distribution of the goods also will depend upon prices, for prices form incomes, and it is with the help of these incomes that the goods produced are distributed amongst the members of society.

Under these assumptions order in the production and distribution of goods is ensured by prices alone.

Self-regulation implies that all production is for sale on the market and that all incomes derive from such sales. Accordingly, there are markets for all elements of industry, not only for goods (always including services) but also for labor, land, and money, their prices being called respectively commodity prices, wages, rent, and interest. The very terms indicate that prices form incomes: interest is the price for the use of money and forms the income of those who are in the position to provide it; rent is the price for the use of land and forms the income of those who supply it; wages are the price for the use of labor power, and form the income of those who sell it; commodity prices, finally, contribute to the incomes of those who sell their entrepreneurial services, the income called profit being actually the difference between two sets of prices, the price of the goods produced and their costs, *i.e.,* the price of the goods necessary to produce them. If these conditions are fulfilled, all incomes will derive from sales on the market, and incomes will be just sufficient to buy all the goods produced.

A further group of assumptions follows in respect to the state and its policy. Nothing must be allowed to inhibit the formation of markets, nor must incomes be permitted to be formed otherwise than through sales. Neither must there be any interference with the adjustment of prices to changed market conditions—whether the prices are those of goods, labor, land, or money. Hence there must not only be markets for all elements of industry,[1] but no measure or policy must be countenanced that would influence the action of these markets. Neither price, nor supply, nor demand must be fixed or regulated; only such policies and measures are in order which help to ensure the self-regulation of the market by creating conditions which make the market the only organizing power in the economic sphere.

To realize fully what this means, let us return for a moment to the mercantile system and the national markets which it did so much to develop. Under feudalism and the gild system land and labor formed part of the social organization itself (money had yet hardly developed into a major element of industry). Land, the pivotal element in the feudal order, was the basis of the military, judicial, administrative, and political system; its status and function were determined by legal and customary rules. Whether its possession was transferable or not, and if so, to whom and under what restrictions; what the rights of property entailed; to what uses some types of land might be put—all these questions were removed from the organization of buying and selling, and subjected to an entirely different set of institutional regulations.

The same was true of the organization of labor. Under the gild system, as under every other economic system in previous history, the motives and circumstances of productive activities were embedded in the general organization of society. The relations of master, journeyman, and apprentice; the terms of the craft; the number of apprentices; the wages of the workers were all regulated by the custom and rule of the gild and the town. What the mercantile system did was merely to unify these conditions either through statute as in England, or through the "nationalization" of the gilds as in France. As to land, its feudal status was abolished only in so far as it was linked with provincial privileges; for the rest, land remained *extra commercium,* in England as in France. Up to the time of the Great Revolution of 1789, landed estate remained the source of social privilege in France, and even after that time in England Common Law on land was essentially medieval. Mercantilism, with all its tendency towards commercialization, never attacked the safeguards which protected these two basic elements of production—labor and land—from becoming the objects of commerce. In England the "nationalization" of labor legislation through the Statute of Artificers (1563) and the Poor Law (1601), removed labor from the danger zone, and the anti-enclosure policy of the Tudors and early Stuarts was one consistent protest against the principle of the gainful use of landed property.

That mercantilism, however emphatically it insisted on commercialization as a national policy, thought of markets in a way exactly contrary to market economy, is best shown by its vast extension of state intervention in industry. On this point there was no difference between mercantilists and feudalists, between crowned planners and vested interests, between centralizing bureaucrats and conservative particularists. They disagreed only on the methods of regulation: gilds, towns, and provinces appealed to the force of custom and tradition, while the new state authority favored statute and ordinance. But they were all equally averse to the idea of commercializing labor and land—the pre-condition of market economy. Craft gilds and feudal privileges were abolished in France only in 1790; in England the Statute of Artificers was repealed only in 1813-14, the Elizabethan Poor Law in 1834. Not before the last decade of the eighteenth century was, in either country, the establishment of a free labor market even discussed; and the idea of the self-regulation of economic life was utterly beyond the horizon of the age. The mercantilist was concerned with the development of the resources of the country, including full employment, through trade and commerce; the traditional organization of land and labor he took for granted. He was in this respect as far removed from modern concepts as he was in the realm of politics, where his belief in the absolute powers of an enlightened despot was tempered by no intimations of democracy. And just as the transition to a democratic system and representative politics involved a complete reversal of the trend of the age, the change from regulated to self-regulating markets at the end of the eighteenth century represented a complete transformation in the structure of society.

A self-regulating market demands nothing less than the institutional separation of society into an economic and political sphere. Such a dichotomy is, in effect, merely the restatement, from the point of view of society as a whole, of the existence of a self-regulating market. It might be argued that the separateness of the two spheres obtains in every type of society at all times. Such an inference, however, would be based on a fallacy. True, no society can exist without a system of some kind which ensures order in the production and distribution of goods. But that does not imply the existence of separate economic institutions; normally, the economic order is merely a function of the social, in which it is contained. Neither under tribal, nor feudal, nor mercantile conditions was there, as we have shown, a separate economic system in society. Nineteenth century society, in which economic activity was isolated and imputed to a distinctive economic motive, was, indeed, a singular departure.

Such an institutional pattern could not function unless society was somehow subordinated to its requirements. A market economy can exist only in a market society. We reached this conclusion on general grounds in our analysis of the market pattern. We can now specify the reasons for this assertion. A market economy must comprise all elements of industry, including labor, land, and money. (In a market economy the last also is an essential element of industrial life and its inclusion in the market mechanism has, as we will see, far-reaching institutional consequences.) But labor and land are no other than the human beings themselves of which every society consists and the natural surroundings in which it exists. To include them in the market mechanism means to subordinate the substance of society itself to the laws of the market.

We are now in the position to develop in a more concrete form the institutional nature of a market economy, and the perils to society which it involves. We will, first, describe the methods by which the market mechanism is enabled to control and direct the actual elements of industrial life; second, we will try to gauge the nature of the effects of such a mechanism on the society which is subjected to its action.

It is with the help of the commodity concept that the mechanism of the market is geared to the various elements of industrial life. Commodities are here empirically defined as objects produced for sale on the market; markets, again, are empirically defined as actual contacts between buyers and sellers. Accordingly, every element of industry is regarded as having been produced for sale, as then and then only will it be subject to the supply-and-demand mechanism interacting with price. In practice this means that there must be markets for every element of industry; that in these markets each of these elements is organized into a supply and a demand group; and that each element has a price which interacts with demand and supply. These markets—and they are numberless—are interconnected and form One Big Market.[2]

The crucial point is this: labor, land, and money are essential elements of industry; they also must be organized in markets; in fact, these markets form an absolutely vital part of the economic system. But labor, land, and money are obviously *not* commodities; the postulate that anything that is bought and sold must have been produced for sale is emphatically untrue in regard to them. In other words, according to the empirical definition of a commodity they are not commodities. Labor is only another name for a human activity which goes with life itself, which in its turn is not produced for sale but for entirely different reasons, nor can that activity be detached from the rest of life, be stored or mobilized; land is only another name for nature, which is not produced by man; actual money, finally, is merely a token of purchasing power which, as a rule, is not produced at all, but comes into being through the mechanism of banking or state finance. None of them is produced for sale. The commodity description of labor, land, and money is entirely fictitious.

Nevertheless, it is with the help of this fiction that the actual markets for labor, land, and money are organized;[3] they are being actually bought and sold on the market; their demand and supply are real magnitudes; and any measures or policies that would inhibit the formation of such markets would *ipso facto* endanger the self-regulation of the system. The commodity fiction, therefore, supplies a vital organizing principle in regard to the whole of society affecting almost all its institutions in the most varied way, namely, the principle according to which no arrangement or behavior should be allowed to exist that might prevent the actual functioning of the market mechanism on the lines of the commodity fiction.

Now, in regard to labor, land, and money such a postulate cannot be upheld. To allow the market mechanism to be sole director of the fate of human beings and their natural environment, indeed, even of the amount and use of purchasing power, would result in the demolition of society. For the alleged commodity "labor power" cannot be shoved about, used indiscriminately, or even left unused, without affecting also the human individual who happens to be the bearer of this peculiar commodity. In disposing of a man's labor power the system would, incidentally, dispose of the physical, psychological, and moral entity "man" attached to that tag. Robbed of the protective covering of cultural institutions, human beings would perish from the effects of social exposure; they would die as the victims of acute social dislocation through vice, perversion, crime, and starvation. Nature would be reduced to its elements, neighborhoods and landscapes defiled, rivers polluted, military safety jeopardized, the power to produce food and raw materials destroyed. Finally, the market administration of purchasing power would periodically liquidate business enterprise, for shortages and surfeits of money would prove as disastrous to business as floods and droughts in primitive society. Undoubtedly, labor, land, and money markets *are* essential to a market economy. But no society could stand the effects of such a system of crude fictions even for the shortest stretch of time unless its human and natural substance as well as its business organization was protected against the ravages of this satanic mill.

The extreme artificiality of market economy is rooted in the fact that the process of production itself is here organized in the form of buying and selling.[4] No other way of organizing production for the market is possible in a commercial society. During the late Middle Ages industrial production for export was organized by wealthy burgesses, and carried on under their direct supervision in the home town. Later, in the mercantile society, production was organized by merchants and was not restricted any more to the towns; this was the age of "putting out" when domestic industry was provided with raw materials by the merchant capitalist, who controlled the process of production as a purely commercial enterprise. It was then that industrial production was definitely and on a large scale put under the organizing leadership of the merchant. He knew the market, the volume as well as the quality of the demand; and he could vouch also for the supplies which, incidentally, consisted merely of wool, woad, and, sometimes, the looms or the knitting frames used by the cottage industry. If supplies failed it was the cottager who was worst hit, for his employment was gone for the time; but no expensive plant was involved and the merchant incurred no serious risk in shouldering the responsibility for production. For centuries this system grew in power and scope until in a country like England the wool industry, the national staple, covered large sectors of the country where production was organized by the clothier. He who bought and sold, incidentally, provided for production—no separate motive was required. The creation of goods involved neither the reciprocating attitudes of mutual aid; nor the concern of the householder for those whose needs are left to his care; nor the craftsman's pride in the exercise of his trade; nor the satisfaction of public praise—nothing but the plain motive of gain so familiar to the man whose profession is buying and selling. Up to the end of the eighteenth century, industrial production in Western Europe was a mere accessory to commerce.

As long as the machine was an inexpensive and unspecific tool there was no change in this position. The mere fact that the cottager could produce larger amounts than before within the same time might induce him to use machines to increase earnings, but this fact in itself did not necessarily affect the organization of production. Whether the cheap machinery was owned by the worker or by the merchant made some difference in the social position of the parties and almost certainly made a difference in the earnings of the worker, who was better off as long as he owned his tools; but it did not force the merchant to become an industrial capitalist, or to restrict himself to lending his money to such persons as were. The vent of goods rarely gave out; the greater difficulty continued to be on the side of supply of raw materials, which was sometimes unavoidably interrupted. But, even in such cases, the loss to the merchant who owned the machines was not substantial. It was not the coming of the machine as such but the invention of elaborate and therefore specific machinery and plant which completely changed the relationship of the merchant to production. Although the new productive organization was introduced by the merchant—a fact which determined the whole course of the transformation— the use of elaborate machinery and plant involved the development of the factory system and therewith a decisive shift in the relative importance of commerce and industry in favor of the latter. Industrial production ceased to be an accessory of commerce organized by the merchant as a buying and selling proposition; it now involved long-term investment with corresponding risks. Unless the continuance of production was reasonably assured, such a risk was not bearable.

But the more complicated industrial production became, the more numerous were the elements of industry the supply of which had to be safeguarded. Three of these, of course, were of outstanding importance: labor, land, and money. In a commercial society their supply could be organized in one way only: by being made available for purchase. Hence, they would have to be organized for sale on the market—in other words, as commodities. The extension of the market mechanism to the elements of industry—labor, land, and money— was the inevitable consequence of the introduction of the factory system in a commercial society. The elements of industry had to be on sale.

This was synonymous with the demand for a market system. We know that profits are ensured under such a system only if self-regulation is safeguarded through interdependent competitive markets. As the development of the factory system had been organized as part of a process of buying and selling, therefore labor, land, and money had to be transformed into commodities in order to keep production going. They could, of course, not be really transformed into commodities, as actually they were not produced for sale on the market. But the fiction of their being so produced became the organizing principle of society. Of the three, one stands out: labor is the technical term used for human beings, in so far as they are not employers but employed; it follows that henceforth the organization of labor would change concurrently with the organization of the market system. But as the organization of labor is only another word for the forms of life of the common people, this means that the development of the market system would be accompanied by a change in the organization of society itself. All along the line, human society had become an accessory of the economic-system.

We recall our parallel between the ravages of the enclosures in English history and the social catastrophe which followed the Industrial Revolution. Improvements, we said, are, as a rule, bought at the price of social dislocation. If the rate of dislocation is too great, the community must succumb in the process. The Tudors and early Stuarts saved England from the fate of Spain by regulating the course of change so that it became bearable and its effects could be canalized into less destructive avenues. But nothing saved the common people of England from the impact of the Industrial Revolution. A blind faith in spontaneous progress had taken hold of people's minds, and with the fanaticism of sectarians the most enlightened pressed forward for boundless and unregulated change in society. The effects on the lives of the people were awful beyond description. Indeed, human society would have been annihilated but for protective countermoves which blunted the action of this self-destructive mechanism.

Social history in the nineteenth century was thus the result of a double movement: the extension of the market organization in respect to genuine commodities was accompanied by its restriction in respect to fictitious ones. While on the one hand markets spread all over the face of the globe and the amount of goods involved grew to unbelievable proportions, on the other hand a network of measures and policies was integrated into powerful institutions designed to check the action of the market relative to labor, land, and money. While the organization of world commodity markets, world capital markets, and world currency markets under the aegis of the gold standard gave an unparalleled momentum to the mechanism of markets, a deep-seated movement sprang into being to resist the pernicious effects of a market-controlled economy. Society protected itself against the perils inherent in a self-regulating market system—this was the one comprehensive feature in the history of the age.

NOTES

1. Henderson, H.D., *Supply and Demand,* 1922. The practice of the market is twofold: the apportionment of factors between different uses and the organizing of the forces influencing aggregate supplies of factors.

2. Hawtrey, G.R., *op. cit.* Its function is seen by Hawtrey in making "the relative market values of all commodities mutually consistent."

3. Marx's assertion of the fetish character of the value of commodities refers to the exchange value of genuine commodities and has nothing in common with the fictitious commodities mentioned in the text.

4. Cunningham, W., "Economic Change," *Cambridge Modern History,* Vol. 1.

WILLIAM J. GOODE

The Family and
Industrialization

Let us now consider another relationship between family factors and social change, the possibility that the family system may have an independent, facilitating effect on the modern shift toward industrialization.

No full-scale research into this hypothesis has been carried out, but a few suggestive facts may be noted here. Negatively, of course, many observers have pointed out that extended and joint family systems prevented a free utilization of talent as well as the easy introduction of innovations against the power and traditionalism of family elders. Positively, it should be kept in mind that the family systems of the West have been different from those of other major civilizations for over a thousand years. Child or early adolescent marriage was not the ideal or the statistically usual. There was no ancestor worship, and *individuals,* not families, were responsible for crimes. There was no lineage or clan system, and the eldest male was not necessarily the leader of the family. Young couples were expected to live independently, for the most part.

Moreover, these differences were accentuated when the individualistic, anti-traditional ideology of ascetic Protestantism began to spread. The Puritans in the U.S., for example, defined husband and wife as loving companions rather than simply part of a family network, and their children had more freedom of marital choice than was possible in the traditional European family systems. Divorce became possible, even though disapproved. It seems likely by the time the new factory jobs opened in the late eighteenth century in England that the family system of at least part of the population was in some harmony with its new demands. Their extended kinship ties and obligations, and their links with family land, did not interfere with the new type of work obligations.

A more striking instance of the importance of family patterns in

Abridged and reprinted from William J. Goode, *The Family* (Englewood Cliffs, N.J.: Prentice Hall, 1964), pp. 108-16. ©1964. Abridged and reprinted by permission of Prentice-Hall, Inc., Englewood Cliffs, New Jersey and the author.

facilitating or hindering social change may be found in the contrast between the success of Japan and China in their attempt to industrialize during the late nineteenth and early twentieth centuries.[1]

Both were opened to the West at about the same time, and both faced a somewhat similar set of problems: threat of conquest, an agrarian economy, a rapid growth of population, extensive bureaucracies that had become corrupt and inefficient, an emphasis on familism not individualism, strains between town and country, and the low prestige of merchants, who would have to assume important roles in any modernizing process.

As against China's essential failure to cope with its problems, within about half a century after 1868 Japan had established heavy industries with almost no outside capital, altered its system of distribution, made both male and female literacy almost universal, and introduced a new set of social relationships, characteristic of the Western market system.

Several differences between the Japanese and Chinese family systems contributed to their varying successes in coping with the problems of industrialization. One was the pattern of inheritance. Under the Chinese family system, all sons inherited equally, so that family capital could not usually be kept intact. In Japan one son (usually the oldest) inherited all the property. Thus wealth could be accumulated, and one person could more easily make a decision to invest it.

Perhaps the most important family differences lay in the relationship between family and state. In China the personal loyalty was owed to the Emperor, but not if conflicted with family loyalty. A man owed his first duty to his father, and through him to clan elders. Being unfilial was the greatest of Chinese sins. Of course, the Japanese man owed loyalty to his father, but the system was *feudalistic* rather than familistic: An unbroken chain of fealty linked each individual through his father and his father's leader or lord, through successively higher ranks to the great princes and the Emperor. Orders from above were backed by family pressure. The radical alterations which the Meiji leaders tried to implement called for much sacrifice—for example, former warriors might be put to work, or used as policemen—but the links of fealty between family and family, and family and state, remained strong.

The Chinese regarded nepotism as a duty. A man could not reject his family if he improved his station in life, and he was expected to carry upward with him as many members as he could. In Japan social mobility was more difficult. Ideally, in contrast to China, people should remain in their places. However, *adoption* was one important mode of social ascent in Japan. A father might even disinherit a son in order to adopt a talented young man. However, the individual so chosen rose alone. He became part of the new family, and was no longer a member of his old family. Both in fact and predisposition this pattern favored innovations under the Meiji leaders: (1) the Japanese were somewhat less handicapped by nepotism, (2) those who rose did not need to help the undeserving members of his family of birth, and (3) men could seek out talented young men for placement in positions of opportunity.

One long-term family process also lowered the capacity of the Chinese to meet the problems of the new era. Since both in fact and ideal the Chinese system permitted social mobility, but accorded the merchant a lowly social rank, a common mobility path was to acquire wealth through commerce, but then to leave that occupation. The gentry were landowners and scholars. Those who acquired wealth sought to achieve prestige and power by becoming members of the gentry or training their sons to become members. The humanistic learning of the mandarins was essentially irrelevant to the problems of the modern era. Thus there was no steady accumulation of a technical and financial tradition by the successful families. By contrast, the Japanese merchant was confined to a narrower type of mobility: financial success. He had little chance of moving out of commerce and into high social ranks. But as a consequence, Japanese merchants and banking families had developed a considerable technical knowledge and tradition and were much better prepared to cope with the complex financial problems that accompanied the rapid industrialization of Japan during the Meiji period.

It must be emphasized that these cases are extremely complex, and family variables cannot be said to be the prime creators of the dramatic contrast. Nevertheless, it seems clear that they did make an important contribution to the striking differences in the industrial achievement of the two countries.

The importance of the family unit in the social mobility system, and thus as a facilitating element in social change, may also be seen in another major historical event, the French Revolution. This connection was commented on in the chapter on stratification. Some bourgeois families had moved into the nobility in the seventeenth and eighteenth centuries, as they had moved into the gentry in China, by acquiring wealth and beginning to live in the style of the upper stratum. This included humanistic education, or at least the support of arts and letters, fine manners, taste in clothing and furniture, and, of course, abandoning the commercial or manufacturing activities of the bourgeoisie. Those who aspired upward had to concede the superiority of the nobles, else there was no reason to move upward; but by definition, to be noble was to have been born noble. The successful bourgeois was caught in an ideological dilemma. It must be emphasized that his aim was not simply to associate with the nobility in government, or to make advantageous deals with those in power. It was rather to move his *family* and thus his family line into the nobility.

When the nobility began, over the course of the eighteenth century, to close gradually the various routes by which some bourgeois families might achieve a validation of noble status, this high stratum began to withdraw its support of the system as a whole, and instead began to view the nobility as a shackle or barrier to national progress, a violation of tenets of freedom. Moreover, the bourgeoisie furnished much of the leadership of the French Revolution in 1789.

NOTES

1. Marion J. Levy "Contrasting Factors in the Modernization of China and Japan," in Simon S. Kuznets, Wilbert E. Moore, and Joseph J. Spengler (eds.), *Economic Growth: Brazil, India, Japan* (Durham, N.C.: Duke University Press, 1955).

WILLIAM LETWIN

Four Fallacies
About
Economic Development

By fallacy I mean a truism that has been misunderstood. It is a statement which, if hedged in by enough qualifications, would be correct, but which, as commonly understood, is false.

It cannot be demonstrated that the human mind is especially given to fallacies when exercising itself on problems of economic development. But the idea of economic development is so vague that it invites confusion. Development is generally understood as the going from an underdeveloped economy to a developed economy, and an underdeveloped economy is generally supposed to be less developed than a developed economy. This circularity in the definition leads to quite unnecessary paradoxes. For instance, the national income of Nepal (the most underdeveloped economy presently on record) has been growing recently; despite that, Nepal must now be considered more underdeveloped than ever before—because the highly developed economy of the United States has been growing faster. Nobody would be satisfied to have it said that a growing boy was becoming less developed because a bigger boy was growing faster. Such a paradox is not essential to the subject.

Economic development can be spoken of simply as the process by which a nation grows richer. An underdeveloped economy, then, is an economy that is poor in a special sense—by comparison with its own economic potential in the foreseeable future. A nation founded on a tiny island in the Antarctic wastes, its land consisting of naked volcanic rock, snow-bound, ice-locked, and wind-swept eleven months of the year; peopled by a race that is unskilled, untaught and unteachable, possessing no capital—that nation would be poor but not underdeveloped, for it might have reached the limits of its economic capacity. Most poor nations are not poor in quite so ultimate and hopeless a sense.

Reprinted and abridged with the permission of the publisher and the author from "Four Fallacies about Economic Development," *Daedalus* (1963): pp. 396-414.

The practical problem of economic development is how to make poor countries richer absolutely. To make them as rich or nearly as rich as the United States or any other rich country is irrelevant and meaningless: are they to be made as rich as the United States is now, was some time ago, or will be hence? We can hope to help the underdeveloped nations eradicate hunger; it is fatuous to hope that the citizens of all nations will some day eat the same amount of food; it is utopian to hope that all men will some day have the same incomes. In any event, to eliminate hunger and misery is a far more commendable and humane goal than to aim for mathematical equality.

The question then is how nations have become richer in the past and how others can become richer in the future. Much is known about this and much more surmised. The four fallacies cover only a small part of the ground, although all alike are fundamental and popular.

The first fallacy: Manufacturing is more productive than agriculture.

This fallacy underlies the widespread belief that the prime or exclusive cure for national poverty lies in industrialization.

Folklore has it that human beings, when they first appeared on the earth, earned their living by hunting. Later, understanding how efficient it would be to keep their prey in easy reach, men supposedly turned to grazing. As communities formed, peace and order were established, and with them the likelihood that a man could reap without hindrance where he sowed; thus cultivation began. And finally—so the legend goes—when farmers had become so proficient that they could raise more food than they needed themselves, the surplus was used to sustain urban workers who earned their claim to food by exchanging for it fabricated things, or manufactures, as they are still called.

Some such broad historical scheme—sketching a development from husbandry to industry—has been borrowed from folklore by social philosophers and social scientists, who by endorsing it and systematizing it have reinforced the public faith. This picture underlies the schematic views on economic history of men as diverse as Adam Smith, Thomas Jefferson and Thorstein Veblen, to mention only a few. It underlies also, for instance, the classification of goods that is part of an economist's everyday vocabulary: "primary" goods being those produced by agriculture and extractive industries; "secondary" goods, manufactures; and "tertiary" goods, those commodities and services generated by "service industries."

Although the notion of the historical priority of agriculture is embedded in folklore, it is not false. On the contrary, the fundamental assertion—leaving aside the details of the story—is more nearly correct than its opposite: it is certain that industry did not predate the extractive occupations, including agriculture. But the historical doctrine in its ordinary form is nevertheless fallacious, for the truth is that agriculture and industry have always coexisted; extraction and fabrication both have gone on together ever since the beginning.

Endless evidence exists for the early practice of manufacturing. Stone-Age arrowheads show that the act of capture was preceded by handicrafts; Stone-Age scrapers and knives show that the act of capture was immediately succeeded by acts of fabrication. Man is, among other things, a tool-making animal; and tools are essential because men are neither strong nor agile enough to capture many animals without tools, and also because Nature does not provide many raw materials that human beings can use, without first transforming them, for food, shelter, or especially clothing. Even the life of men as primitive as can be, is cluttered with spears, knives, pots, bags, huts, ropes and cloths—all fabricated things. Taking things from the earth and molding those things to human ends are equally essential parts of human activity.

History cannot clearly distinguish between agriculture and manufacture according to the order of their appearance; theory cannot more sharply distinguish between their natures. Both activities use land, labor, and capital in the production of commodities. The way each uses them and the character of the commodities that each produces do not fall into the neat and expected categories.

Does manufacture use more capital relative to labor than agriculture? Quite the contrary; it turns out that now, at least, and in many places, agriculture is more capital-intensive than manufacturing. Does manufacture use more power than agriculture? Some forms of it probably do; but on the other hand, the highly mechanized branches of agriculture use more power than an industry as advanced and complex as electronic-components manufacturing. Is the planning period for agricultural production longer than for manufactures? Possibly; but whereas it takes about four or five years from the time a particular automobile model begins to be planned until it comes off the assembly lines, agricultural processes such as mushroom culture take only a few weeks from seed to fruit. Does agriculture produce food, and manufacture other sorts of things? Obviously not, since manufacture produces bread, whereas agriculture produces jute, indigo, and beeswax. Does agriculture produce necessities, and manufacture luxuries? No; manufacture produces boots and brooms, but agriculture produces silk, strawberries, and orchids.

Everyone knows the difference between a farmer and a mill hand, but for the purposes of economic policy too much is usually made of that difference.

These caveats having been entered, it should be pointed out that all underdeveloped economies depend heavily on agriculture, whereas all highly developed economies generate very little of their income by agriculture. Only 5 per cent of the income of the United States arises in agriculture, forestry and fishery; and only 8 per cent of the American labor force is engaged in those activities. In Nepal, by contrast, 93 per cent of the labor force is engaged in agriculture. In India, about half of the national income derives from agriculture, forestry and fishery. But in New Zealand, whose citizens enjoy the third highest average income in the world, only one-sixth of the labor force is engaged in agriculture, and they produce only one-fifth of the national income. The other countries of the world arrange themselves more or less neatly on this scale, neatly enough so that one would be warranted in betting that a country which specializes in agriculture is a poor country and that a country which does not is relatively rich.

That this is not a mere happenstance, but an outcome of the general process of enrichment can be seen by examining the long history of the American economy. In 1840 probably more than half of American output was being produced in the agricultural sector; by the end of the Civil War the contribution of agriculture had shrunk to one-fifth; by the end of World War I to about one-tenth, and by now to less than one twentieth. The same pattern could be exhibited in the history of the United Kingdom or of any other industrialized society. An inevitable concomitant of national enrichment is that agriculture ceases to be the single greatest contributor to national income and in time becomes, instead, one of the lesser contributors.

But the evidence should not be misread. Agriculture ultimately becomes less important when a nation has become fairly rich; although its agricultural output may continue to rise absolutely, the *fraction* of the national income produced by agriculture steadily declines because other forms of production take on greater significance. But this does not mean that agriculture is a crutch that can be abandoned. Although agriculture is superseded in rich nations, there is good reason to think that during the period of its primacy it was agriculture above all, in nations such as the United States or New Zealand or Great Britain, which established the base for enrichment. At some points in the development of any economy, agriculture rather than manufacture *may* be the best means of enrichment.

Agriculture, then, though neither historically prior nor analytically distinguishable, tends to be superseded by manufacture in the course of enrichment. And it should be added, manufacture in turn tends to be displaced somewhat by service industries. For what reason?

The fundamental cause of this sequence is a fairly universal human taste for refinement. In the history of the Western world, for instance, white wheaten bread has always been preferred to whole-grain wheaten bread. But white bread is inevitably more expensive than dark—all else being equal—because the former uses up more wheat per ounce of bread; in consequence, the bread of the rich was always whiter than that of the poor. For similar reasons the linens of the rich have always been finer and whiter, their furnishings more delicate, their manners more elaborate. To refine nature's products to the standards which the human imagination invents requires much transformation, that is, much manufacture, which is costly. Hence, as men's incomes rise, they spend an increasing fraction of their incomes on the manufacturing processes that turn the immediate products of nature into the goods and services that fancy requires.

A poor savage, for want of better, sits in the sand eating meat of the bear that he has himself slain, quartered, and roasted over fire. The wealthy aesthete eats the meat of a duckling that has been reared in domestic tranquility, which has been pressed and cooked with the aid of ingenious machinery and talented labor and in the presence of artfully contrived wines, and which is served to him in a setting far from natural. The former, whose income is small, eats a meal the main ingredient of whose cost is an agricultural or extractive effort. The latter, in paying for his meal, pays mainly for the labor and capital that went into setting the dish before him, the refined dish in its refined setting; only a miniscule part of the cost is accounted for by the effort of producing the duckling, that is, by specifically agricultural costs.

The technical terms describing this behavior are that the income-elasticity of demand for agricultural products is low. It is not, of course, as low as all that. "Food" is not a homogeneous stuff. As their incomes rise, men choose to consume foods of the more tender and delectable sorts: spareribs and lamb forequarters are replaced by tenderloin, in the American version; in France, ordinary wine gives way to Burgundy; among Indian peasants, millet is abandoned in favor of rice. Nevertheless, in all places, the *fraction* of income devoted to the raw—that is, purely agricultural—ingredients of the diet falls as income rises. That is the chief reason why the fraction of income generated by agriculture—as "income" and "agriculture" are defined in national income statistics—is lower in rich countries than in poor countries.

This indisputable fact has been widely misinterpreted after the *post hoc ergo propter hoc* fashion. If rich countries do much manufacturing, does it not follow that a country wishing to be rich should expand its manufactures? Such reasoning is part of the doctrine, albeit only part, which suggests to impoverished nations throughout the world that to erect a steel mill is to make the first step toward national opulence.

It is easy enough to specify circumstances in which it would be anything but reasonable to set up a steel mill, or any other manufacturing enterprise. Imagine a very poor nation, very sparsely settled, absolutely closed off from the rest of the world; and suppose that each inhabitant had the same income, an income hardly sufficient to keep his family alive. In those circumstances agriculture and other extractive occupations would be the only ones; everyone would farm and fish and hunt, and in his spare hours everyone would be busy making clothing and housing, preparing meals, and fashioning implements. In such a setting, were incomes miraculously to rise a bit, nobody would think of spending the increase on anything but extra food. Nobody would think of buying any manufactured goods whatsoever, unless his income were to rise vastly beyond its existing range. Even if a foreign expert could demonstrate that the same effort required to increase the output of rice by one pound could produce instead one hundred pounds of steel, the demonstration would fall on deaf ears— for the inhabitants would want rice so badly that no amount of steel, or gold, would be an acceptable substitute. In a very poor and utterly closed economy, manufacture would be an inimical luxury.

Underdeveloped nations are neither so poor nor so closed as that hypothetical one. Since at least some of their inhabitants are not on the verge of starvation, the nation is already consuming a certain amount of manufactured goods, which may be made inside the country or imported from abroad. At that point it becomes plausible to ask whether the most efficient way to raise the average income of inhabitants is by investing capital—supposing there be some to invest—in agriculture or in manufacturing. The manufactured goods might, of course, find no buyers within the country; but that would be immaterial as long as the goods could be exchanged elsewhere in the world for additional food, if additional food was wanted. On the other hand, the manufactured goods might be of such a sort that they could find no buyers abroad; but that would be no fatal objection if they could be sold domestically to persons who until then had been buying similar goods imported from abroad. Whether the manufactured goods increased the nation's exports or decreased its imports, either way the foreign exchange acquired in the process could be used to buy extra food, if extra food were wanted.

In an open economy, manufacturing may be a better way of getting food than the practice of agriculture. Similarly, agriculture may be a more efficient way of getting manufactured goods. The rational rule, then, is to pursue that activity which is most efficient. A nation that wants steel should not produce steel unless producing it is the cheapest way to get it; the possibility of international trade means that the cheapest way for some nations to get their steel is by producing butter or by catching fish.

Whether manufacturing is more productive than agriculture is therefore a question that cannot be answered in general, but only when one knows which branches of either group are being considered, and where, and when, and at what prices and costs. If an underdeveloped nation can produce radio circuits at a price far below world prices, but cannot produce its staple breadstuff as cheaply as others can, it will enrich itself more quickly by making the former and buying the latter. But which of these two, or of any other form of production it can carry on most efficiently, depends on the intricate relations, at each given moment, between such variables as the levels of income and rates of change of income throughout the world; of wage rates, interest rates, and rents at home and everywhere; of private tastes and diplomatic relations at home and abroad; and many more considerations of that sort.

All such qualifications being made, and in view of the fact that incomes have been rising throughout the world—despite the fears of neo-Malthusians who warn that the world's population will soon outrun the world's capacity to grow food—it is a safe general rule that *eventually* it will pay every nation to devote an increasing fraction of its productive efforts to manufacturing. But this is not all. The day may come when incomes have risen so high everywhere that manufactured goods too, like agricultural goods now, despite being more plentiful become insignificant in the budgets of consumers, who will begin to satisfy increasingly their desire for services.

The second fallacy: More capital is better than less capital.

This fallacy underlies the supposition that the problems of underdeveloped countries can be overcome merely by providing them with more capital.

A simple example will demonstrate the nature of the fallacy. Consider a small farm cultivated by farmer and ox. The man follows the plow from morning until night, under a hot sun: his life is hard. Imagine that the farmer acquires a tractor. The tractor chugs merrily through the day's work in an hour, the farmer driving it comfortably under an awning: his life has become easy and leisurely. The picture rightly comforts all humanitarian observers. The only difficulty is that the farmer is now starving. True, he has more leisure, but his crop is no larger than before, and the cost of keeping up the tractor (including as its main ingredient the interest charges on the loan with which he bought the tractor) is eating up a great deal of the food he previously had. The handy, efficient piece of machinery is impoverishing him.

The case of the farmer and his tractor, translated into technical terms, shows that the use of more rather than less capital is economically rational only if the labor saved by introducing an additional capital good is worth more than the costs added by using the capital good. As underdeveloped economies typically suffer from considerable unemployment, overt or disguised, the labor saved by introducing *certain* capital goods into *certain* occupations has a proper economic value of zero. That is to say that the real economic cost of using an hour's labor in any given enterprise is measured by its "opportunity cost," the additional output which that hour's labor would have produced in alternative employment. If Robinson Crusoe can gather a pound of brambleberries in an hour or catch half a pound of fish, then what the pound of fish really costs him is the two pounds of brambleberries he must forego for it. To return to the peasant and the tractor, the opportunity cost to the peasant of the hours of labor that the tractor saves him may be zero because he cannot use the saved time productively. In that case, the use of labor-saving capital goods is sheer waste.

The more general rule under which the peasant's case falls is that the most efficient combination of resources—efficiency being measured by costs—in the production of any goods is that which uses but little of the most costly resources and much of the cheaper resources. In an economy where wages are high and the use of machinery is cheap, goods that technically could be produced either by hand work or by machine work, will tend to be produced by machine. The converse would naturally hold in an economy where wages are low relative to the price of machinery.

The application of this rule explains, for instance, why Americans buy so many new cars. The American motorists' buying habits are generally thought to be a manifestation of lightheadedness, a proof that the consumer is enslaved by advertisers, and an illustration of conformism. By contrast, the tendency of motorists elsewhere to keep their cars for much longer stretches is supposed to result from a higher sobriety or more elevated taste. All that may be; yet the contrast can be explained simply in terms of economic rationality. In countries where labor is plentiful in comparison with producers' capital goods, the cheapest way to repair a car is by hand labor, that is, labor equipped with a minimal supply of simple tools. In a country like the United States, where labor is more expensive relative to capital goods, the cheapest way to keep a car up to a certain standard of performance is regularly to buy a new one from an automobile factory, where relatively little labor is combined with a vast supply of highly mechanized tools. The most efficient way to repair a car in the United States is to build a new car; the most efficient way to build a new car in most other places is to repair an old one.

In the same way it is equally sensible to build roads in the United States with bulldozers and diesel earthmovers and to build roads in China by using large gangs of laborers shifting gravel with no equipment other than picks, shovels and buckets. From the purely economic standpoint, to save much of that labor in China by using many bulldozers would be a sheer waste.

It is a fallacy, therefore, to believe that using more capital in any given enterprise is economically more efficient than using less. Capital goods, like other productive factors, are efficient only when they are properly allocated among all of the various uses to which they can be put.

The decision as to how much capital should be invested in any particular enterprise cannot be divorced from another decision, how much total capital a nation should accumulate, create or use.

At any given moment, to be sure, the amount of capital at a nation's disposal is not a matter of choice but of fact. Over any stretch of time, however, the amount can be expanded or contracted. Capital goods are produced, like all other goods, by the use of land, labor and capital. The only way a nation can by its own efforts expand its stock of capital goods, therefore, is by using resources that could otherwise have been devoted to making additional consumption goods. This interchangeability, in the production process, of capital goods and consumption goods is illustrated in a farmer's choice between eating his harvest and planting it as seed; the more he eats, the less he can plant; the more he uses for current consumption, the less he can use as capital. The monetary counterpart of this choice is that income can be spent on consumption goods or set aside as savings; and in an economy that is working smoothly, the relative outputs of consumption goods and capital goods will match the ratio of consumption expenditures to savings. All that the people of an underdeveloped economy need do to expand the national stock of capital is to consume less than they produce. Leaving aside economic perturbations and peculiarities, the less they consume relative to current output, the faster their supply of capital will grow.

A slight defect in this prescription is that underdeveloped nations are so poor that they cannot generate much capital. The income of a very poor man hardly suffices for the ordinary needs of life; he cannot be expected to restrict his consumption in favor of future benefits; his needs press too urgently to allow much concern for the future. A man who is twenty and starving would be whimsical to invest in an annuity payable at sixty. A nation full of such men would not rationally do much saving, hence would not generate much capital. It would not, that is, if the voluntary individual choices of its citizens were allowed to prevail.

But the rate of capital formation in an underdeveloped economy can be speeded up by its government. Suppose the citizens are on the average currently saving 5 per cent of their incomes. If the government increases the tax rate and spends the added revenue on capital goods it can push the *national* savings rate, and the national rate of capital formation, up to any level it chooses short of the limit imposed by the size of national income. Programs of forced savings have been instituted by the governments of many underdeveloped nations. Insofar as the tax burden falls on the relatively wealthy citizens of those nations, the policy of forced savings is in effect a program of redistribution, open to approval or disapproval on the grounds generally applicable to schemes for equalizing income and wealth. Unfortunately, however, in very poor economies the national rate of capital formation cannot be raised much by any level of taxation applied to the wealthy few. Where that is the case, and it is probably a fairly typical case, the regime of forced savings may be extended to citizens who are poor absolutely, with the result that those who were already underfed are required to reduce their consumption further. The offer held out to them is that by making this coerced sacrifice now, by foregoing current consumption in order that extra capital may be created, they are guaranteeing themselves a higher income at some future time. But if it would be whimsical or mad for a very poor man voluntarily to save too much, it is surely whimsical or inhumane for a government to force him to save too much. One reads with shock of the aged bachelor brothers discovered lying dead of starvation on mattresses stuffed with money; the spectacle would be hardly more edifying had they died so because the state commandeered their income to build, for the national good, a splendid atomic power station.

There is still another way in which a nation can increase the supply of capital at its disposal, which is to borrow it from foreigners. This method, which has been used by underdeveloped nations for many centuries, is especially suitable since it can put at their disposal, quickly, capital far in excess of the amounts they could generate at home. Moreover, it is made feasible not only by the benevolence of foreign governments; the self-interest of foreign capitalists moves them, too, to invest in underdeveloped countries, for the rate of return in countries that as yet possess little capital is apt to be much higher than the rate capital can earn in richer economies. Unfortunately capital borrowed from private lenders is seldom or never received so warmly by the underdeveloped nation as when it is proffered to the government by other governments or international agencies. The reason is not only that public lenders are more likely to offer bargain rates. More often reluctance is dictated by the feeling that when foreigners invest in and own a country's facilities, especially its public services, they acquire too great a power in its political affairs. Whether this fear is realistic, and if realistic, so compelling that a nation should forego possibilities of more rapid enrichment in order to exclude the threat, is a question fruitless to consider in the abstract. It can be usefully answered, in concrete instances, only by the exercise of fine political prudence. As to the purely economic issue, there is no doubt that foreign financing is the quickest way for underdeveloped nations to expand their supply of capital. It is convenient, also, that transfers of capital, conceived as loans, sometimes end life as gifts.

To accumulate capital, no matter how a nation comes by it, means necessarily to defer current consumption. As men can be short-sighted, so too can they be excessively long-sighted; they can cheat the present as easily as they can cheat the future, and in that sense more capital is no better than less.

(Ed. note: The author discusses two additional fallacies of economic development. The third one is that "more roads are better than fewer roads." The author's arguments apply more generally to communications systems usually provided by governments [though they need not be, he says]: roads, mail service, subways, and railroads. They apply still more generally to the public facilities known as "social overhead capital" or "infrastructure". Because seemingly vast public funds are available for these services, the public may demand more of them than is socially beneficial.

Faced with such demands, may not the government provide too much road? It is possible; to answer whether it is true would require a most exquisite calculation to determine whether the benefits to be realized by the community from an additional dollar invested in roads are at any moment greater or less than the benefits from that dollar's investment in any other capital good. The question cannot be answered.

But since every one who talks about roads says that there are not enough roads, it is important to notice that there *can* be too many roads and that a democratic government may systematically err in favor of too many roads.

The fourth fallacy is that "rapid economic development is better than slow economic development." The argument for rapidity is based on the need to make quick improvements in the standard of living if communism or severe social disorders are to be avoided. The author argues that it is impossible to accomplish simultaneously the greatest possible increase in the standard of living and the speediest increase. The usual means of increasing the standard of living is to increase capital investment. But such investment occurs at the expense of consumption. Therefore, it is virtually impossible to increase both maximally and simultaneously unless unusually large amounts of foreign capital are invested in capital industries.)

ROBERT THEOBALD

Cybernetics and
the Problems of
Social Organization

I do not intend to make an inventory of the identifiable or predictable effects of computer technology and cybernation on our social institutions and then present these as the whole picture of the socioeconomic changes being brought about by the applications of cybernetics. For in addition to these kinds of specific and identifiable changes, there are already occurring other, fundamental changes in the socioeconomic system as a whole. These are being brought about through the drives exerted on the whole social fabric by the applications of cybernetics in the form of computerized systems.

Before discussing these drives we must look at the present state of computer application and its potential development. For some the computer seems the basis of all good, for others, the root of all evil. In these two allegorical roles, as a means of communication, and in a number of other functions, the computer is usurping the place of money. This fact is little understood, even by the informed public.

Computer manufacturers, like computers, increasingly talk among themselves. There is, therefore, a growing gap between the technological realities and public understanding of the potential of the computer and the speed at which developments are occurring.

Speaking before the 1964 Joint Fall Computer Conference, David Sarnoff, Chairman of the Board of the Radio Corporation of America, one of the country's leading computer hardware and software producers, outlined the way in which a universally compatible computer symbol-system will emerge and the unifying and systematizing effect it will have. Implicit in Sarnoff's remarks is the startling revelation that computer systems, not men, will first realize humanity's age-old dream of a universal language, and that the subtleties and nuances of human thought will risk

Reprinted and abridged with the permission of the publisher from Charles R. Dechert, ed., *The Social Impact of Cybernetics* (Notre Dame, Ind.: University of Notre Dame Press, 1966).

being mediated through the restricted and standardized symbols of computer communication.

> We function today in a technological Tower of Babel. There are, by conservative count, more than 1,000 programming languages. And there are languages within languages—in one instance, 26 dialects, and in another, 35 dialects. There are eight computer word lengths in use. There are hundreds of character codes in being, at a ratio of one code for every two machines marketed. Four magnetic tape sizes are employed with at least 50 different tape tracks and codes. Standards have not been accepted even for commonly used symbols, instruction vocabulary, or program development procedures....
>
> ...The interests of the industry and the needs of the user demand a far greater measure of compatibility and standardization among the competing makes of computers and the means by which they receive and transmit information.
>
> Tomorrow's standard computers and their peripheral equipment will instantly recognize a handwritten note, a design or drawing which they will store and instantly retrieve in original form.
>
> The computer of the future will respond to commands from human voices in different languages and with different vocal inflections.
>
> Its vocabulary will extend to thousands of basic words in the language of its country of residence, and machines will automatically translate the speech of one country into the spoken words of another....
>
> The interlocking world of information toward which our technology leads us is now coming closer to realization. It will be possible eventually for any individual sitting in his office, laboratory or home to query a computer on any available subject and within seconds to receive an answer—by voice response, in hard copy, or photographic reproduction, or on a large display screen....
>
> This emerging pattern inevitably will set in motion forces of change within the social order, extending far beyond the present of presently predictable applications of the computer. It will affect man's way of thinking, his means of education, his relationships to his physical and social environment, and it will alter ways of living.

FUNDAMENTAL SOCIOECONOMIC EFFECTS
OF COMPUTER APPLICATIONS

The computer "...will affect man's way of thinking, his means of education, his relationships to his physical and social environment, and it will alter ways of living." This dramatic truth, so clearly set out by Sarnoff, can be expressed even more briefly. We are passing out of the industrial age into the cybernetics era.

No attempt to list the implications of the shift from the industrial age to the cybernetics era can possibly be complete. Up to the present time, we have tended to examine what the introduction of cybernetics can do to and for certain fields: education, medicine, law, police-work, production, sales, administration, etc. While I will touch on many of these fields, I will be concerned primarily with the implications of the theory and practice of cybernetics on the total socioeconomic system.

My chief concern, as a social economist, is to examine the drives which arise from the development of cybernetics and to see how they can be employed to meet our fundamental goals—rather than subvert them. I am not interested in trying to use cybernetics to preserve our existing socioeconomic system. Indeed, I intend to prove that continuation of this system will, in fact, make it impossible to realize our fundamental goals. Put another way, the recruiting of cybernetics to aid in the maintenance of some of our industrial-age values will make it increasingly difficult to realize these more basic goals.

I shall concentrate on four fundamental drives that arise from the application of cybernetics in the form of computer systems: the drive toward unlimited destructive power, the drive toward unlimited productive power, the drive to eliminate the human mind from repetitive activities, and the inherent organizational drive of the computer within a cybernetic system. I shall first examine the components of these drives; I shall then indicate the end results of these drives if we fail to change the present socioeconomic system; and finally, I will set out some of the minimum steps required to enable us to use these drives to achieve our fundamental goals.

Let me take up each of these four drives in turn. First, there is a drive toward unlimited destructive power. This results from the combination of nuclear energy with the control and communication system of the computer plus the activities of those involved in research and development. It is now generally accepted that there are already sufficient nuclear explosives, as well as bacteriological and chemical weapons, available to destroy civilization, if not all life.

Second, there is a drive toward unlimited productive power. This also results from the combination of effectively unlimited energy with the control and communication system of the computer plus the activities of those involved in research and development. While this drive toward unlimited productive power is still denied by the conventional economist, it is fully accepted by those most closely associated with production—the manufacturers and the farmer. American firms now expand their production, both within America and abroad, just as fast as they are able to increase profitable sales. There is no longer any effective limit to our productive abilities. We have passed beyond the dismal science of traditional economics. U Thant, Secretary General of the United Nations, has expressed this reality in the following words: "The truth, the central stupendous truth, about developed countries today is that they can have—in anything but the shortest run—the kind and scale of resources they decide to have.... It is no longer resources that limit decisions. It is the decision that makes the resources. This is the fundamental revolutionary change—perhaps the most revolutionary mankind has ever known." This is the true meaning of abundance: not that goods and services are already available and waiting to be used, but that we possess the technological potential to call forth enough goods and services to meet our needs.

Third, there is a drive to eliminate the human mind from repetitive activities. This results from the fact that the computer is a far more efficient drudge than the human being. We know that the production worker can be replaced by the cybernated system, that the computer controls inventory more effectively than the manager, that the computer handles bank accounts far more cheaply than the clerk. These, however, are primitive developments: in the near future we will see that the computer can take over *any* structured task: that is to say, any task where the decision-making rules can be set out in advance. Thus, for example, the computer will take over the process of granting most types of bank loan, the analysis of stock portfolios and the process of odd-lot trading on Wall Street. The last application is perhaps particularly noteworthy, for it will replace a group of people whose median income is around $50,000 a year.

The computer will force man's mind out of the repetitive productive system just as surely as industrial machinery forced out man's muscle. Gerard Piel, publisher of the *Scientific American,* has stated this truth in the following words:

> The new development in our technology is the replacement of the human nervous system by automatic controls and by the computer that ultimately integrates the functions of the automatic control units at each point in the production process. The human muscle began to be disengaged from the productive process at least a hundred years ago. Now the human nervous system is being disengaged.

Fourth, there is an inherent organizational drive of the computer within a cybernetic system. The initial setting up of computer systems responds to a need to increase economic efficiency or to rationalize operations. But as computer systems become fully operative, a drive emerges toward the reorganization, for purposes of compatability, of interacting systems and institutions. The greater the number of areas of computer application, the greater the force behind this drive. There is now quite clearly a trend toward the emergence of a total computer system organized for maximum efficiency in terms of the coordination of large numbers of specific tasks.

Changes resulting from these four drives have already begun. The transformations taking place around us should not be regarded as the occurrences of random, isolated, nonpredictable events, but rather should be urgently studied to determine developing trends. We must always keep in mind the anthropological insight on culture change: that change brought about in one part of the system will be accompanied by other changes, both predictable and unpredictable, in many parts of the existing socioeconomic system and the entire culture.

It is now clear that the impact of the computer is destroying the industrial-age balance between the economy and the society. We continue, however, to assume that after a period of apparent disorganization, a new, favorable socioeconomic balance will become evident. We have further assumed that if it becomes clear that a satisfactory balance is not emerging, we will be able to intervene at the last moment to correct unfavorable trends. These kinds of assumptions would appear analagous to the economic theories of *laissez-faire* and, later, of precrisis intervention in the economy. But these theories were based on the impossibility of prediction and resulted in the establishment of a policy of remedial, not preventive, action.

Today, the availability of the computer enables us to spot trends long before they would otherwise be visible, to carry out the necessary discussion and to develop policies before the need for action develops. We can thus use these computers to control their own effects. Using information provided by computer systems, we can speed up the observation/discussion/action process so that we can keep up with the developments in our own technology. We can recruit technological drives to aid us in our effort to achieve our fundamental goals. Already information obtained through the use of computers can enable us to perceive rapidly both problems and opportunities. I will now try briefly to outline these problems and these opportunities and the kinds of society that would evolve from our failure or success in taking timely action in response to information already available. I will first discuss the developments that will inevitably follow if we fail to control our driving technology.

The fact that there are now sufficient nuclear explosives available to destroy civilization, if not all life, is now regarded almost as a cliché. New depth and meaning were, however, recently given to this realization in an article published in the *Scientific American* by Herbert York and Jerome Wiesner, both of whom have held high office in recent administrations. They stated: "The clearly predictable course of the arms race is a steady downward spiral into oblivion." The existence of the drive toward unlimited destructive power therefore condemns each country to undermine its own security in the very process of pursuing it.

Let us now turn to the problem posed by the drive toward unlimited productive power. So long as we preserve our present socioeconomic system, internal economic stability is *only* possible if the amount people and institutions are willing and able to buy rises as fast as the amount that we are able to produce. It is necessary that effective demand keep up with potential supply. The viability of our present scarcity socioeconomic system is based on a very simple relationship. It is assumed that it is possible for the overwhelming proportion of those seeking jobs to find them and that the income received from these jobs will enable the jobholder to act as an adequate consumer. The successful functioning of the present socioeconomic system is therefore completely dependent on an ability to provide enough jobs to go round. A continuing failure to achieve this invalidates our present mechanism for income distribution, which operates only so long as scarcity persists. So long as the present socioeconomic system is not changed, abundance is a cancer, and the various parts of the system must continue to do their best to inhibit its growth.

It is for this reason that business firms of all sizes, economists of almost all persuasions, and politicians of all parties agree that it is necessary to keep effective demand growing as fast as potential supply: that those who are still able to act as adequate consumers, because they are still obtaining sufficient incomes from their jobs, be encouraged to consume more and more of the kind of products that the economic system is presently organized to produce. Our economy is dependent on "compulsive consumption" in the words of Professor Gomberg, and manufacturers spend ever increasing sums on consumer seduction to persuade the consumer that he "needs" an ever wider variety of products.

Each of us has his favorite story about the evils of advertising. But a new dimension is being added to the diabolic in advertising by means of new techniques using programmed computers and automatic equipment; for example, a system has already been developed and is presently in use, at least on the West Coast and in Washington, where in a given neighborhood every phone will ring and a tape-recorded sales message will be played when the phone is picked up. The implications for quiet and privacy are too obvious to require comment.

Pressures from the attempt to keep supply and demand in balance are not limited to the mere constant irritative pressure to be aware of sales messages. There is a second type of consequence that is even more serious, for it acts to prevent any effective control of the drive toward unlimited productive power. Economist Paul A. Samuelson has expressed the new reality in the following extreme terms: "In the superaffluent society, where nothing is any longer useful, the greatest threat in the world comes from anything which undermines our addiction to expenditures on things that are useless." It is for this reason that it is difficult to close down obsolete military bases, to limit cigarette consumption, in fact to slow down any form of activity which might in any way create demand or jobs. In these conditions, the need for ever-higher demand will almost inevitably have priority over the needs described by the social worker, the sociologist and the philosopher.

Whatever we do, we can only succeed in delaying the inevitable: the attempt to keep demand growing as fast as supply and thus create enough conventional jobs will inevitably fail. The effects of the computer in developing abundance and eliminating jobs will inevitably exceed our capacity to create jobs.

And even while we continue our effort to maintain the present socioeconomic system, the situation will deteriorate. We will see a continuation of the trends of the past years during which the position of the unskilled and the uneducated has worsened, the plight of the poor has become ever more hopeless. Professor Charles Killingsworth, one of the leading experts on unemployment statistics, has shown that in 1950 the unemployment rate for the least educated group was four times the rate for the most-educated group; by 1962, the "real" rate for the bottom group was 12 times the rate for the top group. In a parallel development, the percentage of income received by the poorest 20% of the population has fallen from 4.9% to 4.7%. It should also be noted that during the five-year period ending in 1962, the income of high school graduates as compared with college graduates dropped from 60% to 52%.

Continuation of *present* trends is leading to a new type of organization of the socioeconomic system within which incomes and work time would be proportional. Starting at the bottom of the scale, there would be a large number of totally unemployed workers subsisting inadequately on resources derived from government schemes merely designed to ensure survival. The greatest proportion of the population would work considerably shorter hours than at present and receive wages and salaries that would provide the necessities and even some conveniences, but would not encourage them to develop a meaningful pattern of activity. A small number of people with the highest levels of education and training would work excessively long hours for very high salaries.

The effects of the drive toward unlimited productive power will, of course, not only be internal but will also affect the prospects of the poor countries. It is now clear that the gap between the rich and the poor countries is continuing to widen and that there is no possible way to reverse this trend until we change the existing socioeconomic system. It is shocking to realize that we have now reached the point where the *annual per capita increase in income* in the United States is equal to the *total income per capita* in some of the poor countries.

The reasons for this disparity are illustrated by the following two quotations. First, from the United Nations Development Decade report: "Taken as a group, the rate of progress of the underdeveloped countries measured by income per capita has been painfully slow, more of the order of 1 percent per annum than 2 percent. Most indications of social progress show similar slow and spotty improvement." And from a statement discussing the situation in India by B. R. Shenoy, director of the School of Social Sciences at Gujerat University: "Per capita consumption of food grains averaged 15.8 ounces per day in 1958, below the usual jail ration of 16 ounces, the army ration of 19 ounces and the current economic plan's target of 18 ounces. Since then, the average has fluctuated downward. Between 1956 and 1960, the annual per capita use of cloth fell from 14.7 metres to 13.9 metres."

The expressed policy of the Western powers is to aid the poor countries to catch up to the rich within an acceptable period of time. It has been generally argued, most explicitly in W. W. Rostow's *Stages of Economic Growth,* that the way the poor countries can attain this goal is to heed the lessons of history, to pass through the Western stages of growth, although hopefully at a faster pace. It is surely time we recognized the inapplicability of this policy.

The rate of economic growth of most poor countries now depends primarily on their being able to export enough goods to pay for their needed imports. It is clear that the poor countries will not be able to increase exports at an adequate rate to pay for the required growth in imports and that they will not be able to attain any reasonable rate of growth. The vast majority of the poor countries have no prospect of achieving an adequate standard of living so long as the present socioeconomic system continues.

Let us now turn to the prospect of freeing the mind of man from involvement in the repetitive productive process. There are a few optimists who persist in arguing that Western man can benefit immediately from the decrease in toil promised by the computer. An analysis of this conclusion suggests that those reaching it have not yet understood that it is typically those people whose life and educational experience ensure that they have the least adequate preparation for imaginative and constructive activities who will receive the largest increase in time not allocated to carrying out conventional jobs. This group is composed of two main categories: those with totally inadequate educations—the "poverty-cycle group," and those whose education and training have been slanted almost entirely toward conformity in order to enable them to perform tasks that will no longer be needed by the socioeconomic system.

Within our social economy a large number of individuals are already manifesting psychopathic symptoms as a response to loss of their roles in the system. Many economic analysts ignore the profound threat which the machines pose to deep-seated individual values and motivations. This threat is not manifest in economic statistics nor even in sociological monographs discussing the "world view" of the poor, but it is already affecting most members of society, both employed and unemployed. It is as all-pervasive as advertising, and, like it, it is constantly exerting pressures upon the individual, whether he be conscious of them or not. Some comments by psychiatrist Jack Weinberg illuminate this issue:

> Complicated machines which perform in intricate and invisible patterns are frightening. They are beyond the common man's understanding and he cannot identify with them. He experiences hostility toward such a machine, as he does toward most things he fails to understand. Furthermore, automation has done something that is unthinkable to a man who values his own self and that which he produces. In a sense, it has removed him from the product which he creates. . . . Work—no matter how odious an implication it

may have to a person—is an enormously prized and meaningful experience to man. It is not all punishment for his transgressions as implied biblically, but it is also a blessing, not only for common-sense, economic reasons... but also because of its varied and unifying psychological implications.

Psychiatrists in clinical practice report increasingly that their patients are concerned because they feel that they function in an inferior way compared to machines, that their limbs are not acting as efficient machine-parts. They also report fantasies, such as dreams in which the patient is being backed into a corner by a computer. The popular arts—cartoons, comedy routines, and folk-songs—increasingly reflect these fears and influences of advanced technology and, above all, of the computer.

A. R. Martin, chairman of the American Psychiatric Association Committee on Leisure Time and Its Use, has summarized this problem in the following terms in a discussion of the role of medicine in formulating future public health policy:

> Symptoms of individual maladaption are: excessive guilt, compulsive behavior (especially compulsive work), increase of anxiety, depression, psychosomatic symptoms and suicide.. We must face the fact that a great majority of our people are not emotionally and psychologically ready for free time. This results in unhealthy adaptations which find expression in a wide range of sociopathologic and psychopathologic states. Among the social symptoms of this maladaption to free time are: low morale, civilian unrest, subversiveness and rebellion.

We are all aware of the manifest acceleration of past trends which bears out Martin's statement: let me briefly recall a few of them:

The crime rate is presently rising at about 10% a year as compared with a population increase of less than 2% a year.

Drug addiction grows not only in the ghettoes but in the well-to-do suburbs, and young people are especially vulnerable to the activities of those who seek new recruits to the army of addicts.

America, as a society, tolerates over 40,000 deaths in automobile accidents a year, despite the fact that techniques of accident reduction are available for use.

There is a fascination with violence. This was dramatically illustrated by a recent event in New York when 40 interested spectators remained indifferent to the appeals of an 18-year-old bruised and bloodied office worker as she tried to escape from a rapist. Similarly in Albany, a crowd gathered to urge a mentally disturbed youth to jump to his death. Two comments reported in *The New York Times* are hardly believable: "I wish he'd do it and get it over with. If he doesn't hurry up we're going to miss our last bus." And another: "I hope he jumps on this side. We couldn't see if he jumped over there."

The problem of increased violence and crime was raised in the recent presidential campaign, but a meaningful discussion never developed. The growing extent of the problem was underlined by the police chief of Los Angeles, William H. Parker, in a question and answer interview in *U.S. News and World Report* in April 1964:

Question: Has the crime picture changed much in [the last 37 years?]

Answer: Not only has the crime picture changed, but the entire attitude of the American people toward crime, I think, has undergone quite a definite change. I think there is a tendency to accept crime as part of the American scene, and to tolerate it. . . .

Question: America might have the choice, eventually between a criminal state and a police state.

Answer: I believe that will become the option before us if crime becomes so troublesome that we are no longer able to control it.

I have been discussing societal and psychological deterioration primarily with reference to the removal of the human mind from repetitive productive activity as a result of the installation of computer systems. To many it will appear that I have overstated my case in casting the computer in the role of the root of all evil. I would therefore like to emphasize that my point here is only that it *can* be just that in the future, for it can accelerate existing disfunctional socioeconomic trends.

It is true that these societally disfunctional trends began long before the computer appeared on the socioeconomic scene, but it is also true that our attempts to reverse these trends will be frustrated if we continue to regard the ability of the computer to act with maximum efficiency in carrying out an immediate task as more important than all of our fundamental values put together. As long as we regard these values as of minor importance, to be upheld only when it is convenient to do so, we will be unable to recruit the computer to help us to attain our fundamental goals.

Whether increasing violence and social disorder can fairly be laid at the door of the computer is, however, peripheral to the possibility of the development of a police state. The only question is whether we will become convinced that our predominant need is for greater control over the individual and the means we will use to achieve it.

We have so far failed to perceive that the types of control made possible by the inherent organizational drive of the computer within a cybernetic system have no common measure with our past experience in organization. The generalized use of the computer as a means of societal control threatens to destroy at least the privacy, and very probably *all* the present rights, of the individual unless we change the socioeconomic system. Let us be very clear: the only way to run the complex society of the second half of the twentieth century is to use the computer. The question is to determine the rights of the individual under these circumstances and then to ensure that they are respected by the computer-using authorities.

The danger is imminent. Government already holds very substantial dossiers on a major part of the population. These are either in computer memories or can be placed in computer memories. Information on the financial affairs of each individual will soon be available through the development of the Internal Revenue Service Computer System. It is now planned that the records of the Job Corps will be placed on computers, a step which will inevitably be extended to cover *all* those that the government considers to be in need of help to find or regain a place in society. In the area of the exercise of socially sanctioned force and compulsion, it is significant that New York State is developing a statewide police information network: a network which all authorities agree could be extended nationwide within a brief period of years.

It is no longer possible to dismiss such works as *Brave New World* and *1984* as mere literary nightmares. I do not believe that I exaggerate when I say that almost all those who have looked not simply at one, but rather at all four of the drives I have discussed, agree that some form of dehumanized, impersonal world is inevitable in the next 10 years unless we make major changes in our socioeconomic system. In particular, I remember very clearly the comment of one individual very heavily involved in the development of new computer applications, who said to me that the only thing wrong with the descriptions of the internal police state in *1984* was that the date was at least 10 years too late.

Unless we consciously develop new policies, we will destroy all the goals we have striven so long to achieve. Only the working out of a new socioeconomic balance with the aid of society's servants—computer systems—will enable us to meet our fundamental societal goals.

I have been discussing the effect of the drives exerted by the application of computers in reinforcing certain industrial-age values and thus inhibiting our forward movement into the cybernated era. I will now turn to a consideration of the potential of these drives as aids in the effort to move toward the realization of our fundamental societal goals in the new context of a cybernetics-based socioeconomy. It is my contention that the positive potential of these drives will not become a reality as long as we continue to subordinate efforts to correct socioeconomic ills to the goal of the continuation of an outmoded industrial-age system, with its now inappropriate set of restraints and freedoms. If we are to have a more fulfilling way of life in the cybernetics-based abundance era, we must take conscious steps to enable us to arrive at a new set of restraints and freedoms and a new balance between them.

I will attempt to indicate briefly some of the steps which I consider to be of first importance. Those who are interested in a fuller discussion of these and related subjects will find more detailed descriptions in my books *The Rich and the Poor, The Challenge of Abundance,* and *Free Men and Free Markets.*

Let us begin with a consideration of the drive toward unlimited destructive power. It is now generally accepted that this can only be prevented from destroying mankind if we renounce force, and that this requires that negotiation and arbitration become the means of settling disputes. In effect, nations will have to move toward world cooperation and world law. We are, at the present time, witnessing the early efforts of institutions which could become the creators and administrators of world law, but we continue to view such efforts as primarily aimed at peace-keeping. Our perception of the role of world cooperation in achieving socioeconomic advances remains very dim, for we still allow language and cultural barriers to impede the free flow of information. The physical barriers to communication are being lifted. New channels are opening. Our role is to insure that we use them, not allow ourselves to be persuaded that we should block them once again.

The drive toward unlimited productive power can result in vast benefits, both internationally and domestically, but only if we change the methods presently used to distribute rights to resources. It is, of course, impossible to determine the final pattern that will emerge, but I believe that the need for three steps can already be seen.

1. The rich countries should accept an unlimited commitment to provide the poor countries of the world with all the resources they can effectively employ to help them to move into the cybernetics-based abundance era. Let me state explicitly, however, that such a commitment should not be accompanied by the right to dump unwanted surplus industrial-age products and machinery into the poor countries. Rather, the poor countries must move as directly as possible from the agricultural era to the cybernetics era, without being forced to pass through the industrial-age process of socio-cultural and economic realignments.

Domestically, we should adopt the concept of an absolute constitutional right to an income through provision of basic economic security. This would guarantee to every citizen of the United States, and to every person who has resided within the United States for a period of five consecutive years, the right to an income from the federal government sufficient to enable him to live with dignity. No government agency, judicial body, or other organization whatsoever should have the power to suspend or limit any payments assured by these guarantees.

2. A second principle, committed spending, should also be introduced. This would embody the concept of the need to protect the existing middle-income group against abrupt and major declines in their standard of living, for a very substantial proportion of this group will lose their jobs in the next decade. This principle is based on the premise that in the process of transition between the industrial age and the cybernetics-based abundance era, socioeconomic dislocation should be avoided wherever possible, whether caused by sudden large-scale reduction in demand or by

sudden withdrawal of economic supports for valid individual and social goals.

Let me remind you that the validity of the classic objection—"we cannot afford it"—has been destroyed by the drive toward unlimited productive power. We can afford to provide the individual with funds that will encourage and enable him to choose his own activities and thus increase his freedom, and, *at the same time,* increase, to the required extent, expenditures on community needs: particularly education, medical services, housing, recreation facilities, and conservation.

3. There is now general agreement that if we are to profit from the drive to eliminate the human mind from repetitive tasks we must greatly increase our emphasis on education. We have been unwilling to face up to the fact that the school and the university were designed to serve the requirements of the industrial age. We have therefore concentrated our attention on longer periods of education for more and more people, rather than on changing the educational system to make it appropriate for the cybernetics era.

An attempt to lengthen the time spent in school and college will not be enough. We must find ways to develop the creativity and to enlarge the capacity of each individual in terms of his own uniqueness. We will have to teach people to think for themselves, rather than to absorb and then regurgitate with maximum efficiency the theories of past thinkers. I believe the best way to do this is to change our educational process from being discipline-oriented to being problem-oriented: to set up educational systems which will force people to face all the implications of each problem and to evaluate the individual's potential in terms of his ability to perceive new interconnections between aspects of the problem.

We must do this in such a way as to avoid the "new education" emphasis on means, the smoothly interacting group or seminar, and concentrate on ends, the kind of problems that will be studied. I think this can probably best be achieved through what we can call the two-dimensional seminar technique. Here the choice is up to the individual; he enters the systems at the first level with a multiple choice of seminars; he can then go on to specialize by movement up the levels of complexity in one problem area or he can choose to gain wider knowledge by horizontal movement, through participation in many seminars.

Education along problem-oriented lines is the prime necessity of the future and it is also the prime reason why we cannot preserve our present industrial-age values nor return to the simple values of the agricultural era. The set of values of the cybernetic era will be unique; attitudes toward time and space, production and consumption, will have to be appropriate to the realities of this era. In the future we are going to value those who can take a systems approach in all fields—not only about the problems of society but also about the individual. For example, the patient will respect his doctor on the basis of his ability to understand him as a biological system rather than value his seeming quasi-magical techniques as in our agricultural past.

I am sure that many humanists will be shocked by my acceptance of systems-thinking, for they fear that man will be destroyed by the rationality implicit in it. In this view the rational is synonymous with the logical solution to any problems inherent in a task, the choice of the one best way to do something, the constant search for the efficient. Compared to any system or smoothly running organization, man's thought processes are less rational, more subject to accident and distortion. According to this thesis, it follows that man must inevitably end by acting according to the instruction of the efficient decision-making mechanisms which he himself created for his service, to carry out his wishes, to fulfil his needs. But the efficient, knowledgeable servant becomes the administrator and thus the master. This is the case put forward by Jacques Ellul in his book originally published in France in 1952 under the title of *La Technique,* and recently published in the United States under the title *The Technological Society.* It is impossible not to concede the immense strength of Ellul's argument even though it was based on the organizational efficiency drives existing before the emergence of the computer and its accelerating drive toward maximum efficiency.

Up to the present time, automation, which should be described as advanced industrial mechanization *not* involving the use of computer systems, has been predominant in industrial reorganization. Automation sets up a few inherent drives for system-linkage. As cybernation—the combination of advanced machinery with the computer—develops on the factory floor and as cybernetic systems develop within organizations, the drive toward linking of systems will grow rapidly stronger. Cybernation has its *own inherent* drives which demand the linkage of systems. This was the prime fact made clear in Sarnoff's recognition that the absence of a single computer language is now the major impediment to large-scale systems link-up and that the efforts of the computer industry must be directed to rapid elimination of this barrier.

My acceptance of systems-thinking is based on reality: on my willingness to face up to the fact that there is no way to avoid the development of large-scale computerized systems in the second half of the twentieth century. Our only hope is to accept this reality and to use all of man's energy to recruit technological drives for the attainment of our fundamental goals.

The increasing efficiency of organization permits greater output with less energy input. In the industrial scarcity age, this process worked to our advantage because demand exceeded supply and energy sources were always insufficient. In the cybernetics-based abundance era, however, we are being confronted with the need to place restraints on both production and on new energy sources, lest their drives destroy us. The danger of exploding production is no less real than that of destructive explosions. It is incorrect to assume that because presently we have unfulfilled global production needs, we can absorb any extra amount, and rapidly.

We are living in a world of exponential growth. But Dennis Gabor, professor at the Imperial College of Science and Technology in London, has pointed out:"...exponential curves grow to infinity only in mathematics. In the physical world they either turn round and saturate, or they break down catastrophically. It is our duty as thinking men to do our best toward a gentle saturation, instead of sustaining the exponential growth, though this faces us with very unfamiliar and distasteful problems."

For many people the most distasteful of all these problems is the fact that there is already insufficient toil to go round—that it is now necessary to allow vast numbers of people to do what *they want to do* simply because they personally believe that their activity is important. The guaranteed income proposal mentioned above recognizes this reality, and it has therefore been attacked from both ends of the political spectrum, and from every point in between, on the grounds that the proposal would promote the lazy society. For example, August Heckscher, who served as President Kennedy's special assistant for cultural affairs, declared: "The very idea of large populations doing nothing but pleasing themselves goes against the American grain," and then went on to make proposals for job allocations and income distribution which Gerard Piel has described as "instant feudalism."

We have not yet been willing to recognize the true extent of the challenge posed by the drive toward unlimited destructive power, unlimited productive power, the elimination of the human mind from repetitive tasks, the organizing drive of the computer within a cyber-netiated system. We have not yet been willing to recognize that we live today in the truly lazy society—a society where we allow technological trends to make our decisions for us because we have no mechanisms to allow us to control them. We have not yet been willing to recognize that man's power is now so great that the minimum requirement for the survival of the human race is individual responsibility.

Man will no longer need to toil: he must find a new role in the cyber-netics era which must emerge from a new goal of self-fulfillment. He can no longer view himself as a superanimal at the center of the physical universe, nor as a super-efficient taker of decisions self-fashioned in the model of the computer. He must now view himself as a truly creative being in the image of a creative God.

PART III

Bureaucratization

THE GROWTH OF CITIES AND FACTORIES
exposed ever greater numbers of people to the problems and
the disciplines that they created. Most Americans and almost
all of the British now live in urban areas. America's old rural
economy in which three-fourths of the employed people
earned their living in 1840 has become an industrial and
service oriented economy in which only ten percent of the
labor force earns its living from agriculture: a percentage
which is about twice as high as it should be if all farm families
were to earn a comfortable living. But the people in the industrialized societies have experienced yet another organizational
change which has also had profound effects on their lives: the
bureaucratization of a broad range of human activities.

In the last section we saw that industrialization involved the
growth of factories from the small company with a few
workers and crude machinery to large factories with complex
and expensive machinery and dozens or even hundreds of
employees. This growth, which has continued to the present
day, was dictated by a number of economic and human
considerations. Some owners wanted larger factories simply
because they desired personal power or because they found

security in largeness or for any of a number of personal and complex motivations. But even if no personal motivations or emotions were involved, growth was dictated by rational economics. The cost of the newer and increasingly complex machines was very great; only large factories with extensive markets could afford them. Further, in many industries the greater the volume of goods produced, the lower the cost per unit because certain fixed costs, such as machinery and buildings, are spread over more units. A factory producing a large volume of goods has a competitive advantage over a smaller manufacturer because it can produce the product more cheaply and either sell it for less or take a larger profit. Mindful of this economic truism industrialists sought safety in size, and if the cost problem were not sufficient to encourage them to increase their factory's productive capacity, the threat that their competitors would was incentive enough.

The United States, like other Western societies, has become a nation of large business organizations. Over half of the steel produced in the United States is made by the four largest companies.[1] Similarly, 78 percent of the canned milk, 94 percent of the baby food, 80 percent of the cigarettes, 90 percent of the finished thread for home use, 96 percent of the linoleum, 99 percent of the passenger cars, 90 percent of the electric lights, 95 percent of the window glass, and 64 percent of the zippers manufactured in this country are produced by the four largest companies in each industry. There are, of course, a great many businesses where the degree of concentration is not that great, but they are usually making products for which there is no competitive advantage to concentration.

This phenomenal growth in size is not restricted to business organizations; witness the growth of giant unions. The structure of unions *has* to parallel that of the businesses

---

[1] Committee of the Judiciary, United States Senate, *Concentration Ratios in Manufacturing Industry*, 1958: Part I (Washington, U.S. Government Printing Office, 1962).

whose workers it represents. If a union represented the workers in only one plant in a large corporation, it would be in an extremely poor bargaining position. The threat to strike would not bother management particularly, because production could be shifted to another plant where a different union represented the workers. Thus logic dictates that unions must represent not only all of the plants in a company, but also all of the companies that manufacture the same products. Today over eighteen million people are affiliated with labor unions, and all but one-sixth of them are affiliated with the three largest.

But perhaps the most spectacular example of growth has been in the area of government. All levels—city, state, and federal—have grown enormously. The total expenditures of the federal government during Andrew Jackson's ad-ministration averaged around 20 million dollars per year. Today the total federal budget is 200 billion dollars per year which is about one-fifth of the Gross National Product. The budget for the National Weather Service is four times as large as Jackson's annual expenditures. As recently as 1935 the largest department in the federal government was the Department of Agriculture with 6,000 employees. Today the federal government has over 2 million employees and a number of departments now have more employees than the Department of Agriculture.

This growth is part of an important trend in many societies: more and more human activities are being performed or guided by large organizations. Where the old farmer and seaman had only their personal experiences and lore from their fathers, friends, and almanacs with which to gauge the weather, today the National Weather Service provides 90 million dollars worth of predictions. That same farmer learned to farm from his father, but today there is the Agricultural Extension Service and the County Agent system to advise him on farming techniques and state-financed universities where his son can major in agriculture.

Responsibility for a great many human activities has been assumed by very large and ever growing organizations with highly bureaucratized structures. What are the effects of bureaucratization on the people who work in them and on those who use them? The articles in this section are intended to look at some answers to these questions and, as we have done in earlier sections, to consider some thoughts about the future.

The first two selections in this section are partly concerned with the reasons for the development of bureaucracies. The conception of Miller and Swanson is broader than Galbraith's. The former are talking about the emergence of a new way of life which they label "welfare bureaucracy" in which the economic security of people working in large, bureaucratized organizations is guaranteed. The reasons for the emergence of this new ethic are discussed. In other parts of the book not included here the authors relate the child-rearing practices of parents to their adherence to either the welfare-bureaucratic or entrepreneurial ethic and they find important differences between the two groups.

Departing from the same point, Galbraith takes another avenue. Because large organizations have unique needs for specialization, rational planning, and coordination, Galbraith says that the power becomes lodged in groups rather than with individuals and at levels in the organizations well below the top; he calls this the technostructure. The implications for organizations and society are discussed elsewhere in the author's book. Two of the basic points that Galbraith is making are problematic. First while it is true that many organizations have grown to enormous size, was it necessary that they grow to such size in order to achieve the advantages of division of labor, competitive security and so forth? Or is it possible that they could have been just as successful at a considerably smaller size? Second, while the decisions may have been formulated in the technostructure, can it be said that they were unshaped by the values of top management?

The next two articles also discuss problems commonly associated with bureaucracies. Alvin Gouldner takes a fresh look at the problem of red tape, procedures that slow the bureaucracy's response to requests for action. Ordinarily, red tape is conceived as a characteristic of insensitive, procedure-oriented, self-absorbed bureaucracies. Gouldner does not deny that red tape can be a characteristic of bureaucracies, but he shows that it can also be related to the client's situation. If the client believes he has a *right* to a certain action from a bureaucracy and his objective is frustrated, he is likely to see the situation as arbitrary and fraught with red tape. Suspicion of the bureaucracy and a sense of relative powerlessness are other client characteristics Gouldner finds related to the accusation of red tape.

The theme of powerlessness is central to Seeman's article on alienation. The alienated person feels separated not only from himself, but also from others, organizations, and his society. In this existential state he feels powerless to achieve his ends or to affect the actions of others. He also loses his motivation to acquire knowledge that might help him to control the situation he is in. But Seeman shows that the way out of the cycle of alienation requires learning how to control situations and working through unions and associations is the way to gain that control.

The final two articles discuss ways that bureaucracies should be modified to make them more responsive to the needs of members and clients alike. Reuss and Munsey propose to adopt the European concept to assist clients in getting their problems addressed by the bureaucracy. Warren Bennis argues that the problems of alienation and the loss of creativity among workers could be solved by the workers' participation in making decisions about the organization's objectives. In an argument similar to Galbraith's he says that groups of specialists need to be organized to cope with the complexity of modern problems and technologies. Therefore, organizations must abandon their notions of graduated

authority structures and individual decision making and
reconceive themselves as collections of temporary groups that
change as problems change.

DANIEL R. MILLER
GUY E. SWANSON

The Emergence of
Welfare-Bureaucratic
Society

Toward the end of the nineteenth century and the beginning of the twentieth, new organizational trends appeared that were to transform much of the life of all Americans and to produce a new kind of middle class. These new trends are modifying the older and more individuated society of the United States just as the latter took the place of village and rural ways of life. For this emerging pattern of social life, we shall use the term "welfare bureaucracy." This new pattern of life is bureaucratic because it is characterized by large organizations employing many kinds of specialists and coordinating their activities by supervisors who follow a codified set of rules of practice. Its flavor is that of "welfare" bureaucracy because it can and must provide a large measure of security for its participants. Since the white-collar workers—the middle classes—are more likely to be highly specialized than the blue-collar employees, they are also more likely to be the first to feel the impact of these new conditions. Our purpose here is to describe these conditions, to contrast them with those of a more individuated period, and to show some of their effects on parents and children.

As we see it, four essential conditions are bringing about the change from individuated-entrepreneurial to welfare-bureaucratic (or, as we shall speak of it, bureaucratic) organization. These are: (a) the increase in the size of the organization of production, (b) the growth of specialization in organization, (c) the great increase in the real incomes of the population, and (d) the enlarged power in the hands of lower-middle and lower-class workers.[1]

The increase in the size of organizations and in the proportion of their personnel who are specialists of some kind are the two defining characteristics of bureaucracy. Organizations are bureaucratic to the extent that

---

Reprinted and abridged with the permission of the publisher and the authors from "Changes in Society and Child Training in the United States," in Daniel R. Miller and Guy E. Swanson, *The Changing American Parent* (New York: John Wiley & Sons, 1958), pp. 30-60.

they exhibit these features. Much that we shall have to say about the newer methods of child care will be explained as flowing from the experiences which parents encounter in a bureaucratized society.

We feel that American prosperity and the enlarged power of the lower middle and lower classes are important for our story because these two developments provide crucial aspects of the setting in which we expect bureaucratic influences to modify techniques of rearing children. These two conditions underlie our conception of welfare bureaucracy. Prosperity not only represents greater income, but it means, in our day, that there is a considerable shortage of workers. That shortage, in turn, forces employers to give active attention to the problem of keeping their personnel happy and satisfied. We shall try to show how this makes an important modification in the amount of impersonality and insecurity experienced by bureaucratic employees.

The political strength of the American people, like prosperity, seems to us to affect the consequences of bureaucratization. It has forced the creation of governmental welfare measures which, like prosperity, enhance the economic security of the labor force. And, like prosperity, it provides a measure of freedom for employees that enables them to make demands of the organizations for which they work to the end that mutual respect and satisfaction are underwritten between employer and worker.

Each of these four conditions of welfare bureaucracy will now be discussed. Then we shall turn to the way of life and the methods of rearing children we believe to be consistent with them.

The decline of small business in all fields of endeavor and the shift toward larger and larger units have many sources. The population has been growing. Larger scale manufacturing and commerce can serve that population with greater economies on each unit sold than can small concerns. Because such large-scale concerns are working over vast regional, national, and international markets, they are not so susceptible to the ill effects of purely local drops in purchasing power; their profits are more stable. Not only can they compete successfully for existing markets, but they can create new ones through their ability to sponsor research, conduct massive advertising campaigns, and produce a greater variety of goods and services tailored to the desires of small, but significant, groups of purchasers. All of these potential advantages have been helped on their way to reality by the continuing development of machinery that increases the amount that can be produced and by such organizational inventions as assembly-line production, the corporation, and the holding company. By breaking production into small parts, the assembly line permits a considerable increase in the volume of work turned out. The corporation, owned by large numbers of investors, with each liable for its debts only to the extent of his investment, allows for gigantic increases in the amount of capital available to start and expand production.

We have spoken of the growth of factories before the twentieth century as a growth of large organizations. In relative terms this is true. It was experienced as such by the people at the time. Yet, in a modern sense, most of these factories would not be considered large. The difference may be illustrated this way. It is estimated that the typical American urban manufacturing concern in the first half of the nineteenth century employed from fifty to one hundred persons. We may contrast this situation with estimates for 1948. Based on reports from establishments paying wages taxable under the Old-Age and Survivor's Insurance plan, a program covering the vast majority of employees in manufacturing concerns, we find that 75 per cent of all employees in manufacturing were employed in firms having 100 or more persons. Some 47.5 per cent worked in firms numbering 500 or more employees, and 34.9 per cent were in establishments of 1000 or more workers.[2]

GROWTH OF SPECIALIZATION

Luther Gulick has given a succinct statement of the causes of specialization:[3]

1. men differ in nature, capacity, and skill.
2. no man can be in two places at the same time.
3. no man can do two things at the same time.
4. no man knows everything.

Most of the jobs that have become specialized did so for one of the first three reasons listed by Gulick. The classic illustration is the establishment of assembly-line procedures.

Specialization has made important changes in the characteristics of the labor force. . . . Several important trends have appeared since the 1890's. Especially striking are the decline of laborers and the steady rise of semiskilled workers and of "clerks and kindred" types of employees. The percentage of professional and semiprofessional persons increased steadily but slowly in the non-farm labor force. Skilled workers and foremen showed a decline of similar proportions[4]. Servants and the broad group of proprietors, managers, and officials held relatively steady positions over these years.

These changes sharpen our picture of the results of a growth in the size and specialization of economic enterprise. Increasingly, machines have provided skills that in an earlier period would have been found in the talents of workmen. The machine tender, a semiskilled worker, does not have the kind of technical knowledge that he can take with him from job to job. His skill lies in "his ability to adjust quickly to the sequence and timing of his operation and to the attainment of an acceptable volume and quality of output"[5]. Simultaneously, however, technological development has opened new jobs for skilled workers, and the demand for their services has shown only a slow decline.

Greater size and specialization of organizations have meant somewhat different things for white-collar employees. First, the proportion of white-collar workers has risen sharply. Second, although their numbers are small in relation to the total work force, increased demands for specialized skills have produced a rise in the proportion of professional workers in the population.... There has been an increase in the percentage of salaried corporation officers and a decline in the proportion of proprietors and members of firms in the total labor force. This last pair of tendencies reflects the larger requirements of big organizations for specially trained management. This growing separation of ownership and administration has been dramatized as the "managerial revolution."

Broad data from the census mask some of the sharpness of the increase in managerial and other professionals as a proportion of the labor force. If, for example, we look only at some professions most closely connected with economic production, the change is clearer. Thus, from 1890 to 1940 the number of gainful workers per college-trained engineer employed in manufacturing, mining, construction, transportation, and public utilities dropped from about 300 to less than 100 [6].

INCREASE IN REAL INCOME

One of the phenomenal differences between the lot of most Americans in the nineteenth and those of the twentieth centuries is the rise in income, not only in terms of dollars, but of buying power. Despite a great depression and the inflation that accompanied two global wars, there has been a steady rise in the buying power of the American people at about the rate of 2 per cent a year [7]. Even over shorter periods, the rise in real income is most impressive. From 1929 to 1951, real income rose 131 per cent [8]. Another way to see the size of American prosperity is to compare real income in the United States with that in other Western, industrial countries. In 1949 [9] real income was $1450 *per capita* in the United States. By contrast, it was $870 in Canada, $780 in Sweden, $770 in the United Kingdom, and $230 in Italy. Asian and African peoples fared even less well by comparison. For example, the estimated figure for Korea is $35, for Japan, $100, for Communist China, $30, and for Ethiopia, Kenya, Liberia, and Northern Rhodesia, $40.

Again it is impressive that in recent years the percentage increase in American incomes has been greatest for those in the lower income groups. On every hand are signs that there has been a progressive equalization of income within the population through the rise in the amount of money in the hands of the least well paid [10].

ENLARGED POWER OF THE LOWER-MIDDLE
AND LOWER CLASSES

The final condition that has led to what we call welfare bureaucracy is the increased power in the hands of lower-middle and lower-class people in the United States[11]. The sources of this trend are complex, but its presence is reflected in the progressive enfranchisement of all the American people, and in the greater sensitivity of the Federal government to their needs and wishes. The trend is also mirrored in the success of such organizations as the labor unions which (whether or not actually providing the forces responsible for the rise in workers' incomes) seem to have gained greater job security for their members, to have helped them mobilize for political action, and to have represented them as effective pressure groups in the nation's councils.

We have been looking at the changes from an individuated-entrepreneurial to a welfare-bureaucratic society as if they happened in smooth transitions without overlap or conflict. This is not the case. An English economic historian[12] could say that his country at the turn of the century embodied most of the previous economic systems of her history with sizable portions of the population employed in each organizational setting. It is easy to find examples of such a variety of economic patterns in contemporary America. The small businessman still exists. The unorganized worker in fields oversupplied with labor can be found. The employee in the small establishment, depending on his employer's good will and clinging precariously to the uncertain fortunes of the little store or shop lives in the same towns as do the employees of welfare bureaucracies. Sons and daughters from both backgrounds often work in the same establishments and, with their very different expectations of the future and interpretations of the present, find it difficult to understand one another[13]. We shall find integrations of both the entrepreneurial and bureaucratic varieties in the Detroit area.

THE DEMANDS OF BUREAUCRATIC ORGANIZATIONS

The whole development of welfare bureaucracy changes the world for the middle-class citizens who join its ranks. No longer need they struggle and strive so hard. They must still be circumspect and respectable, but their incomes do not depend on manipulating a host of risks and investments.

The early picture that observers had of the likely consequences of bureaucratization for the middle classes took its cues primarily from the educational and governmental bureaucracies of Europe and the United States where this form of organization first matured. The employee in a bureaucratic situation should, it was felt, be more secure than his fellow in an individuated situation. The large organization had resources enabling it to continue operation without becoming disorganized through the minor ups and downs of the business cycle. Therefore it could provide job security.

Bureaucracies also embodied other sources of employee security. It takes time to train a man for a specialized type of work. To lose trained men costs money. They are hard to replace. Large organizations could keep their employees providing them with tenure and pension plans and by guaranteeing them advancement on the basis of seniority.

Seniority not only worked to keep employees with a particular company, but it solved another problem of bureaucracies as well. A large, complex, organization requires the continued, faithful performance of duties. Payrolls must come out. A product must flow from the production lines. A sales force has to be advised, stimulated, and coordinated. And these functions must be performed on an hourly and daily basis. They do not allow for drastic or continuous tampering. Steady morale must underlie steady performance. An employee with unusual imagination and energy who tries to institute drastic changes can cause the whole complex machine to grind to a halt. Such enterprising efforts are desirable, but need to be kept under control. To retain a high level of staff morale and to discourage excessive drive and ambition, a regular system of promotion through seniority provides an answer.

Just as size and complexity of organization can lead to employee security, they also exact a price from their personnel. The ideal worker must be precise and conscientious in performance. He must keep to his assigned task and not stray off into the provinces of others even if he has some new ideas for the performance of their work. He must always "clear" ideas and problems "through channels" with his superiors. Because he may leave the company or die, his work and plans must be reported on paper so that someone else may take his place and continue where he left off. He must, like the individuated middle-class worker, be rational, looking to the consequences of his action and curbing momentary desires until their consequences can be examined and evaluated. He must not be aggressive or too ambitious for these qualities disturb the organization's course.

Thus it is clear, even though entrepreneurial and bureaucratic organizations make some similar demands of their personnel, they also differ in critical ways. In particular, bureaucratic organizations find unnecessary or undesirable the rather extreme self-control and self-denial and the active, manipulative, ambition that entrepreneurial organizations exalt. This difference is one that we expect to find influential in determining how children are reared.

This takes us a little ahead of our story. There is one feature of bureaucracy as described by the early writers on European and American developments that we feel has undergone considerable modification in the contemporary United States. Because the interpretation of this feature of bureaucracy makes a difference in the account of how the newer middle classes rear their children, we shall take it up in some detail. It is the stress in the earlier accounts on the theme that bureaucratic organizations force people to deal impersonally with one another[14].

Those accounts say that the size and complexity of bureaucratic organizations force employees to see each other, the organization's clients, and themselves as parts of an organization, not as people. Bureaucratic personnel, these descriptions asserted, must learn to treat each other, not as living, feeling flesh that might make demands for special treatment or that might have idiosyncratic needs, but as human machines who might legitimately require only those things necessary for playing their parts in the organization. Each participant, these accounts continued, has a job to do, with limited but compulsory responsibilities and requirements. Other considerations must not be allowed to interfere with this impersonal order.

If these early descriptions of bureaucracy were correct about the unadulterated impersonality of the human relations in such organizations, we would have to conclude that bureaucracy exacerbates rather than relieves the individuating tendencies of urban life. In its impersonality it would be yet another way of isolating people from one another and should promote a wary self-control. However accurate these early accounts may have been as descriptions of the governmental and military bureaucracies on which they are based, we feel that they do not describe the growing spirit of large organizations in the United States today. This is the reason that we speak not simply of "bureaucracy" but of "welfare bureaucracy" as characterizing our place and time.

What difference does that adjective "welfare" make? We use it to represent developments having the effect of reducing impersonality; of doing much toward transforming the relation of employees to their employers and to each other from one based on a formal job contract to one based on a shared moral relationship. All of this has consequences for the interpretation we want to make of the newer developments in child care, so we shall elaborate our meaning before presenting that interpretation.

The language of employer-employee relations tells much of the story. In the entrepreneurial organization and in the earlier and more authoritarian bureaucracy, management defined its relations to the work force in terms of employee discipline. It was assumed that the worker came haltingly to his tasks. He was seen as resisting or lazy or stubborn and the problem of the supervisor was that of providing him with direct and effective rewards and deprivations which would force him, in his own self-interest, to behave as desired. It was also implicit that supervisors had the power to perform such a task. One magazine much favored among entrepreneurs still describes its model for labor relations with the telling analogy of the donkey that can be persuaded only by the proper, but minimal, rewards of the carrot and, simultaneously, proper and judicious prods from the master's stick. But even *Time* is not always timely. The day of forcing the worker to his desk or machine passed. The day of fitting him to the job took its place.

Shortly before the First World War, a student of industrial management, Frederick J. Taylor, published his epochal *The Principles of*

Scientific Management[15]. He pointed out that workers "soldiering" on the job hurt their company's competitive position. Labor discontent was costly. Taylor urged on management the adoption of procedures that would minimize such discontent. If unruly impulses could not be eliminated, they could be managed. The way to do it was to fit the worker's needs to his job by a program of determining the demands the job would make, by simplifying jobs through breaking them into tasks "anyone" could perform, and by hiring employees who would find these jobs congenial. This theory became a great modern impetus for the personnel man—a man defined as one who could analyze jobs and administer tests to find workers whose personalities and skills fitted the work situation.

However, even Taylor's scientific management was not adequate to the newer problems of contemporary organization. It assumed a degree of managerial dominance that was already passing in his time. The latest step has been the adaptation of the job to the worker. Pressures for such a move were inherent in welfare bureaucracy. They were, as we remarked earlier, enhanced by the growing political power of employees and by their prosperity. From the assumptions of the disciplining of labor, the social relations of management moved to adapting the worker to his tasks, and from that to the maintenance of his morale. This last step needs some elaboration.

A concern with worker morale suggests that managerial skills are now directed toward enlisting worker desires and aspirations. But it also assumes that it is in the worker's power to grant or to refuse such enlistment. If he refuses, management will have to continue trying to gain his support. Within the limitations set by technology, the worker's loyalty can be had by adjusting the conditions of work to his desires. The word "loyalty" is central. He must be prevented from disturbing the routines of production by transferring to another company. If he is highly specialized in tasks such as those of business operation or design or sales or any of the pyramiding number of others in which there is no clear and rapid index available by which his performance may be judged, supervision is extremely difficult. He must be self-supervised. He must want to perform with high proficiency. An essential part of that performance is set by the way he gets along with other people. For many reasons the older conceptions of control and decision-making in giant organizations have broken down[16]. Again, there is required a devotion to the welfare of the enterprise and a satisfaction with its procedures if the irritations of human interaction are to be minimized. No known techniques of supervision could compel such behavior[17].

This kind of natural loyalty and devotion does not come solely from good pay and a feeling of dominance over one's employer. It represents the experience of a fundamentally moral relationship. Morals, in turn, are the code of social rules that grow up to preserve a situation in which people find each other's presence to be so mutually rewarding and, simultaneously, so lacking in threat, that they feel wholly comfortable and spontaneous and seek to preserve their happy and productive state. The problem of management is to establish such a moral relationship with its workers without losing its authority over them. There has been a persistent and analogous problem for parents in dealing with their children—how to be both authority and benefactor. The management solution, like that of many parents, is one of seeking avidly for benefits it can give without jeopardizing control. The pastel-colored washrooms, the coffee breaks, the use of first names on the job, the company banquet, the employee picnic, the practice of consultation with employees on those decisions where a crucial management postion will not be compromised are examples of the important devices to be used. The change of the personnel man and the vice-president in charge of employee relations from, respectively, giving tests and settling disputes on a legal, contractual basis to the roles of counselors and liaison men is part of the same movement. What once was accomplished in small informal groups in the little communities and in the countryside now is the subject of planning and of the construction of elaborate formal organizational devices. Moral relations in large institutions, like the daily quota of parts produced, must be planned.

The benefits, not the planning, must be the conspicuous thing in the worker's experience. He must feel that what was done occurred because management was genuinely interested in his welfare, not because the benefits would result in higher productivity. Since there are always suspicions of management's motives, there are persistent tests of the genuineness of the employer's concern. The limits of his willingness to fraternize and spend time on non-productive employee interests are sought. Walkouts that seem irrational to workers, union leaders, and supervisors alike may occur to determine whether management will be punitive or understanding. Morale may be the overt subject of discussion, but morality is its central object.

These paragraphs on the moral nature of relations in a welfare bureaucracy have been broad and descriptive. They have sought, in the absence of more systematically gathered evidence, to bring together a picture of a new and potent and, in good measure, incipient style of life. They emphasize our view that the competitive and amoral world of the individuating metropolis is being changed. The consequence, we believe, is yet another force that makes striving and extreme and rigid self-control less necessary than before. Further, it seems to us that the reestablishment of moral relations makes such striving and self-control less desirable than formerly for they interfere with the development of supportive and moral relations among employees. Now we must examine some of the effects of moralization and the other features of welfare bureaucracy on the training of children.

NOTES

1. The development of automation may have as profound effects on the organization of American life as any of these, but its role is in the future and has no consequences for our present study.

2. Wladimir S. Woytinsky and others, *Employment and Wages in the United States* (New York: The Twentieth Century Fund, 1953).

3. Luther Gulick, "Notes on the Theory of Organization," in Luther Gulick and L. Urwick (eds.), *Papers on the Science of Administration* (New York: Institute of Public Administration, Columbia University, 1937), 3.

4. Because of the nature of the categorization of data by the United States Census, it is likely that this trend should not be applied to skilled laborers. There is evidence that the proportion of skilled laborers in the urban labor force is rising.

5. Harry Ober, "The Worker and His Job," *Monthly Labor Review,* 71 (July, 1950), 15.

6. "Employment Outlook for Engineers," *Monthly Labor Review,* 69 (July, 1949), 15.

7. See, for example, Elizabeth E. Hoyt and others, *American Income and Its Use* (New York: Harper and Bros., Publishers, 1954), 87-91; and William F. Ogburn, "Technology and the Standard of Living in the United States," *The American Journal of Sociology,* 60 (January, 1955), 380-386.

8. Hoyt, *op. cit.,* xvi.

9. *Ibid.,* xii.

10. *Ibid.,* 132-135.

11. For the story of this change see Richard Hofstadter's *The American Political Tradition and the Men Who Made It* (New York: Alfred Knopf, Inc., 1948). Also useful are: Charles A. and Mary R. Beard, *The Rise of American Civilization* (New York: The Macmillan Company, 1930) and their *America in Midpassage* (New York: The Macmillan Co., 1939).

12. George Unwin, *Industrial Organization in the Sixteenth and Seventeenth Centuries* (Oxford: The Clarendon Press, 1904), 1-15.

13. David Riesman and others, *The Lonely Crowd: A Study of the Changing American Character* (New Haven: Yale University Press, 1950), 3-35.

14. For a convenient summary of the literature describing bureaucratic characteristics, see: Robert K. Merton and others (eds.), *Reader in Bureaucracy* (Glencoe, Illinois: The Free Press, 1952).

15. *The Principles of Scientific Management* (New York: Harper and Brothers, 1911).

16. A book written largely in the course of attempts to identify the newer problems of organizational functioning is Herbert A. Simon and others, *Public Administration* (New York: Alfred A. Knopf, Inc., 1950).

17. A summary of many studies of the relation of the newer attempts at supervision to overcome this problem appears in Edward A. Shils' article "The Study of the Primary Group," in Daniel Lerner and Harold D. Lasswell (eds.), *The Policy Sciences: Recent Developments in Scope and Method* (Stanford University Press, 1951), 44-69. See also: Riesman and others, *op. cit.*

JOHN KENNETH GALBRAITH

The
Technostructure

"...the prevalence of group, instead of individual, action is a striking characteristic of management organization in the large corporation."

R.A. Gordon, *Business Leadership in the Large Corporation*

The individual has far more standing in our culture than the group. An individual has a presumption of accomplishment; a committee has a presumption of inaction.[1] We react sympathetically to the individual who seeks to safeguard his personality from engulfment by the mass. We call for proof, at least in principle, before curbing his aggressions against society. Individuals have souls; corporations are notably soulless. The entrepreneur—individualistic, restless, with vision, guile and courage—has been the economists' only hero. The great business organization arouses no similar admiration. Admission to heaven is individually and by families; the top management even of an enterprise with an excellent corporate image cannot yet go in as a group. To have, in pursuit of truth, to assert the superiority of the organization over the individual for important social tasks is a taxing prospect.

Yet it is a necessary task. It is not to individuals but to organizations that power in the business enterprise and power in the society has passed. And modern economic society can only be understood as an effort, wholly successful, to synthesize by organization a group personality far superior *for its purposes* to a natural person and with the added advantage of immortality.

The need for such a group personality begins with the circumstance that in modern industry a large number of decisions, and *all* that are important, draw on information possessed by more than one man. Typically,

---

Reprinted from *The New Industrial State* (Boston: Houghton Mifflin, 1967) pp. 60-71. Copyright © 1967 by John Kenneth Galbraith. Reprinted with the permission of the publishers, Houghton Mifflin Company and Hamish Hamilton, Ltd.

they draw on the specialized scientific and technical knowledge, the accumulated information or experience and the artistic or intuitive sense of many persons. And this is guided by further information which is assembled, analyzed and interpreted by professionals using highly technical equipment. The final decision will be informed only as it draws systematically on all those whose information is relevant. Nor, human beings what they are, can it take all of the information that is offered at face value. There must, additionally, be a mechanism for testing each person's contribution for its relevance and reliability as it is brought to bear on the decision.

2

The need to draw on, and appraise, the information of numerous individuals in modern industrial decision-making has three principal points of origin. It derives, first, from the technological requirements of modern industry. It is not that these are always inordinately sophisticated; a man of moderate genius could, quite conceivably, provide himself with the knowledge of the various branches of metallurgy and chemistry, and of engineering, procurement, production management, quality control, labor relations, styling and merchandising which are involved in the development of a modern motor car. But even moderate genius is in unpredictable supply, and to keep abreast of all these branches of science, engineering and art would be time-consuming even for a genius. The elementary solution, which allows of the use of far more common talent and with far greater predictability of result, is to have men who are appropriately qualified or experienced in each limited area of specialized knowledge or art. Their information is then combined for carrying out the design and production of the vehicle. It is a common public impression, not discouraged by scientists, engineers and industrialists, that modern scientific, engineering and industrial achievements are the work of a new and quite remarkable race of men. This is pure vanity; were it so, there would be few such achievements. The real accomplishment of modern science and technology consists in taking ordinary men, informing them narrowly and deeply and then, through appropriate organization, arranging to have their knowledge combined with that of other specialized but equally ordinary men. This dispenses with the need for genius. The resulting performance, though less inspiring, is far more predictable.

The second factor requiring the combination of specialized talent derives from advanced technology, the associated use of capital, and the resulting need for planning with its accompanying control of environment. The market is, in remarkable degree, an intellectually undemanding institution. The Wisconsin farmer, aforementioned, need not anticipate his requirements for fertilizers, pesticides or even machine parts; the market stocks and supplies them. The cost of these is substantially the same for the man of intelligence and for his neighbor who, under medical examination, shows daylight in either ear. And the farmer need have no price or selling strategy; the market takes all his milk at the ruling price. Much of the appeal of the market, to economists at least, has been from the way it seems to simplify life. Better orderly error than complex truth.

For complexity enters with planning and is endemic thereto. The manufacturer of missiles, space vehicles or modern aircraft must foresee the requirements for specialized plant, specialized manpower, exotic materials and intricate components and take steps to insure their availability when they are needed. For procuring such things, we have seen, the market is either unreliable or unavailable. And there is no open market for the finished product. Everything here depends on the care and skill with which contracts are sought and nurtured in Washington or in Whitehall or Paris.

The same foresight and responding action are required, in lesser degree, from manufacturers of automobiles, processed foods and detergents. They too must foresee requirements and manage markets. Planning, in short, requires a great variety of information. It requires variously informed men and men who are suitably specialized in obtaining the requisite information. There must be men whose knowledge allows them to foresee need and to insure a supply of labor, materials and other production requirements; those who have knowledge to plan price strategies and see that customers are suitably persuaded to buy at these prices; those who, at higher levels of technology, are so informed that they can work effectively with the state to see that it is suitably guided; and those who can organize the flow of information that the above tasks and many others require. Thus, to the requirements of technology for specialized technical and scientific talent are added the very large further requirements of the planning that technology makes necessary.

Finally, following from the need for this variety of specialized talent, is the need for its coordination. Talent must be brought to bear on the common purpose. More specifically, on large and small matters, information must be extracted from the various specialists, tested for its reliability and relevance, and made to yield a decision. This process, which is much misunderstood, requires a special word.

3

The modern business organization, or that part which has to do with guidance and direction, consists of numerous individuals who are engaged, at any given time, in obtaining, digesting or exchanging and testing information. A very large part of the exchange and testing of information is by word-of-mouth—a discussion in an office, at lunch or over the telephone. But the most typical procedure is through the committee and the committee meeting. One can do worse than think of a business organization as a hierarchy of committees. Coordination, in turn, consists in assigning the appropriate talent to committees, intervening on occasion to force a decision, and, as the case may be, announcing the decision or carrying it as information for a yet further decision by a yet higher committee.

Nor should it be supposed that this is an inefficient procedure. On the contrary it is, normally, the only efficient procedure. Association in a committee enables each member to come to know the intellectual resources and the reliability of his colleagues. Committee discussion enables members to pool information under circumstances which allow, also, of immediate probing to assess the relevance and reliability of the information offered. Uncertainty about one's information or error is revealed as in no other way. There is also, no doubt, considerable stimulus to mental effort from such association. One may enjoy the luxury of torpor in private but not so comfortably in public at least during working hours. Men who believe themselves deeply engaged in private thought are usually doing nothing. Committees are condemned by the cliché that individual effort is somehow superior to group effort; by those who guiltily suspect that since group effort is more congenial, it must be less productive; and by those who do not see that the process of extracting, and especially of testing, information has necessarily a somewhat undirected quality— briskly conducted meetings invariably decide matters previously decided; and by those who fail to realize that highly paid men, when sitting around a table as a committee, are not necessarily wasting more time than, in the aggregate, they would each waste in private by themselves.[2] Forthright and determined administrators frequently react to belief in the superior capacity of individuals for decision by abolishing all committees. They then constitute working parties, task forces, assault teams or executive groups in order to avoid the one truly disastrous consequence of their action which would be that they should make the decisions themselves.

Thus decision in the modern business enterprise is the product not of individuals but of groups. The groups are numerous, as often informal as formal, and subject to constant change in composition. Each contains the men possessed of the information, or with access to the information, that bears on the particular decision together with those whose skill consists in extracting and testing this information and obtaining a conclusion. This is how men act successfully on matters where no single one, however exalted or intelligent, has more than a fraction of the necessary knowledge. It is what makes modern business possible, and in other contexts it is what makes modern government possible. It is fortunate that men of limited knowledge are so constituted that they can work together in this way. Were it otherwise, business and government, at any given moment, would be at a standstill awaiting the appearance of a man with the requisite breadth of knowledge to resolve the problem presently at hand. Some further characteristics of group decision-making must now be noticed.

4

Group decision-making extends deeply into the business enterprise. Effective participation is not closely related to rank in the formal hierarchy of the organization. This takes an effort of mind to grasp. Everyone is influenced by the stereotyped organization chart of the business enterprise. At its top is the Board of Directors and the Board Chairman; next comes the President; next comes the Executive Vice President; thereafter come the Department or Divisional heads—those who preside over the Chevrolet division, the large-generators division, the computer division. Power is assumed to pass down from the pinnacle. Those at the top give orders; those below relay them on or respond.

This happens, but only in very simple organizations—the peacetime drill of the National Guard or a troop of Boy Scouts moving out on Saturday maneuvers. Elsewhere the decision will require information. Some power will then pass to the person or persons who have this information. If this knowledge is highly particular to themselves then their power becomes very great. In Los Alamos, during the development of the atomic bomb, Enrico Fermi rode a bicycle up the hill to work; Major General Leslie R. Groves presided in grandeur over the entire Manhattan District. Fermi had the final word on numerous questions of feasibility and design.[3] In association with a handful of others he could, at various early stages, have brought the entire enterprise to an end. No such power resided with Groves. At any moment he could have been replaced without loss and with possible benefit.

When power is exercised by a group, not only does it pass into the organization but it passes irrevocably. If an individual has taken a decision he can be called before another individual, who is his superior in the hierarchy, his information can be examined and his decision reversed by the greater wisdom or experience of the superior. But if the decision required the combined information of a group, it cannot be safely reversed by an individual. He will have to get the judgment of other specialists. This returns the power once more to organization.

No one should insist, in these matters, on pure cases. There will often be instances when an individual has the knowledge to modify or change the finding of a group. But the broad rule holds: If a decision requires the specialized knowledge of a group of men, it is subject to safe review only by the similar knowledge of a similar group. Group decision, unless acted upon by another group, tends to be absolute.[4]

5

Next, it must not be supposed that group decision is important only in such evident instances as nuclear technology or space mechanics. Simple products are made and packaged by sophisticated processes. And the most massive programs of market control, together with the most specialized marketing talent, are used on behalf of soap, detergents, cigarettes, aspirin, packaged cereals and gasoline. These, beyond others, are the valued advertising accounts. The simplicity and uniformity of these products require the investment of compensatingly elaborate science and art to suppress market influences and make prices and amounts sold subject to the largest possible measure of control. For these products too, decision passes to a group which combines specialized and esoteric knowledge. Here too power goes deeply and more or less irrevocably into the organization.

For purposes of pedagogy, I have sometimes illustrated these tendencies by reference to a technically uncomplicated product, which, unaccountably, neither General Electric nor Westinghouse has yet placed on the market. It is a toaster of standard performance, the pop-up kind, except that it etches on the surface of the toast, in darker carbon, one of a selection of standard messages or designs. For the elegant, an attractive monogram would be available or a coat of arms; for the devout, at breakfast there would be an appropriate devotional message from the Reverend Billy Graham; for the patriotic or worried, there would be an aphorism urging vigilance from Mr. J. Edgar Hoover; for modern painters and economists, there would be a purely abstract design. A restaurant version would sell advertising or urge the peaceful integration of public eating places.

Conceivably this is a vision that could come from the head of General Electric. But the systematic proliferation of such ideas is the designated function of much more lowly men who are charged with product development. At an early stage in the development of the toaster the participation of specialists in engineering, production, styling and design and possibly philosophy, art and spelling would have to be sought. No one in position to authorize the product would do so without a judgment on how the problems of inscription were to be solved and at what cost. Nor, ordinarily, would an adverse finding on technical and economic feasibility be overridden. At some stage, further development would become contingent on the findings of market researchers and merchandise experts on whether the toaster could be sold and at what price. Nor would an adverse decision by this group be overruled. In the end there would be a comprehensive finding on the feasibility of the innovation. If unfavorable this would not be overruled. Nor, given the notoriety that attaches to lost opportunity, would be the more plausible contingency of a favorable recommendation. It will be evident that nearly all powers—initiation, character of development, rejection or acceptance—are exercised deep in the company. It is not the managers who decide. Effective power or decision is lodged deeply in the technical, planning and other specialized staff.

6

We must notice next that this exercise of group power can be rendered unreliable or ineffective by external interference. Not only does power pass into the organization but the quality of decision can easily be impaired by efforts of an individual to retain control over the decision-making process.

Specifically the group reaches decision by receiving and evaluating the specialized information of its members. If it is to act responsibly, it must be accorded responsibility. It cannot be arbitrarily or capriciously overruled. If it is, it will develop the same tendencies to irresponsibility as an individual similarly treated.

But the tendency will be far more damaging. The efficiency of the group and the quality of its decisions depend on the quality of the information provided and the precision with which it is tested. The last increases greatly as men work together. It comes to be known that some are reliable and that some though useful are at a tacit discount. All information offered must be so weighed. The sudden intervention of a superior introduces information, often of dubious quality, that is not subject to this testing. His reliability, as a newcomer, is unknown; his information, since he is boss, may be automatically exempt from the proper discount; or his intervention may take the form of an instruction and thus be outside the process of group decision in a matter where only group decision incorporating the required specialized judgments is reliable. In all cases the intrusion is damaging.

It follows both from the tendency for decision-making to pass down into organization and the need to protect the autonomy of the group that those who hold high formal rank in an organization—the President of General Motors or General Electric—exercise only modest powers of substantive decision. This does not mean that they are without power. This power is certainly less than conventional obeisance, professional public relations or, on occasion, personal vanity insist. Decision and ratification are often confused. The first is important; the second is not. Routine decisions, if they involve a good deal of money, are also invariably thought important. The nominal head of a large corporation, though with slight power, and, perhaps, in the first stages of retirement, is visible, tangible and comprehensible. It is tempting and perhaps valuable for the corporate personality to attribute to him power of decision that, in fact, belongs to a dull and not easily comprehended collectivity.[5] Nor is it a valid explanation that the boss, though impotent on specific questions, acts on broad issues of policy. Such issues of policy, if genuine, are pre-eminently the ones that require the specialized information of the group.

Leadership does cast the membership of the groups that make the decisions and it constitutes and reconstitutes these groups in accordance witn changing need. This is its most important function. In an economy where organized intelligence is the decisive factor of production this is not unimportant. On the contrary. But it cannot be supposed that it can replace or even second-guess organized intelligence on substantive decisions.

7

In the past, leadership in business organization was identified with the entrepreneur—the individual who united ownership or control of capital with capacity for organizing the other factors of production and, in most contexts, with a further capacity for innovation.[6] With the rise of the modern corporation, the emergence of the organization required by modern technology and planning and the divorce of the owner of the capital from control of the enterprise, the entrepreneur no longer exists as an individual person in the mature industrial enterprise.[7] Everyday discourse, except in the economics textbooks, recognizes this change. It replaces the entrepreneur, as the directing force of the enterprise, with management. This is a collective and imperfectly defined entity; in the large corporation it embraces chairman, president, those vice presidents with important staff or departmental responsibility, occupants of other major staff positions and, perhaps, division or department heads not included above. It includes, however, only a small proportion of those who, as participants, contribute information to group decisions. This latter group is very large; it extends from the most senior officials of the corporation to where it meets, at the outer perimeter, the white and blue collar workers whose function is to conform more or less mechanically to instruction or routine. It embraces all who bring specialized knowledge, talent or experience to group decision-making. This, not the management, is the guiding intelligence—the brain—of the enterprise. There is no name for all who participate in group decision-making or the organization which they form. I propose to call this organization the Technostructure.

NOTES

1. "Of the various mechanisms of management, none is more controversial than committees.... Despite their alleged shortcomings, committees are an important device of administration. Paul E. Holden, Lounsbury S. Fish and Hubert L. Smith, *Top Management Organization and Control* (New York, McGraw, 1951). p. 59.

2. Also committees are not, as commonly supposed, alike. Some are constituted not to pool and test information and offer a decision but to accord representation to diverse bureaucratic, pecuniary, political, ideological or other interests. And a particular committee may have some of both purposes. A committee with representational functions will proceed much less expeditiously, for its ability to reach a conclusion depends on the susceptibility of participants to compromise, attrition and cupidity. The representational committee, in its present form, is engaged in a zero sum game, which is to say what some win others lose. Pooling and testing information is nonzero sum—all participants end with a larger score.

3. He was head of the Advanced Development Division of the Los Alamos Laboratory. His slightly earlier work was central to the conclusion that a self-sustaining chain-reaction was possible. Cf. Henry De Wolf Smyth, *Atomic Energy for Military Purposes* (Princeton: Princeton University Press, 1943), Chapter VI.

4. I reached some of these conclusions during World War II when, in the early years, I was in charge of price control. Decisions on prices—to fix, raise, rearrange or, very rarely, to lower them—came to my office after an extensive exercise in group decision-making in which lawyers, economists, accountants, men knowledgeable of the product and industry, and specialists in public righteousness had all participated. Alone one was nearly helpless to alter such decisions; hours or days of investigation would be required and, in the meantime, a dozen other decisions would have been made. Given what is commonly called an "adequate" staff, one could have exercised control. But an adequate staff would be one that largely duplicated the decision-making group with adverse effect on the good nature and sense of responsibility of the latter and the time required for decision. To have responsibility for all of the prices in the United States was awesome; to discover how slight was one's power in face of group decision-making was sobering. President Kennedy enjoyed responding to proposals for public action of one sort or another by saying: "I agree but I don't know whether the government will agree."

5. I return to these matters in the next chapter.

6. "To act with confidence beyond the range of familiar beacons and to overcome that resistance requires aptitudes that are present in only a small fraction of the population and [they] define the entrepreneurial type as well as the entrepreneurial function." Joseph A. Schumpeter, *Capitalism, Socialism and Democracy.* Second Edition (New York: Harper, 1947), p. 132.

7. He is still, of course, to be found in smaller firms and in larger ones that have yet to reach full maturity of organization. I deal with his evolution in the next chapters.

ALVIN W. GOULDNER

Red Tape as
a Social Problem

"These clients came to plead with us. Instead of storming the office and knocking everything to smithereens, they came to plead." Franz Kafka

It is now something more than a century since the term "red tape" was introduced into the English language in its figurative sense. Sidney Smith (1771-1845), an Englishman who could not make up his mind whether he wished to be remembered as a clergyman or as a wit, did much to popularize the satirical connotations of the term.

In 1838, Lord Lytton averred that "the men of dazzling genius began to sneer at the red-tape minister as a mere official manager of details." The redoubtable Carlyle once described someone as "little other than a red-tape talking machine." Probably the first person to give red tape its sociological baptism was Herbert Spencer (about 1873). It was not, however, until 1889 and 1890 that the term began to appear in American newspapers and periodicals.

Present day interest in red tape on the part of sociologists largely derives from studies in bureaucratic structure. Alexander Leighton[1] and Robert Merton have analyzed it as a dysfunctional behavioral pattern which impairs the persistence or continuity of an organization.[2]

Here, and in similar approaches to the subject, red tape is interpreted as being the actual behavior engaged in by the bureaucrat, or of its consequences, interpreted in terms of the ends of the *organization*.[3]

There is, however, one set of observations which this approach to red tape was not designed to encompass. Namely, that red tape is a popular and widespread complaint which is explicitly articulated. There is, then, a second, not an alternative but an additional, context in terms of which red tape may be analyzed—i.e., as a "social problem" taken cognizance of by large numbers of laymen.

The implications of this further analysis may be clarified if two questions are asked:

(1) Why is it, for example, that not all means which have become transformed into ends are thought of as red tape, e.g., the American Constitution?

(2) Why is it, also, that the very same procedures or practices which one group may characterize as red tape may be viewed by another group as deserving no invidious label? The latter may, in fact, attach an approving (possibly, "green-tape") label to the procedure. For example, some land-lords but few tenants characterize rent control procedures as red tape.[4]

Commonplace as those observations are, they, nevertheless, suggest that red tape involves phenomena of two orders: (1) the perceiving individual who, with a given frame of reference, comes into some relationship with (2) objective, perhaps bureaucratic, practices or behavior patterns.

Thus red tape as a social problem cannot be explained unless the frame of reference employed by the individual who uses this label is understood, as well as the objective attributes of the situations with which he comes into contact. Both elements are interrelated and changes in either alter the scope and formulation of the problem.

This analysis of red tape as a social problem does not seek to attach a new meaning to a familiar term. Rather, it seeks to identify the frame of reference of people who are hostile to red tape and for whom it therefore comprises a problem, as well as to describe the structural context and the social functions of red tape.

The data upon which this tentative account is partly based are of two kinds: first, secret ballot, group interviews, qualitatively analyzed; second, interviews with a small sample of 124 respondents stratified in terms of status and ethnic group.[5]

RED TAPE AS THE UNNECESSARY

As might be expected, the meanings ascribed by our interviewees to the term "red tape," as indicated both by their general definitions and concrete illustrations, are most often stated in the language of efficiency. For example, "going through a lot of unnecessary beating around the bush." Another: "Red tape is something which disagrees with the theory that the shortest distance between two points is a straight line." And again: "It means a lot of unnecessary rigamarole and delay in filling out forms."

The language of efficiency is not a valueless and detached judgment on the part of people in our society. "Efficiency"—the choice of those alternatives that maximize the realization of objectives, or minimize expenditures in their pursuit—is widely regarded as a good in and of itself. It is in this sense that a belief in efficiency is one critical element in the frame of reference for the perception and judgment of red tape.

Since efficiency is a widely acknowledged value in a society priding itself upon its "technique" and "know-how," it is apparently employed to mask negative judgments based on less universally accredited values or less easily articulated sentiments. It is not merely that there are other non-rational elements in the red-tape frame of reference, but that these may be implicit in seemingly rational judgments expressed in terms of efficiency.[6] This will be evident from the discussion following.

THE SEPARATION OF PUBLIC AND PRIVATE SPHERES

In describing the meaning red tape has for them, interviewees tend to emphasize presumably "unnecessary" or dispensable features. These, however, are condemned not solely because they violate the canons of efficiency, but because they transgress less easily expressed values. One of the most important of these is the sacredness of privacy, or a belief that the individual should be privileged to withhold certain information about himself from anyone. In this context, the unnecessary is that which violates privacy.

The clichés and commonplaces of complaints regarding red tape repeatedly strike this same keynote: too many people have a chance to observe something of a nature which the respondent deems private; he feels that he is being forced to divulge matters construed as intimate. For some, red tape means: "filling out forms," "going through many hands," "too many details asked," "being investigated," or "too many interviews needed."

One respondent remarks: "When I wanted to withdraw $300 from my bank account, they wouldn't let me take it out unless I first saw a vice-president. They could see that I had the money in my account from my bank book. He wanted to know what I wanted the money for, and I had to explain I was moving and buying new furniture. Why was it his business?" This theme is compactly summarized by another: "Many questions that are asked are of a personal nature and should not be the ordinary business of a stranger."

Not only is the individual's privacy invaded by the information demanded of him, but he is himself investigated, and thus placed on the defensive. One respondent, describing an experience with what he called red tape, reports:

"A commercial vehicle struck my automobile. To settle the matter, I had to give a report to my insurance company. They had to send out a man to inspect my damage to see if the estimate I have given them was correct. . . ." Another says that a "mild example" of red tape "would be in the attempt to borrow money from a finance company. All your references have to be *checked,* your source of income *checked,* your honesty, reliability, etc." A respondent describing efforts of a married couple to adopt a child says: "They must undergo *investigation* for moral and financial reasons. After they finally get a child, they must be *investigated* again before they can legally adopt the child...." Finally a respondent complains that "You are asked questions which have to be *verified* by so and so and so and so."

In these instances regarded as red tape, the individual's ego is challenged on two counts: (1) A claim which he believes legitimate is not taken "at face value." He must either supply proof or allow it to be investigated. He is, as one remarked, "treated as a criminal"—he may feel his worth is questioned, his status impugned. (2) Not only are his claims and assertions challenged, but other details of his "private life" are investigated. The individual enters the situation on "official," "technical," or "public business, and feels that he ends up by being investigated as a person.

It seems clear that this conception of red tape would turn up only if the individual accepted the current value which insists upon the division of social activity into the spheres of the public and private.[7] In such cases, the individual responds to the violation of the value by feeling, as some expressed it, that "he is getting involved;" that he is experiencing the fusion of spheres which should be kept separated.

THE BELIEF IN EQUALITY

The foregoing comments of interviewees may have suggested that the situation is defined as red tape when pursuit of an end is obstructed and especially so when the ends themselves are defined in a particular way—namely, as rights. One respondent mentions that veterans encounter red tape when "trying to get the V. A. to approve dental work to a veteran who is *entitled to it*...." Another tells of his difficulty in obtaining an army promotion when he was "due for" it. A third speaks of his difficulty in collecting back flying pay, even though "I had papers with me verifying my *entitlement* to the flying pay...."

It is not necessarily the absolute, but rather the relative complexity of demands made by an organization upon its clientele which leads these to be regarded as red tape. Ordinary routines are so regarded if there is the suspicion that special privilege exempts others from these routines. A commercial aviator thus considers the customs procedures encountered in international flights as red tape, going on to declare that if you belong to the "right organizations" you pass through customs much more quickly. A respondent speaking of banks says that they "act as if they are doing you a favor to take your money. When you first open your account, they keep you waiting until they are ready.... They really don't want a small account. They're interested in the big accounts."

The democratic creed with its accent on equality of rights may thus provide a value component of the red tape frame of reference,[8] one which would presumably not be common in a nondemocratic society.

POWERLESSNESS

Sensitivity to disparities of power seems to be another element in the red tape frame of reference. A veteran refers to his army experiences to illustrate his conception of red tape: "If a soldier wishes to go on leave, first of all the G.I. must present the claim to his platoon sergeant. Then it is referred to the top sergeant who, in turn, goes over the request and gives either his approval or disapproval. He then presents this to the C.O. who will either approve or disapprove your request."

Another: "In factories, when persons have grievances, they are usually sent to many different persons before 'hitting' the particular one who will handle the case, rather than being sent directly to the person who will give you the satisfaction."

A student discussing an encounter with what he calls red tape says:

"To secure permission to use school records for the purpose of doing an attendance survey, I was first directed to an employee at the Board of Education, then to another employee, then to the deputy superintendent, the superintendent, the first employee asked, the superintendent again, then to the attendance director and, finally, permission to use the records was obtained."

These and similar statements suggest that the individual who decries red tape feels that he is unable to "get to" the people who have the power, or get to them readily enough. You first have to go before the powerless people—they seem to be saying—who though they may be able to deny your request, are often unable to approve it finally. They can say, "no," but not "yes." Power centers are felt to be out of reach and the individual experiences himself and those with whom he can have some face to face contact as powerless.[9] This feeling of powerlessness may in some cases be a character trait rather than an artifact of a social situation.

SUSPICION AND THE INABILITY TO DEFER GRATIFICATIONS

Two further character traits of clients apparently encourage them to perceive red tape where others do not. These are suspiciousness and an apparent inability to defer gratifications. The prevalence of suspicion manifests itself in the motives that respondents ascribe to those who present them with the red tape obstacles. "Apparently the only thing to be gained in making this application complicated, which resulted in many applications rejected," said one informant, "was the increase and duration of political jobs." Red tape, says another, "seems to be used in order to have only the very anxious ones receive whatever they're after and discourage those who are not too eager." These remarks, among others, seem to imply that there exists deliberate intent to frustrate the client. For some, the world of red tape is not merely "unnecessary," "complicated," or "meaningless"; it becomes meaningful as willful maliciousness when viewed in the context of suspicion.[10]

Those who are particularly sensitive to "waiting," when they emphasize the time it takes to comply with their requests or to get a decision on them, may include some whose capacity to defer gratification has become weakened. It would seem that suspicion and an inability to defer gratifications are closely interlocked. For, to the extent that the world is felt to be peopled with those who would do us harm and who cannot be trusted, safety lies only in the *immediate* satisfaction. The satisfaction that has to be deferred is imperiled by all manner of hostile forces that may prevent its realization.

INADEQUATE "SUBSTANTIAL RATIONALITY"

One further characteristic of the red-tape-sensitive frame of reference deserves special mention: its apparent inhibition of an "intelligent insight into the interrelations of events in a given situation," what Karl Mannheim called[11] "substantial rationality." Persons complaining of red tape often say, in effect, that the things they experience are meaningless and make no sense to them. They describe red tape as "complicated," "unnecessarily complex," a "mix-up" or "befuddlement."

We need not presuppose that the demands placed upon a client, or the procedures with which he is forced to comply, are actually necessary or unnecessary. The only question of interest here is whether anything can be learned about the client and his frame of reference from his repeated references to red tape as "confused" or "mixed-up." Our data do not permit us to say whether, in some objective sense, the situation is really "befuddled." We can be reasonably certain, however, that it does "confuse" the client, and that it provides him with experiences which are meaningless in his frame of reference.

As Lundberg has indicated,[12] the degree to which a situation appears complicated or simple is not only determined by the situation itself. It is also influenced by the frame of reference through which it is viewed. Thus individuals coming upon a situation which they label "red tape" and finding it confusing are likely to have a frame of reference that cannot make sense of their experience.

What are some reasons for this eclipse of substantial rationality and for the inadequacy of the red-tape-sensitive frame of reference? Some clues may be provided by examining the kinds of organizations alleged to have the least red tape. Most respondents mention nonprofit, private associations, as having least red tape. These include churches, Y's, the American Legion, the Salvation Army, fraternities, and trade unions. In part, these groups are distinguished by their relatively personalized and informal relationships. The tendency to choose "least red tape" groups on the basis of this criterion is epitomized by one person who nominated, "the home."

A second criterion apparently used by respondents involves the effectiveness of the possible cash transactions. Thus one respondent, who declared that second-hand car dealers have little red tape, went on to say, "Here, money talks!"

The organizations listed as having least red tape in general appear to have well-developed, personalized, and informal relations or effective cash relationships. Among privately owned businesses believed to have little red tape, *small* businesses were prominent. These, providing "service with a smile," also effectively fuse informal and pecuniary ties.

Apparently, many individuals in our society expect organizations to operate on one or both of these bases. But a distinctive feature of contemporary bureaucracies is their use of relationships which are neither personalized nor pecuniary, neither informal nor contractual. Instead, they are attuned to abstract and impersonal rules. These considerations suggest that those who pronounce red tape to be a "mix-up" and "befuddlement" are utilizing a frame of reference which relies upon somewhat outmoded techniques for realizing goals. A frame of reference which depends upon market and informal arrangements as instrumentalities will be less and less effective as bureaucratic organization invades ever-widening spheres of the society.

RED TAPE AS "RESENTMENT"

Other social sources of the red-tape-sensitive frame of reference are indicated in Max Scheler's concept of "resentment." According to Scheler, "resentment" is a compound of envy and suppressed aggression, a compound which sometimes bursts into the open and is directed against some diffusely defined group or object. Scheler maintains that, "The wider the gulf existing between the juridical condition of divergent social groups established by the political system or tradition, on the one side, and their actual power on the other, the more powerful will be the charge of psychological explosiveness implicit in the situation." [13]

In certain major respects the red tape frame of reference and Scheler's description of resentment converge. Both involve a belief in equality which is violated by a sense of powerlessness. Like the "man of resentment," the individual hostile to red tape also feels that there are things to which he is entitled but never receives. Essentially, however, what distinguishes the man of resentment is not his frustration, but his feeling of powerlessness. He has little hope of rectifying the situation. It would appear, therefore, that a full analysis of the social roots of the red-tape-sensitive frame of reference must link up with the phenomenon of alienation.

ALIENATION OF THE CONSERVATIVE

If this is so, it is likely that we are confronted with the alienation of a distinct ideological group, roughly characterizable as "conservatives." For it is the conservatives, rather than the "radicals," who seem most concerned with red tape as a social problem. [14] To designate this group simply as "conservative," without specifying its other attributes, especially its status properties, is clearly inadequate. Further analysis of our data is required, however, before the other characteristics of this group can be stated with confidence.

For the present, a tentative formulation might hold that red tape, as a culturally familiar epithet, has largely developed under conservative sponsorship.[15] This may explain why those indignant at red tape frequently direct their aggression against clerks at the bottom of a structure, while higher echelons escape unscathed. Their hostility is, moreover, aimed at *means*—e.g., forms and questionnaires—rather than at group *ends*. Criticisms embodied in the term "red tape" enable the individual to express aggression against powerful and prestige-laden organizations, while still permitting him to be "counted in." As such, "red tape" is a social critique readily acceptable to conservatives.

The significance of the red tape stereotype seems, however, to be even deeper. Social institutions during the last century or so have undergone profound changes partly describable as bureaucratization. The red tape stereotype gives compact but blurred expression to the resentment against the alienation, the impersonalization, and the dull routines that afflict bureaucracy. This suggests that the growth of concern with "red tape" may indicate new types of social problems.

NOTES

1. *The Governing of Men* (Princeton University Press, 1945), p. 309.

2. "Bureaucratic Structure and Personality" reprinted in *Reader in Bureaucracy.*

3. We have, elsewhere, suggested the possibility of analyzing this phenomenon in theoretical contexts other than the means-end schema. Alvin W. Gouldner, "Discussion of 'Industrial Sociology: Status and Prospects.' " *American Sociological Review,* XIII (August, 1948), p. 399, reprinted in part in *Reader in Bureaucracy* under the title of "On Weber's Analysis of Bureaucratic Rules."

4. "When at the threshold of World War II motormaker William Knudsen assumed a post of great importance in the defense effort of the nation, he said of Washington red tape, 'In Detroit we call it system.' " John A Vieg. "Bureaucracy—Fact and Fiction," in Fritz Morstein Marx (ed.), *Elements of Public Adminstration* (New York: Prentice-Hall, Inc., 1946), p. 54.

5. Preliminary statistical analyses of these are reported in footnotes. Only suggestive at best, these are intended to indicate that further study is warranted.

6. Proportion of Respondents Using Differing Values in Defining and Illustrating Red Tape:

Value	Per Cent of Respondents*
Efficiency	74
Equality	17
The separation of private and public spheres	10
	(N = 124)

*Some, of course, use more than one value: 61 percent of the respondents use "efficiency" alone; 17 percent of those using "efficiency" use it in conjunction with either or both of the other values.

7. Respondents were asked: "On the whole, do you feel that: (a) Most of the red tape you came across is really necessary, (b) Some of the red tape you came across is necessary but some is not, (c) Practically none of the red tape you came across is necessary?" Respondents choosing either (a) or (b) were classified as "tolerant" toward red tape; those choosing (c), as "hostile." Among a battery of questions designed to explore their values, they were asked to indicate their agreement or disagreement with the following statement, (which was used as an index of their belief in the value of maintaining a separation of private and public spheres) "A man's business and private life should be kept strictly separated." Cross-tabulation of answers to the first and second questions gave the following table ("no answers" and "don't knows" eliminated).

	Attitude Toward Separation of Private and Public Spheres		
Attitude Toward Red Tape	*Agree*	*Disagree*	
Tolerant	62	19	
Hostile	24	2	
Total	86	21	107

The probability of the correct chi square for this table is between 0.10 and 0.20.

8. Responses to the following statement were used as an index for the respondent's attitude toward equality: "All people are born equal and should be treated that way."

	Attitude Toward Equality		
Attitude Toward Red Tape	*Agree*	*Disagree*	
Tolerant	61	19	
Hostile	26	3	
Total	87	22	109

Probability for the corrected chi square is about 0.02.

9. Agreement with the following statement (here selected from several others of like kind) was used as an index of the respondent's feeling of powerlessness: "An awful lot of people are getting stepped on these days."

	Sense of Powerlessness		
Attitude Toward Red Tape	+	—	
Tolerant	53	20	
Hostile	27	2	
Total	80	22	

Probability for the corrected chi square is between 0.05 and 0.02.

10. Responses to the following statement were used as an index to the respondent's feeling of suspicion: "Lots of people seem to be friendly and sincere but many of them only pretend to be that way."

	Suspiciousness		
Attitude Toward Red Tape	+	—	
Tolerant	11	65	
Hostile	10	19	
Total	21	84	105

Probability for the corrected chi square is about 0.05.

11. *Man and Society in an Age of Reconstruction* (Harcourt, Brace and Company, 1941), p. 53.

12. George A. Lundberg, *Foundations of Sociology* (Macmillan Company, 1938), p. 138.

13. As quoted in Gerard de Gré, *Society and Ideology* (Columbia University Bookstore, 1943), p. 11.

14. The question here is: in what kind of a political orientation is red tape ascribed the *most importance*. To ascertain this we asked: "How important a problem would you say red tape is?" Respondents could check one of the following answers: (a) of great importance, (b) of some importance, (c) not very important, (d) not sure. Responses to the following

statement were used as a crude index of "radicalism-conservatism": "The country would be better off if the trade unions had more power." Omitting those without a definite opinion the following table was obtained:

Importance Ascribed to Red Tape	*Political Orientation*	
	"Radical"	"Conservative"
High (a, b)	19	43
Low (c)	15	8
Total	34	51

Probability for the corrected chi square is better than 0.01.

15. It is an interesting fact of intellectual history that those passages of Karl Marx's writings in which he castigates alienation, impersonalization, and dull, routine work find little echo among the present Marxian epigoni.

MELVIN SEEMAN

Antidote to Alienation— Learning to Belong

Most of us in the United States now live in the great faceless conglomerates of population—the large metropolitan areas with their strung-out suburban belts—where who one's neighbors are is largely a matter of accident, and it usually doesn't pay to get closely involved with them because they keep changing. Parents and children are close— perhaps even closer than before—as long as they live in the same house; but older generations and other relatives drift away, take jobs in other cities, go to retirement homes, have their own interests and associates. Often it seems painful but realistic to conclude that, in the last analysis, you and your family are alone, and the only ones you can really count on for help and support are yourselves. No one else cares.

The American legend has it that not much more than a generation ago it used to be very different. Our fathers lived, mostly, in a golden age of belonging, in the traditional tree-shaded small town or closely-knit neighborhood (complete with the *Saturday Evening Post* version of a colonial-style church at the end of the block). Everyone was friendly and solicitous, and in case of need neighbors by the tens and cousins by the dozens would come running.

For most of us this dream, to the extent that it ever was real, is dead.

It is the dominant theme of "mass theory" in social psychology that such social and personal ties cannot be cut or seriously weakened without major damage—both to us and to the democratic process. Torn loose from so many of our emotional supports and roots—from the guidelines that remind us who we are and what we are worth—we must, so the theme goes, become prey increasingly to feelings of isolation, helplessness, and alienation.

But a theme is not yet a theory. It becomes a theory by being specific about processes—by describing the step-by-step development from cause to effect. How do the feelings of isolation, helplessness and alienation come about and what is their consequence? Mass theory becomes useful when it combines (a) history and social structure with (b) a description of the psychological effects of that structure, those alienative effects which in turn lead to (c) predicted behavior. *Alienation* is the center and the key to mass theory—it is produced by the structure of society, and it produces distinctive behavior.

To describe this process in greater detail:

Historically and *structurally* the old roots and close relationships have practically disappeared and been replaced by anonymity and impersonality in social and personal life, and by bureaucracy and mechanization at work.

Psychologically this must result in *alienation*. Alienation can take a number of forms: feelings of powerlessness, rootlessness, lack of standards and beliefs, and "self-estrangement" (having no clear idea of your personality or place, not even "belonging" to yourself).

Alienation in turn results in *alienated behavior,* such as political passivity, racial and religious prejudice, taking part in movements that promise to usher in the millenium (but have little immediate or practical effect) and the like.

SUCCESS AND FAILURE

Since personal alienation is the key element, psychological theory is crucial to its understanding. In trying to understand and explain these psychological processes, I have found the social learning theory of Julian B. Rotter very helpful. (*Social Learning and Clinical Psychology,* Prentice-Hall, 1954) Rotter's principal contention is that human behavior depends on (1) the degree to which a person *expects* that the behavior will have a successful outcome, and (2) the *value* of that success to the person trying to achieve it. If these factors are powerful, separately or together, the behavior is most likely to occur. Specifically, if a person expects that learning something will help him achieve some goal, and/or he values that goal, he is more likely to learn.

Rotter's theory helps clarify the different meanings of alienation. Let us concentrate on what is probably the most important aspect of alienation in mass society—feelings of *powerlessness,* a person's belief that there is little he can do to bring about what he wants. People conceive of success and failure as being not only due to *external* factors—those that work on a man essentially from the outside and are usually considered beyond his control (luck, fate, "city hall," or "they")—but also *internal* factors, coming from within, which often do give him some control (skills, motives, determination, work).

Rotter and his co-workers argue that most experimental studies in learning usually unwittingly emphasize *external* control—the experimenter himself controls most of the pressures and conditions of the situation, and the subject is really not independent at all. If the subject could feel that he had some personal control over the learning, could relate it to his own needs and self-respect, then the patterns and amounts of learning might be very different.

A number of recent studies have supported this principle. These studies show that when the same learning task is performed in two separate ways, with two sets of instructions—one, for instance, emphasizing the skill and energy required from the learner, and the other stressing the luck or chance aspect of the task (*internal* versus *external* control)—there are striking differences in learning and retention. A person will definitely learn *less* from experiences he conceives to be dominated by outsiders, or by chance, which he feels he cannot influence.

This finding parallels the argument of the followers of mass theory that the isolated individual in "the lonely crowd," subordinated to and intimidated by bureaucracy, becomes convinced of his powerlessness and gives up learning about those things that might affect his future. As a specific example, he becomes apathetic and indifferent to politics—"You can't fight city hall."

Thus, mass society theory and Rotter's social learning theory agree that those persons with greater feelings of powerlessness will not learn as much or as well as those who feel they exercise some control over the factors that influence their lives.

UNIVERSAL ALIENATION

The statement that feelings of powerlessness inhibit knowledge is a basic conclusion about human beings. If true, it should be true not only of a few people, but of many; not only of those in our country but in other nations as well. It should be true not only about one type of learning, but throughout a wide spectrum of learning situations. Providing always, of course, that the learning is *relevant to control*—that it seems to the learner to be giving him a tool he can use to change his condition. Thus, an unemployed man learning how and where best to apply for a job is acquiring *control-relevant* information—while one learning baseball batting averages is not. The alienated can presumably learn escapist and irrelevant information as quickly as anyone—perhaps more quickly.

To test the hypothesis that the connection between feelings of powerlessness and inhibition of learning was generally true of mankind, we conducted several studies on powerlessness and alienation:

in different institutions (a hospital and a reformatory);

with different degrees of belonging to a work organization (unorganized versus unionized workers in Columbus, Ohio);

and in different nations (Sweden and the United States).

Although specific items used in the several studies (hospital, reformatory, Columbus, and Sweden) varied somewhat, in all cases the person was offered a choice between an expression of mastery and one of powerlessness. For example:

"Many times I feel that I have little influence over the things that happen to me" or "I do not believe that chance and luck are very important in my life";

"Becoming a success is a matter of hard work; luck has little or nothing to do with it" or "Getting a job depends mainly on being in the right place at the right time."

The study of the hospital, published by John W. Evans and myself in the *American Sociological Review* (1962), and of the reformatory in *American Journal of Sociology* (1963), may be considered as a pair. They were both done in the United States. They sought to find out how feelings of powerlessness are related to lack of knowledge and information, in places where knowledge and information might give the individual some understanding and control of his fate. The hospital study dealt with tuberculosis patients; we found that those with the strongest feelings of powerlessness knew less about health matters than those not so alienated. In the reformatory study, inmates with greater feelings of helplessness learned relatively little when given information about parole, even though it might have helped shorten their confinement.

A third American study with Arthur G. Neal (*American Sociological Review*, 1964) was designed to test whether, as predicted, members of a formal occupational organization, such as a union or professional association, would feel less powerless than non-members. In form and feeling (if not always in fact) joining a vocational association apparently dedicated to a common goal should give a member some feeling of control over his job destiny, and perhaps over broader socio-economic matters as well. Mass theory postulates that the great centers of power—government and the major corporations—are rapidly increasing in size and impersonality. At the same time, and as a consequence, jobs are becoming more specialized, more interchangeable, and the workers are moving more and more from job to job and city to city. This breakdown of personal identification with his work is supposed to make the worker feel more insignificant, expendable, and isolated ("just another cog"). The labor organizations that mediate between him and the great bureaucracies should therefore become more and more important to him, especially as a means of providing him with some sense of control.

ORGANIZED FOR POWER

We picked at random about 800 adult male names from the Columbus, Ohio, city directory, and mailed questionnaires to them designed to explore this relationship between union membership and feelings of powerlessness. About 57 percent answered—245 manual workers and 216 non-manuals.

The results of the Columbus study were definite. When factors such as age, income, education, and type of job are equal, unorganized workers *do* feel more powerless. This was true of both manual and non-manual workers. (The powerlessness was a little greater for workers who changed jobs most often.) Further, these results were *specific* to powerlessness; that is, a test of the workers' generalized unhappiness (anomie) showed that the unorganized do not feel significantly more despairing about everything (or even most things) than the organized—it is apparently a rather specific sense of *mastery* but not of wellbeing in general, that organization membership provides

On the basis of the Columbus study we could state that feelings of powerlessness do arise among unorganized workers in the United States. But a further demonstration seemed necessary—one that could combine all three elements—organization, powerlessness and knowledge—into a single study; that could show whether these findings were peculiar to America; and that could concentrate on a broader field than health or corrections—the field of politics and international affairs.

Accordingly, a study was designed for Sweden to fulfill these needs, and was carried out by interview (in Swedish) with a sample of the male work force in Malmo. (Malmo is Sweden's third largest city, population about 240,000, with a heavy concentration of commercial and seaport oc- cupations.) A random sample of males aged twenty to seventy-nine was drawn from the official register maintained by government authorities. A total of 558 workers were interviewed.

The interview contained questions on three major variables:

Feelings of powerlessness. (The individual's expectations of control), proferring the usual choice between items expressing mastery and powerlessness.

Organization membership. Apart from simple membership in a union or other work organization, evidence was gathered on (a) the person's *degree* of participation, and (b) his *involvement* in organizations outside of work.

Political knowledge. A sixteen-item information test dealt with both Swedish politics and international affairs.

When the Swedish data had been collected, checked and evaluated, the differences were found to be consistently and significantly as predicted: *high feelings of powerlessness and low political knowledge were found together among the unorganized workers.* Second, there was a relatively small but predictable difference between those who were officials and those who were simply members of unions.

MASTER OF THE POLITICAL SHIP

These results are clearly consistent with the learning and mass society theses. But before they can be accepted without question, other complicating factors must be eliminated. What about education? Could differences in education be the real underlying cause of the differences in feelings of powerlessness? What about other factors, such as age or job prestige? A close examination of the data, correcting for education and the other elements, makes the result even more emphatic. In Sweden as in the United States, neither education nor other differences obliterated the trend. High powerlessness among the workers appeared to flow from lack of union membership and was intimately related to low political knowledge.

The officers of the unions were shown to have the lowest feelings of powerlessness, and to be highest in political knowledge. But was this due to the fact that they were *officers,* and therefore a special kind of member (and also, perhaps, a special breed of cat with different personality characteristics); or was it primarily because they were more involved—"more engaged"—in the affairs of the union, and therefore more capable of exerting control? Would other "more engaged" members (who were non-officers) also be less alienated, and have greater capacity for learning control-relevant information?

"Engaged" members, we decided, would be those who attended meetings regularly, considered the union to be important in their lives, and thought individual members were important and influential in the union. Pitting the scores of such rank-and-file members against the "less engaged" we found a parallel with the overall comparison of organized versus unorganized workers. The relationship is modest but consistent: the greater the personal involvement in union meetings and affairs, the less the feelings of powerlessness; and for the manual workers (who would generally tend to have less education) involvement and amount of political knowledge go together as well. (This picture calls to mind the old socialist ideal of the politically-wise proletarian who spent much time in study and discussion of the political and economic factors that controlled his life, and then organized to do something about them.)

We found, too, that the person's *interest* in political affairs is part of the same picture. Of course, those with more interest in politics have greater knowledge of it; but more important here is the fact that strong feelings of powerlessness go along with low interest. Those who do not feel mastery do not develop interest and do not learn.

This interest, or lack of it, is directly related to union membership—to belonging to an organization that could exert job control. Organized workers were significantly more interested in political affairs than the non-union workers. And this interest, again, was *specific* to what we call *control-relevant* information. The unorganized were *not* totally withdrawn or apathetic; they were just as interested as the organized workers in personal and local affairs and in discussing their work. But the unorganized felt powerless to control their larger destinies—and politics and international affairs represented these larger destinies.

So far, these conclusions agree with both learning theory and mass theory. Men with little hope for success feel powerless, lose interest in, and have difficulty learning control-relevant information.

However, it must be recalled that Rotter's learning theory made a distinction between a person's *expectation* that he can achieve a goal, and the *value* he places on that goal. Theoretically at least, a person will not try very earnestly for a goal he does not value, no matter how sure he is he can get it; contrariwise, he may try very hard, even with little hope of achievement, if he wants the goal badly enough.

In the American reformatory study, knowledge which might have helped the inmate have some control over his future (parole information) and non-control knowledge (descriptive information about the institution) were both offered to the inmates tested. We split the subjects into two groups—those who tended to conform to what prison authorities wanted of them, who seemed to value the officially approved goals and behavior set for them (working hard, obeying regulations, making no trouble, trying to meet parole requirements) and those who would not conform. We reasoned that if the inmate did not value parole (as part of the prison system) very highly, then whether or not he believed he could achieve it was not very important in determining whether he would learn parole information; however, if he did value parole, his expectation (or lack of it) that he could determine his own life should affect how much he would study and learn about parole. The results were consistent with this view: generally, those inmates who valued the conventional standards of how to get ahead in the reformatory world, who "conformed," learned more of the parole information than did the "unconventionals." But even in this conforming group, those who felt powerless learned less. We may conclude then that both the *value* of the goal and the *expectation* of achieving it will be reflected in how much learning a man will acquire that relates to the goal.

RISING EXPECTATIONS

Summarizing the overall conclusions of all four studies:

Powerlessness and organization. A person's feelings of self-reliance and power are tied up with whether he belongs to an organization that has some control over his occupational destiny. If he does belong to such an organization—union, business or professional association—his further feelings of mastery are directly tied up with how actively he works in it— whether he has some control over *its* destiny.

Powerlessness and learning. The ability to learn and retain knowledge which has some connection with control over an individual's future (politics, parole, or health information) is also directly affected by belonging to a union or other relevant organization, and to a person's alienation. To the extent that he feels powerless to affect his future, he will not learn as well what he needs to know to affect it. And he will not be as interested in it—he may even reject it.

To the degree that he *expects* to achieve his goal, he will attend to the associated learning; to the degree that he *values* the goal, he will also be oriented to learn.

The connection between organization membership and powerlessness holds true from nation to nation—it is as true in Sweden, for example, as in the United States.

The connection between powerlessness and learning holds true through many different kinds of organizations (reformatories, hospitals, unions) and many different kinds of control information (parole and health information, politics, international affairs).

These studies are perhaps more important for what they promise than for what they presently accomplish. The promise is that controlled studies of this kind, carried out in various cultures and settings, can establish the validity of arguments and theories about contemporary life which depend upon the idea of alienation. There is much literature of this kind, both inside and outside of social science; and it deals with a wide range of subjects—for example, mass movements, inter-group prejudice, mass communication, and politics. It is a literature which touches a powerful array of basic human values: normlessness and trust, meaninglessness and understanding, self-estrangement and integrity.

The promise is that we can concern ourselves with such large questions about the individual in modern society and test long-held theories that have highly practical consequences—learning what it really means, under various circumstances, to exert control, to sink roots, to find understanding, or even to be oneself.

WARREN G. BENNIS

Post-Bureaucratic Leadership

In an early issue of this magazine (*Trans*-action, June-July 1965), I forecast that in the next 25 to 50 years we would participate in the end of bureaucracy as we know it and in the rise of new social systems better suited to the 20th century demands of industrialization. The prediction was based on the evolutionary principle that every age develops an organizational form appropriate to its genius, and that the prevailing form today—the pyramidal, centralized, functionally specialized, impersonal mechanism known as *bureaucracy*—was out of joint with contemporary realities.

This breakdown of a venerable form of organization so appropriate to 19th century conditions is caused, I argued, by a number of factors, but chiefly the following four: 1) rapid and unexpected change; 2) growth in size beyond what is necessary for the work being done (for example, inflation caused by bureaucratic overhead and tight controls, impersonality caused by sprawls, outmoded rules, and organizational rigidities); 3) complexity of modern technology, in which integration between activities and persons of very diverse, highly specialized competence is required; 4) a change in managerial values toward more humanistic democratic practices.

Organizations of the future, I predicted, will have some unique characteristics. They will be adaptive, rapidly changing *temporary systems,* organized around problems-to-be-solved by groups of relative strangers with diverse professional skills. The groups will be arranged on organic rather than mechanical models; they will evolve in response to problems rather than to programmed expectations. People will be evaluated, not in a rigid vertical hierarchy according to rank and status, but flexibly, according to competence. Organizational charts will consist of project groups rather than stratified functional groups, as is now the

Reprinted with the permission of the publisher and the author from "Post-Bureaucratic Leadership," by Warren Bennis, TRANS-action, July-August 1969, pp. 44-51, 61.

case. Adaptive, problem-solving, temporary systems of diverse specialists, linked together by coordinating executives in an organic flux—this is the organizational form that will gradually replace bureaucracy.

Ironically, the bold future I had predicted is now routine and can be observed wherever the most interesting and advanced practices exist. Most of these trends are visible and have been surfacing for years in the aerospace, construction, drug, and consulting industries as well as professional and research and development organizations, which only shows that the distant future now has a way of arriving before the forecast is fully comprehended.

A question left unanswered, however, has to do with leadership. How would these new organizations be managed? Are there any transferable lessons from present managerial practices? Do the behavioral sciences provide any suggestions? How can these complex, ever-changing, free-form, kaleidoscopic patterns be coordinated? Of course there can be no definitive answers, but unless we can understand the leadership requirements for organizations of the future, we shall inevitably back blindly into it rather than cope with it effectively.

Accepted theory and conventional wisdom concerning leadership have a lot in common. Both seem to be saying that the success of a leader depends on the leader, the led, and the unique situation. This formulation—abstract and majestically useless—is the best that can be gleaned from over 100 years of research on "leadership."

On the other hand, any formulations may be inadequate and pallid compared to the myths and primitive psychological responses that surround such complexities as leadership and power. Our preoccupation with the mystiques of the Kennedys is sufficient reminder of that.

Thus, leadership theory coexists with a powerful and parallel archetypal reality. But in what follows, we shall see that it is the latter myth that is threatened—the aggressive, inner-directed 19th century autocrat. For the moment, though, I want to quickly review some of the key situational features likely to confront the leader of the future.

The overarching feature is change itself, its accelerating rate and its power to transform. The phrase "the only constant is change" has reached the point of a cliché, which at once anesthetizes us to its pain and stimulates grotesque fantasies about a Brave New World with no place in the sun for us. Change is the "godhead" term for our age as it has not been for any other. One has only to recall that the British Parliament was debating in the last part of the 19th century whether to close up the Royal Patent Office, as it was felt that all significant inventions had already been discovered.

SITUATIONAL FEATURES

But what are the most salient changes affecting human organization, the ones with most relevance to their governance? Foremost is the changing nature of our institutions. In 1947, employment stood at approximately 58 million and now is at about 72 million. According to V.K. Fuchs, "Virtually all of this increase occurred in industries that provide services, for example, banks, hospitals, retail stores, and schools." This nation has become the only country to employ more people in services than in production of tangible goods. The growth industries today, if we can call them that, are education, health, welfare, and other professional institutions. The problem facing organizations is no longer manufacturing—it is the management of large-scale sociotechnical systems and the strategic deployment of high-grade professional talent.

There are other important correlates and consequences of change. For example, the working population will be younger, smarter, and more mobile. Half of our country's population is under 25, and one out of every three persons is 15 years of age or younger. More people are going to college; over half go to college in certain urban areas. The United States Postal Department reports that one out of every five families changes its address every year.

Most of these changes compel us to look beyond bureaucracy for newer models of organizations that have the capability to cope with contemporary conditions. The general direction of these changes—toward more service and professional organizations, toward more educated, younger, and mobile employees, toward more diverse, complex, science-based systems, toward a more turbulent and uncertain environment—forces us to consider new styles of leadership. Leading the enterprise of the future becomes a significant social process, requiring as much, if not more, managerial than substantive competence. Robert McNamara is a case in point. Before he came to Washington, he was considered for three Cabinet positions: Defense, State, and Treasury. His "only" recommendation was that he was a superior administrator. Chris Argyris has concluded that success or failure in the United States Department of State depends as much or more on one's interpersonal and managerial competence as one's substantive knowledge of "diplomacy." It can also be said that leadership of modern organizations depends on new forms of knowledge and skills not necessarily related to the primary task of the organization. In short, the pivotal function in the leader's role has changed away from a sole concern with the substantive to an emphasis on the interpersonal and organizational processes.

MAIN TASKS OF LEADERSHIP

One convenient focus for a discussion of leadership is to review the main problems confronting modern organizations, and to understand the kinds of tasks and strategies linked to the solution of these problems.

CONTRIBUTIONS AND INDUCEMENTS

A simple way to understand this problem is to compute the ratio between what an individual gives and what he gets in his day-to-day transactions. In other words, are the contributions to the organization about equivalent to the inducements received? Where there is a high ratio between inducements and contributions, either the organization or the employee gets restless and searches for different environments, or different people.

There is nothing startling or new about this formulation. Nevertheless, organizations frequently do not know what is truly rewarding, especially for the professionals and highly trained workers who will dominate the organizations of the future. With this class of employee, conventional policies and practices regarding incentives, never particularly sensitive, tend to be inapplicable.

Most organizations regard economic rewards as the primary incentive to peak performance. These are not unimportant to the professional, but, if economic rewards are equitable, other incentives become far more potent. Avarice, to paraphrase Hume, is *not* the spirit of industry, particularly of professionals. Professionals tend to seek such rewards as full utilization of their talent and training; professional status (not necessarily within the organization, but externally with respect to their profession); and opportunities for development and further learning. The main difference between the professional and the more conventional, hourly employee is that the former will not yield "career authority" to the organization.

The most important incentive, then, is to "make it" professionally, to be respected by professional colleagues. Loyalty to an organization may increase if it encourages professional growth. (I was told recently that a firm decided to build all future plants in university towns in order to attract and hold on to college-trained specialists.) The "good place to work" resembles a super-graduate school, alive with dialogue and senior colleagues, where the employee will not only work to satisfy organizational demands, but, perhaps primarily, those of his profession.

The other incentive is self-realization, personal growth that may not be task-related. I'm well aware that the remark questions four centuries of an encrusted Protestant ethic, reinforced by the indispensability of work for the preservation and justification of existence. But work, as we all must experience it, serves at least two psychic functions: first, that of binding man more closely to reality; and secondly, in Freud's terms, "of displacing a large amount of libidinal components, whether narcissistic, aggressive, or even erotic, onto professional work and onto human relations connected with it. . . ."

It is not at all clear as to how, or even if, these latter needs can be deliberately controlled by the leadership. Company-sponsored courses, sensitivity training sessions, and other so-called adult education courses may, in fact, reflect these needs. Certainly attitudes toward "continuing education" are changing. The idea that education has a terminal point and that college students come in only 4 sizes—18, 19, 20, and 21—is old-fashioned. A "dropout" should be redefined to mean anyone who hasn't *returned* to school.

Whichever way the problem of professional and personal growth is resolved, it is clear that many of the older forms of incentives, based on the more elementary needs (safety-economic-physiological) will have to be reconstituted. Even more profound will be the blurring of the boundaries between work and play, between the necessity to belong and the necessity to achieve, which 19th century mores have unsuccessfully attempted to compartmentalize.

THE PROBLEM OF DISTRIBUTING POWER
There are many issues involved in the distribution of power: psychological, practical, and moral. I will consider only the practical side, with obvious implications for the other two. To begin with, it is quaint to think that one man, no matter how omniscient and omnipotent, can comprehend, let alone control, the diversity and complexity of the modern organization. Followers and leaders who think this is possible get trapped in a child's fantasy of absolute power and absolute dependence.

Today it is hard to realize that during the Civil War, "government" (Lincoln's executive staff) had fewer than 50 civilian subordinates, and not many executives at that, chiefly telegraph clerks and secretaries. Even so recent an administration as Franklin Roosevelt's had a cozy, "family" tone about it. According to his doctor, for example, Roosevelt "loved to know everything that was going on and delighted to have a finger in every pie."

"Having a finger in every pie" may well be an occupational disease of presidents, but it is fast becoming outmoded. Today's administration must reflect the necessities imposed by size and complexity. In fact, there has been a general tendency to move tacitly away from a "presidential" form of power to a "cabinet" or team concept, with some exceptions (like Union Carbide) where "team management" has been conceptualized and made explicit. There is still a long-standing pseudomasculine tendency to disparage such plural executive arrangements, but they are on the increase.

This system of an "executive constellation" by no means implies an abdication of responsibility by the chief executive. It should reflect a coordinated effort based on the distinct competencies of the individual. It is a way of multiplying executive power through a realistic allocation of effort. Of course, this means also that top executive personnel are chosen not only on the basis of their unique talents but on how these skills and competencies fit and work together.

Despite all the problems inherent in the executive constellation concept—how to build an effective team, compatibility, etc.—it is hard to see other valid ways to handle the sheer size and overload of the leader's role.

THE CONTROL OF CONFLICT

Related to the problem of developing an effective executive constellation is another key task of the leader—building a climate in which collaboration, not conflict, will flourish. An effective, collaborative climate is easier to experience and harder to achieve than a formal description of it, but most students of group behavior would agree that it should include the following ingredients: flexible and adaptive structure, utilization of individual talents, clear and agreed-upon goals, standards of openness, trust, and cooperation, interdependence, high intrinsic rewards, and transactional controls—which means a lot of individual autonomy, and a lot of participation making key decisions.

Developing this group "synergy" is difficult, and most organizations take the easy way out—a "zero-synergy" strategy. This means that the organization operates under the illusion that they can hire the best individuals in the world, and then adopt a Voltairean stance of allowing each to "Cultivate his own garden." This strategy of isolation can best be observed in universities, where it operates with great sophistication. The Berkeley riots were symptomatic of at least four self-contained, uncommunicating social systems (students, faculty, administration, regents) without the trust, empathy, and interaction—to say nothing of the tradition—to develop meaningful collaboration. To make matters worse, academics by nature, reinforced by tradition, see themselves as "loners." They want to be independent together, so to speak. Academic narcissism goes a long way on the lecture platform, but may be positively dysfunctional for developing a community.

Another equally pernicious strategy with the same effects, but different style (and more typical of American business institutions), is a pseudodemocratic "groupiness" characterized by false harmony and avoidance of conflict.

Synergy is hard to develop. Lack of experience and strong cultural biases against group efforts worsen the problem. Groups, like other highly complicated organisms, need time to develop. They need a gestation period to develop interaction, trust, communication, and commitment. No one should expect an easy maturity in groups any more than in young children.

Expensive and time-consuming as it is, building synergetic and collaborative cultures will become essential. Modern problems are too complex and diversified for one man or one discipline. They require a blending of skills and perspectives, and only effective problem-solving units will be able to master them.

RESPONDING TO A TURBULENT, UNCERTAIN ENVIRONMENT

> In the early days of the last war when armaments of all kinds were in short supply, the British, I am told, made use of a venerable field piece that had come down to them from previous generations. The honorable past of this light artillery stretched back, in fact, to the Boer War. In the days of uncertainty after the fall of France, these guns, hitched to trucks, served as useful mobile units in the coast defense. But it was felt that the rapidity of fire could be increased. A time-motion expert was, therefore, called in to suggest ways to simplify the firing procedures. He watched one of the gun crews of five men at practice in the field for some time. Puzzled by certain aspects of the procedures, he took some slow-motion pictures of the soldiers performing the loading, aiming, and firing routines.
>
> When he ran those pictures over once or twice, he noticed something that appeared odd to him. A moment before the firing, two members of the gun crew ceased all activity and came to attention for a three-second interval extending throughout the discharge of the gun. He summoned an old colonel of artillery, showed him the pictures, and pointed out this strange behavior. What, he asked the colonel, did it mean? The colonel, too, was puzzled. He asked to see the pictures again. "Ah," he said when the performance was over, "I have it. They are holding the horses." (Elting Morison, *Man, Machines and Modern Times, 1966*)

This fable demonstrates nicely the pain with which man accommodates to change. And yet, characteristically and ironically, he continues to seek out new inventions which disorder his serenity and undermine his competence.

One striking index of the rapidity of change—for me, the single, most dramatic index—is the shrinking interval between the time of a discovery and its commercial application. Before World War I, the lag between invention and utilization was 33 years, between World War I and World War II, it was 17 years. After World War II, the interval decreased to about nine years, and if the future can be extrapolated on the basis of the past, by 1970 it will be around five to six years. The transistor was discovered in 1948, and by 1960, 95 percent of all the important equipment and over 50 percent of *all* electronic equipment utilized them in place of conventional vacuum tubes. The first industrial application of computers was as recent as 1956.

Modern organizations, even more than individuals, are acutely vulnerable to the problem of responding flexibly and appropriately to new information. Symptoms of maladaptive responses, at the extremes, are a guarded, frozen, rigidity that denies the presence or avoids the recognition of changes that will result most typically in organizational paralysis; or, at the opposite extreme, an overly receptive, susceptible gullibility to change resulting in a spastic, unreliable faddism. It is obvious that there are times when openness to change is appropriate and other times when it may be disastrous. Organizations, in fact, should reward people who act as counterchange agents to create forces against the seduction of novelty for its own sake.

How can the leadership of these new style organizations create an atmosphere of continuity and stability amidst an environment of change? Whitehead put the problem well:

> The art of society consists first in the maintenance of the symbolic code, and secondly, in the fearlessness of revision...Those societies which cannot combine reverance to their symbols with freedom of revision must ultimately decay....

There is no easy solution to the tension between stability and change. We are not yet an emotionally adaptive society, though we are as close to having to become one as any society in history. Elting Morison suggests in his brilliant essay on change that "we may find at least part of our salvation in identifying ourselves with the adaptive process and thus share some of the joy, exuberance, satisfaction, and security...to meet... changing times."

The remarkable aspect of our generation is its commitment to change in thought and action. Executive leadership must take some responsibility in creating a climate that provides the security to identify with the adaptive process without fear of losing status. Creating an environment that would increase a tolerance for ambiguity and where one can make a virtue out of contingency, rather than one that induces hesitancy and its reckless counterpart, expedience, is one of the most challenging tasks for the new leadership.

CLARITY, COMMITMENT, AND CONSENSUS

Organizations, like individuals, suffer from "identity crises." They are not only afflictions that attack during adolescence, but chronic states pervading every phase of organizational development. The new organizations we speak of, with their bands of professional problem-solvers, coping within a turbulent environment, are particularly allergic to problems of identity. Professional and regional orientations lead frequently to fragmentation, intergroup conflicts, and power plays and rigid compartmentalization, devoid of any unifying sense of purpose or mission.

UNIVERSITIES SURPASS BUSINESS IN SUBTERFUGE

The university is a wondrous place for advanced battle techniques, far surpassing their business counterparts in subterfuge and sabotage. Quite often a university becomes a loose collection of competing departments, schools, institutes, committees, centers, programs, largely non-communicating because of the multiplicity of specialist jargons and interests, and held together, as Robert Hutchins once said, chiefly by a central heating system, or as Clark Kerr amended, by questions of what to do about the parking problem.

The modern organizations we speak of are composed of men who love independence as fiercely as the ancient Greeks; but it is also obvious that they resist what every Athenian, as a matter of course, gave time and effort for: "building and lifting up the common life."
Thucydides has Pericles saying:

> We are a free democracy. . . . We do not allow absorption in our own affairs to interfere with participation in the city's. We regard men who hold aloof from public affairs as useless; nevertheless we yield to none in independence of spirit and complete self-reliance.

A modern version of the same problem (which the Greeks couldn't solve either, despite the lofty prose) has been stated by the president of a large university:

> The problem with this institution is that too few people understand or care about the overall goals. Typically they see the world through their own myopic departmental glasses; i.e., too constricted and biased. What we need more of are professional staff who can wear not only their own school or departmental "hat" but the overall university hat.

Specialism, by definition, implies a peculiar slant, a skewed vision of reality. McLuhan tells a good joke on this subject. A tailor went to Rome and managed to get an audience with his Holiness. Upon his return, a friend asked him, "What did the Pope look like?" The tailor answered, "A 41 regular."

Having heard variations of this theme over the years, a number of faculty and administrators, who thought they could "wear the overall university hat" formed what later came to be known as "the HATS group." They came from a variety of departments and hierarchical levels and represented a rough microcosm of the entire university. The HATS group has continued to meet over the past several years and has played an important role in influencing university policy.

There are a number of functions that leadership can perform in addition to developing HATS groups. First, it can identify and support those persons who are "linking pins," individuals with a psychological and intellectual affinity for a number of languages and cultures. Secondly, it can work at the places where the different disciplines and organizations come together (for example, setting up new interdisciplinary programs), in order to create more intergroup give and take.

The third important function for leadership is developing and shaping identity. Organizations, not only the academic disciplines, require philosophers, individuals who can provide articulation between seemingly inimical interests, and who can break down the pseudospecies, transcend vested interests, regional ties, and professional biases. This is precisely what Mary Parker Follett had in mind when she discussed leadership in terms of an ability to bring about a "creative synthesis" between differing codes of conduct.

Chester Barnard in his classic *Functions of the Executive* (1938) recognized this, as well as the personal energy and cost of political process. He wrote, "it seems to me that the struggle to maintain cooperation among men should as surely destroy some men morally as battle destroys some physically."

THE PROBLEM OF GROWTH AND DECAY

For the leader, the organization has to take a conscious responsibility for its own evolution; without a planned methodology and explicit direction, the enterprise will not realize its full potential. For the leader, this is the issue of revitalization and it confronts him with the ultimate challenge: growth or decay.

The challenge for the leader is to develop a climate of inquiry and enough psychological and employment security for continual reassessment and renewal. This task is connected with the leader's ability to collect valid data, feed it back to the appropriate individuals, and develop action planning on the basis of the data. This three-step "action-research" model sounds deceptively simple. In fact, it is difficult. Quite often, the important data cannot be collected by the leader for many obvious reasons. Even when the data are known, there are many organizational short circuits and "dithering devices" that distort and prevent the data from getting to the right places at the right time. And even when data-gathering and feedback are satisfactorily completed, organizational inhibitions may not lead to implementation.

In response to the need for systematic data collection, many organizations are setting up "Institutional Research" centers that act as basic fact-gathering agencies. In some cases, they become an arm of policy-making. Mostly, they see as their prime responsibility the collection and analysis of data that bear on the effectiveness with which the organization achieves its goals.

Fact-gathering, by itself, is rarely sufficient to change attitudes and beliefs and to overcome natural inertia and unnatural resistance to change. Individuals have an awesome capacity to "selectively inattend" to facts that may in their eyes threaten their self-esteem. Facts and reasons may be the least potent forms of influence that man possesses.

Some progressive organizations are setting up organizational development departments that attempt to reduce the "implementation gap" between information and new ideas and action. These OD departments become the center for the entire strategic side of the organization, including not only long-run planning, but plans for gaining participation and commitment to the plans. This last step is the most crucial for the guarantee of successful implementation.

NEW CONCEPTS FOR LEADERSHIP

In addition to substantive competence and comprehension of both social and technical systems, the new leader will have to possess interpersonal skills, not the least of which is the ability to defer his own immediate desires and gratifications in order to cultivate the talents of others. Let us examine some of the ways leadership can successfully cope with the new organizational patterns.

UNDERSTANDING THE "SOCIAL TERRITORY"

"You gotta know the territory," sang "Professor" Harold Hill to his fellow salesmen in *The Music Man*. The "social territory" encompasses the complex and dynamic interaction of individuals, roles, groups, organizational and cultural systems. Organizations are, of course, legal, political, technical, and economic systems. For our purposes, we will focus on the social system.

Analytic tools, drawn primarily from social psychology and sociology, are available to aid in the understanding of the social territory. But we need more than such tools to augment and implement these un-derstandings. Leadership is as much craft as science. The main in-strument or "tool" for the leader-as-a-craftsman is *himself* and how creatively he can use his own personality. This is particularly important for leaders to understand, for, like physicians, they are just as capable of spreading as of curing disease. And again, like the physician, it is im-portant that the leader heed the injunction "heal thyself" so that he does not create pernicious effects unwittingly. Unless the leader understands his actions and effects on others, he may be a "carrier" rather than a solver of problems. Understanding the social territory and how one in-fluences it is related to the "action-research" model of leadership men-tioned earlier: 1) collect data, 2) feed it back to appropriate sources, and 3) action-planning. The "hang-up" in most organizations is that people tend to distort and suppress data for fear of real or fancied retaliation. (Samuel Goldwyn, a notorious martinet, called his top staff together after a par-ticularly bad box-office flop and said: "Look, you guys, I want you to tell me exactly what's wrong with this operation and my leadership—even if it means losing your job!")

THE CONCEPT OF "SYSTEM INTERVENTION"

Another aspect of the social territory that has key significance for leadership is the idea of *system*. At least two decades of research have been making this point unsuccessfully. Research has shown that productivity can be modified by what the group thinks important, that training effects fade out and deteriorate if they do not fit the goals of the social system, that group cohesiveness is a powerful motivator, that conflict between units is a major problem in organizations, that individuals take many of their cues and derive a good deal of their satisfaction from their primary work group, that identification with the small work group turns out to be the only stable predictor of productivity, and so on.

The fact that this evidence is so often cited and rarely acted upon leads one to infer that there is some sort of involuntary reflex that makes us locate problems in faulty individuals rather than in malfunctioning social systems. What this irrational reflex is based upon is not altogether clear. But individuals, living amidst complex and subtle organizational conditions, do tend to oversimplify and distort complex realities so that people rather than conditions embody the problem. This tendency toward personalization can be observed in many situations. In international affairs, we blame our troubles with France on deGaulle, or talk sometimes as though we believe that replacing Diem, or Khanh, or Ky will solve our problems with the Saigon government. Other illustrations can be seen when members of organizations take on familial nicknames, such as "Dad," "Big Brother," "Man," "Mother Hen," "Dutch Uncle," etc. We can see it in distorted polarizations such as the "good guy" leader who is too trusting, and his "hatchet man" assistant who is really to blame. Those grotesques seem to bear such little resemblance to the actual people that one has to ask what psychological needs are being served by this complex labeling and stereotyping.

One answer was hinted at earlier in the Freud quote. He said that work provides an outlet for displacing emotional components onto professional work and the human relations associated with work. If there were no "Big Daddys" or "Queen Bees," we would have to invent them as therapeutic devices to allay anxieties about less romantic, more immediate mothers and fathers, brothers and sisters.

Another reason for this tendency toward personalization is related to the wounded narcissism leaders often suffer. Organizations are big, complex, wondrous—and hamstrung with inertia. Impotence and alienation imprison the best of men, the most glorious of intentions. There is a myth that the higher one goes up the ladder, the more freedom and potency one experiences. In fact, this is frequently not the case, as almost any chief executive will report: the higher he goes the more tethered and bound he may feel by expectations and commitments. In any case, as one gets entrapped by inertia and impotence, it is easier to blame heroes and villains than the system. For if the problems are embroidered into the fabric of the social system, complex as they are, the system can be changed. But if the problems are people, then the endemic lethargy can be explained away by the difficulty—the impossibility—of "changing human nature."

If management insists on personalizing problems that arise from systems, serious repercussions must result. In the new organizations— where roles will be constantly changing and ambiguous, where changes in one subsystem will clearly affect other subsystems, where diverse activities have to be coordinated and integrated, where individuals work simultaneously in many different jobs and groups—a system viewpoint must be developed. Just as psychotherapists find it difficult to treat a "problem child" without treating the entire family, it will be more difficult to influence individual behavior without working with his particular subsystem. The leader will be compelled to intervene at the system level if the intervention is to last and serve its purpose.

AN AGRICULTURAL MODEL OF LEADERSHIP

I have not found the right word or phrase that accurately portrays the concept of leadership I have in mind—which can be summarized as follows: *an active method for producing conditions where people and ideas and resources can be seeded, cultivated, and integrated to optimum effectiveness and growth.* The phrase "other-directedness," unfortunately, has taken on the negative tone of "exclusively tuned into outside cues." For awhile I thought that "applied biology" might capture the idea, for it connotes an ecological point of view; a process of observation, careful intervention, and organic development. I have also noticed that many biologists and physicians (particularly those physicians who either have no practices or went into public health, psychiatry, or research) are excellent administrators. Socrates used a close and congenial metaphor to symbolize the role of the teacher, the "midwife," someone who helped others to give birth to creations.

The most appropriate metaphor I have found to characterize adaptive leadership is an "agricultural" model. The leader's job, as I have stated, is to build a climate where growth and development are culturally induced. Roy Ash, an astute industrialist and chairman of Litton Industries, remarked recently, "If the larger corporations, classically viewed as efficient machines rather than hothouses for fomenting innovation, can become both of these at once, industrial competition will have taken on new dimensions." I think Ash captures exactly the shift in metaphor I am getting at, from a mechanical model to an organic one. Up until very recent times, the metaphor most commonly used to describe power and leadership in organizations derived from Helmholtz's laws of mechanics. Max Weber, who first conceptualized the model of bureaucracy, wrote, "Bureaucracy is like a modern judge who is a vending machine into which the pleadings are inserted along with the fee and which then disgorges the judgment with its reasons mechanically derived from the code."

The language of organizational dynamics in most contemporary writings reflects the machine metaphor: social engineering, equilibrium, friction, resistance, force-field, etc. The vocabulary for adaptive organizations requires an organic metaphor, a description of a *process,* not structural arrangements. This process must include such terms as open, dynamic systems, developmental, organic, adaptive, etc.

All of these strategic and practical considerations lead to a totally new concept of leadership. The pivotal aspect of this concept is that it relies less on the leader's substantive knowledge about a particular topic than it does on the understanding and possession of skills summarized under the agricultural model.

This new concept of leadership embraces four important sets of competencies: 1) knowledge of large, complex human systems; 2) practical theories of intervening and guiding these systems, theories that encompass methods for seeding, nurturing, and integrating individuals and groups; 3) interpersonal competence, particularly the sensitivity to understand the effects of one's own behavior on others and how one's own personality shapes his particular leadership style and value system; and 4) a set of values and competencies which enables one to know when to confront and attack, if necessary, and when to support and provide the psychological safety so necessary for growth.

It is amusing and occasionally frustrating to note that the present view of leadership which I have referred to as an agricultural model, is often construed as "passive" or "weak" or "soft" or more popularly "permissive," and generally dismissed with the same uneasy, patronizing shrug one usually reserves for women who try, however clumsily, to play a man's game. The fact is that the role of leadership described here is clearly more demanding and formidable than any other historical precedent, from king to Pope.

It may be that the common tendency to give this new leadership role such passive and effeminate names betrays the anxiety that many must feel at the final downfall of that distant, stern, strict Victorian father, whose surrogate has led us so often as teacher, military commander, and corporation president. Perhaps that is the only kind of authority we have experienced first hand, or know intimately, or even consider legitimate. But if this new man of power—other-directed and interpersonally competent—takes over the dominant role, as he now seems to be doing, then not only will new myths and archetypes have to substitute for the old, family ones, but new ways—perhaps new legends—will have to be developed to dramatize the rise of new heroes. Let us hope that this new tradition of leadership is not only more potent, but in the long run more gratifying.

HENRY S. REUSS
EVERARD MUNSEY

The Ombudsman:
A Proposed Scheme for
the United States

In the years since the Great Depression, the United States government has assumed unprecedented social and economic responsibilities. Since the end of World War II, it has had to administer the affairs of a vastly increased number of veterans and operate a huge "peacetime" defense establishment. The American economy has become more complex.

A result of these events has been an expansion of the federal bureaucracy and a great increase in the contact between the average citizen and the federal government. For the United States, as for other Western nations, this has emphasized the old problem of how to give the administrators the power and discretion they require to act effectively and, at the same time, to provide avenues for checking abuses and excesses and means of correcting errors and misjudgments.

One American solution to this problem has been the evolution of the member of Congress as a mediator between citizens and the bureaucracy. Congressmen receive and look into citizens' complaints about social security matters or veterans' benefits, about alleged discrimination in the granting of government contracts, mistreatment in the military, and countless other subjects. The public image of the Congressman as the citizens' advocate against governmental abuse is so widespread that members of Congress continually receive pleas for assistance in state and local matters that are beyond their power. On the other hand, the Congressman also has the role of explaining the bureaucracy to the citizen in many cases where the bureaucracy has been too wrapped up in jargon or technicalities to explain itself. Foreign parliamentarians are continually amazed to see members of the U.S. House of Representatives equipped with three-room suites and up to ten aides, and members of the Senate

Reprinted with the permission of the Toronto Press and George Allen & Unwin Ltd. from *The Ombudsman,* Donald C. Rowat. ed. (Toronto: University of Toronto Press, 1965).

Mr. Reuss is a member of the US House of Representatives (5th District, Wisconsin), and Mr. Munsey is his Legislative Assistant.

with an even more lavish allocation of human and material resources. This paraphernalia is in no small measure due to the Congressman's role as mediator.

It is sometimes argued that the American Congressman has no business in such a role and should be remodeled after the example of his British counterpart. Whether this is correct or not—and we do not believe it is— the role of Congressman as mediator is a well-entrenched and virtually unalterable part of the American system of government. It is a principal means of resolving the conflicts between administrative power and efficiency on one hand and civil liberties and individual rights on the other. It is a way of humanizing the bureaucracy and making it responsible.

The real political problem is to assure a reasonable balance between this function as mediator and other vital Congressional duties. Unfortunately, the balance in recent years has swung to a disproportionate emphasis on mediation, on activities that Congressmen call their "casework". The volume of casework has mounted steadily—perhaps more than proportionately—as the role of the federal government has expanded. In response, Congressional staffs were increased, the Legislative Reorganization Act of 1946 banned several types of private bills to redress citizens' complaints that formerly consumed much time and effort, quasi-judicial review boards were established in some executive agencies, and the General Accounting Office, an arm of Congress, was created to audit the legality of government expenditures. Yet, almost every Congressman finds himself spending more time on casework and, inevitably, less on his other duties. This development has coincided with an increase in the complexity of legislation before the Congress. Although bills are demanding more and more attention, less and less time for this is available.

The Congressman does not needlessly divert time from legislation to casework. Even if a Congressman should prefer to be rid of his mediating function, neglect of casework can have a political repercussion that will rid him of all the burdens of office. One astute reporter of Congressional affairs hardly exaggerated when he wrote recently that:

> The plain fact is that a man's legislative work is commonly a matter of indifference—if not outright suspicion—for his constituents. What can hurt politically is the charge that he has failed to look after his district. Neglect of correspondence, of constituent services or of vital local needs lies behind the defeat of a vast majority of those few in Congress who fail of re-election. [1]

Under existing circumstances Congress is doubly hampered. The impediment of an excessive casework burden is added to the impediment resulting from unrepresentative districting and intolerable rules. Both impediments must be removed to make Congress really effective. Lightening the casework burden is not a cure-all but it is one of several positive steps that need to be taken.

1. PROPOSAL FOR AN ADMINISTRATIVE COUNSEL

The need is clear, then, for a new device to aid the Congressman in helping his constituents so that he can continue to be a protector of their rights and still have time to be a thoughtful legislator. A further expansion of the Congressman's staff might be one answer. But, for reasons to be presented later, we do not believe it would be the best solution. Instead, we have proposed (in HR7593, introduced on July 16, 1963) the creation of an Administrative Counsel of the Congress. The proposal represents an attempt to adapt to the American governmental system the institution of Ombudsman. Naturally, substantial changes have been necessary because of constitutional and political realities.

The Administrative Counsel would be appointed by the Speaker of the House of Representatives and the President *pro tempore* of the Senate "without reference to political affiliation and solely on the basis of his fitness to perform the duties of his office." His term of office would normally expire at the beginning of the Congress following the Congress in which he was appointed except that, if the two appointing officers could not agree, an Administrative Counsel could continue in office until the end of the Congress following that in which he was appointed. In the absence of a prolonged deadlock between the Speaker and the President *pro tempore,* this provision would avoid any period in which there would be no Administrative Counsel in office.

Constituents' complaints against the administrative departments and agencies would continue to come to members of Congress. Congressmen would, in turn, be able to refer such complaints to the Administrative Counsel who "shall review the case of any person who alleges that he is being subjected to any improper penalty, or that he has been denied any right or benefit to which he is entitled, under the laws of the United States, or that the determination or award of any such right or benefit has been... unreasonably delayed as a result of any action or failure to act on the part of any officer or employee of the United States."

The Administrative Counsel, who will be assisted by an adequate staff, would look into the claim on the basis of material submitted by the complainant and through inquiries to government officials, investigations of records, or any other necessary fact-finding procedures. He is given powers of inquiry comparable to those of Congressional committees, which exceed the investigatory authority of a single Congressman. His inquiry could extend to all aspects of good administrative practice as well as to the correctness of the administrative decision. All governmental officers and employees are required to co-operate with him and to give him full information and access to any books or records.

The right of Congress to obtain information from the executive branch is well established. One cloud on this right, however, has been the claim of "executive privilege" as a basis of withholding information from Congress.

The House Government Operations Committee has consistently maintained that claims of "executive privilege" are without foundation in law, but such claims have been made from time to time, occasionally by minor officials. Although the question will remain in doubt until a Supreme Court decision is obtained, President Kennedy at least declared that "executive privilege" can be invoked only by the President himself. Access to information should not prove a serious problem to the Administrative Counsel.

The Counsel's area of activity would include departments, agencies or instrumentalities of the United States. Specifically excluded from his jurisdiction, however, are the President, the Congress and its employees, the federal judiciary, the government of the District of Columbia, and of course state and local governments. In addition, he would be empowered to exclude "any...officer or employee of the United States whose activities are of such a nature that...the application of this Act thereto would be contrary to the public interest." One instance of the application of this provision almost certainly would be a determination by him that he should stay out of matters involving the intelligence agencies. Undoubtedly, there will be other areas he should stay out of, but it seems better not to try to foresee and specify them.

After completing his investigation, the Administrative Counsel would report his findings and his recommendation, if any, to the Congressman concerned. If his recommendation were in favor of the constituent, in many instances the erring administrative agency would have rectified the matter in the course of the investigation. If the error had not been rectified, the member would undoubtedly wish to transmit the Counsel's recommendation to the agency concerned, with his own request for remedial action. An administrative agency would be more likely to respond to a member's request for relief if it were accompanied by the Counsel's recommendation; a member's request by itself can sometimes be laughed off as "political pressure." However, if the member preferred, he would not need to refer a matter to the Administrative Counsel at all, but could handle it himself as at present. Moreover, if he did refer a matter and the Counsel upheld the administrative agency rather than the constituent, the member could always, if he wished, pursue the matter further on his own.

In addition to the reports on specific cases, the Administrative Counsel is directed to make an annual report to the House and Senate and may make specific reports to either body at any time. These provisions should be of great value because the Counsel will be able to obtain an unprecedented insight into administrative practices, the lack of sufficient or competent staff, and the laws and regulations that are the sources of numerous, recurring problems between the bureaucracy and the citizenry. At present, with the casework divided among 535 congressional offices, the breeding grounds of citizens' problems are not readily spotted. In his general report to Congress, the Counsel should be able to recommend action to eliminate the roots of much friction between the bureaucracy and the citizenry.

In many cases, legislative action by Congress will not be needed. If the Administrative Counsel is a person of high qualification and unquestioned standing, as the Nordic Ombudsmen have been, his criticisms in reports to the Congress should acquire the same capacity as theirs to bring prompt remedial action by the administration. Indeed, he will be able to make the remedy fit the administrative crime: a report to the referring Congressman, with or without recommendations, in individual cases; a public report criticizing poor administrative practices or a recommendation for legislative action, where that seems desirable. He will be able to investigate, recommend, criticize and publicize. He is given complete discretion in making special reports to Congress, and they may deal with individual cases as well as groups of cases. Although his reports to individual Congressmen will not be published, his annual and special reports to Congress will be printed as House or Senate documents and will undoubtedly receive widespread press coverage. The sanction of public opinion could become a powerful force for the improvement of administration.

2. ADVANTAGES OF THE SCHEME

Two major advantages to be obtained from establishment of the Administrative Counsel have already been set forth: (1) Congressmen would be relieved of some of the burden of casework and allowed to spend more time on legislation, and (2) problems between the bureaucracy and citizens could be more readily spotted and eliminated. In addition, such an office would make the Congressman's mediation between citizens and the bureaucracy more effective. It would provide centralized, expert handling of casework. At present no one congressional office can afford to maintain true experts in even the most common type of cases. Much time is wasted by staff members of an individual Congressman who lack adequate knowledge in the subject of a constituent's complaint and thus cannot discuss the matter with the administrative technician concerned on anything like an equal basis. Centralizing the operation in the Office of the Administrative Counsel would permit specialization, just as has been done for the supervision of financial transactions by creating the Office of Comptroller General in the General Accounting Office. The handling of citizens' problems by the new office should promote efficiency and reduce the need for continual, costly increases in congressional staff and office space.

An Administrative Counsel of the Congress would be in harmony with the system of separation of powers and of checks and balances that characterizes the American government. For he would represent Congress in exercising a check upon the executive branch. Yet he would neither act with respect to nor in any way supplant the function of the judiciary.

The congressional-constituent relationship, it should be emphasized, would not be impaired by the work of such an officer. The Congressman would still retain control of the beginning and end of each case. He would have the option of referring the case to the Administrative Counsel or not. He could pursue the matter further after receiving the Counsel's report. And the benefits of specialization in the Counsel's staff should result in better service to constituents.

The Counsel's effectiveness will largely depend upon the confidence that Congressmen repose in him. To gain and maintain this confidence, he will of course have to operate so that Congressmen do not have to "follow up" cases referred to him in the same manner as inquiries they send directly to agencies of the executive branch.

The success of this new office will also depend in large measure upon its holder being, as the Swedish statute requires of the Ombudsman, of "conspicuous integrity." That he should also have extraordinary ability and judgment is of first importance. The proposed legislation provides that he be paid a salary of $22,500, equal to members of Congress, in order to give him the status and prestige that he needs to operate effectively.

3. POSSIBLE OBJECTIONS

What may be said in objection to the proposals? It will no doubt be said that the Administrative Counsel will require such a large staff that this will merely mean the creation of another bureaucracy. But because of the efficiency that can be obtained through specialization, this staff should be considerably smaller than the total of congressional staff members saved from handling casework.

It may be objected that the Administrative Counsel will become a "fixer," a powerful favor-seeker, a leader of contract-seeking Chamber of Commerce delegations. Congressmen, it may be said, will try to use his power to bludgeon unjustified concessions from the administration. But, in virtually all cases handled by Congressmen, they attempt nothing more than to assure that the constituent obtains his due, after full and fair consideration. Congressmen who wish to "pressure" the administration will be able to do so whether the new office exists or not. Moreover, the Counsel will have a legal right to refuse to be used in such a way. The statutory language limiting the Counsel's power to review of cases in which citizens allege that they have been subjected to improper penalties or deprived of rights or benefits should help prevent his office from degenerating into a general information bureau. The provision allowing him, at his discretion, to exclude from his jurisdiction any official "whose activities are of such a nature that. . .the application of this Act would be contrary to the public interest" will allow the Counsel to stay out of areas where policy considerations are dominant and where political pressure is most likely.

It may be asked whether the Counsel should make recommendations directly to administrators. However, under the separation of powers system, it seems better that he make his reports to Congress formally. The Legislative Counsel believes that the legality of direct recommendations to officers of the executive branch by an appointed agent of the legislative branch is questionable. But in practice the legal distinctions are not likely to be important. The Administrative Counsel will be able to make informal recommendations to administrators, and his formal reports to individual Congressmen and to Congress will be sent to the administrators concerned. Often when the Counsel makes a recommendation in favor of a citizen, his recommendation by itself will bring corrective action. Less frequently in such cases officials will not respond promptly to the Counsel's recommendation, and action by the individual Congressman concerned will be necessary and effective. Action by Congress as a whole will usually occur only when citizens would be subjected to severe inequities or injustice, or where a need for general remedial action has been revealed.

Finally, it may be complained that the Counsel deviates most markedly from the other Ombudsmen in that citizens may not approach him directly but only through a member of Congress. A Congressman could, of course, refuse to submit a complaint to the Counsel, even as he may now ignore a constituent's problem. But a desire to be returned to office may be depended upon to make such behavior a rarity. Besides, each citizen has three Congressmen—one representative and two Senators—each of whom has a particular interest in being of service to him. In addition, a citizen can write to any of the other 532 members of Congress, who may refer the matter to the Administrative Counsel. Practically, it would seem that any citizen wishing to bring a matter before the Counsel would be able to do so, with little difficulty.

The requirement that citizens approach the Counsel through a member of Congress results from the decision to use an Ombudsman-like official to strengthen an existing American means of harmonizing relations between the citizenry and the bureaucracy—Congressional mediation. Any arrangement providing for direct access to the Counsel would inevitably have the effect of weakening the Congressman's role as mediator. Of course, the Counsel could be in direct communication with the complainant *after* the case is referred, just as Congressional staff members now telephone or interview complainants on occasion. In any case, it is doubtful whether Congressmen would support any proposal to remove them from their role as champions of citizens' rights against the federal bureaucracy. For, although this role is burdensome, it is a source of great strength at the polls. The scheme proposed, then, can make a valuable contribution to democratic government in the United States without a radical alteration of our institutions and traditions of government.

NOTES

1. David S. Broder, "Portrait of a Typical Congressman," *New York Times Magazine,* October, 7, 1962, 31.